Gloucestershire Road
A history of Gloucestershire County Cricket Club

Frontispiece. Gloucestershire County Cricket Club above *1877 and below 1977.*

GRAHAME PARKER

Gloucestershire Road
A history of Gloucestershire County Cricket Club

Published in association with
♻ National Westminster Bank PLC

PELHAM BOOKS
LONDON

For Mary, Jennifer, Jane and Tony.

First published in Great Britain by
Pelham Books Ltd
44 Bedford Square
London WC1B 3DU
1983

British Library Cataloguing in Publication Data

Parker, Grahame
   The Gloucestershire Road: a history of the
   Gloucestershire County Cricket Club.
   1. Gloucestershire County Cricket Club – History
   I. Title
   796.33′863   GV921G5

   ISBN 0-7207-1454-0

Printed and bound in Great Britain by
Butler & Tanner Ltd, Frome and London

Contents

Illustrations

CREDITS

Most of the photographs are from the archives of Gloucestershire County Cricket Club and in some cases it has not been possible to ascertain the copyright holders. It is hoped that any such omissions will be excused.

The author and publishers are grateful to the following for permission to reproduce photographs; numbers refer to photograph numbers: Barratt's Photo Press Ltd. 71, 73; T. R. Beckett, 77, 81, 88; *Bristol Evening Post* 66, 99, 105; *Cape Argus* South Africa, 91; Central Press 54, 57, 93; Cheltenham Newspaper Co. Ltd., 85; *Daily Star* 127; Patrick Eagar 72, 109, 128; Foto-Prints (Bristol) Ltd. 131; Fox-Waterman Photography Ltd. 120; George P. Herringshaw 100; The Rev. Gilbert Jessop 39, 40, 43 and back cover; Marylebone Cricket Club 1, 30, 32, 36, 47; Press Association 59, 68, 92; Bill Smith frontispiece (bottom), 101, 104, 116, 122, 124, 129; Sport and General 79, 80, 82, 84, 87; Robert Tedder 121.

My family has been associated with Gloucestershire County Cricket Club since its earliest days and I am delighted to write this short foreword to Grahame Parker's 'Gloucestershire Road'.

The pages will remind readers of the long diverse history and characters of the County's cricket club. The great number of cricketers who have left their foot steps on the Road must be a surprise to us all. We are reminded fittingly of some of the great names of the past - Grace, Jessop, Hammond - and the outstanding endeavours of many others. Also we must remember countless supporters of the club and the generations of members of the Regional Committees and the Council who have given their selfless work for its welfare. This story also reflects the happy comradeship that has existed throughout Gloucestershire cricket.

We are indeed grateful to the National Westminster Bank for their assistance in this project. This is fitting, for they have been associated with the Club for most of its 112 years.

Gloucestershire, and indeed cricket itself, may be experiencing some formidable problems but this book, whilst concentrating our thoughts on the past, must surely encourage us to face the future.

Beaufort.

PATRON.

Preface

I first came into direct involvement with Gloucestershire County Cricket Club in 1931. I was invited to the pre-season nets, joined Alf Dipper, Tom Goddard and Dick Stephens at the now demolished Gloucester L.M.S. station and unable to play their auction bridge sat in my corner watching the telegraph poles go by. The other three played with a dummy until Berkeley Road where Billy Neale got in. At Temple Meads we all trundled into a tram for the Centre, changed into another skirting the basin for the uphill journey to Nevil Road and the County Ground.

The years passed. After my return to Gloucestershire cricket in 1968 and the Centenary Year in 1970 I became increasingly absorbed with what had happened during the Club's history. My sketchy outline of the great names and events of the past became more clearly defined. I was delighted when in 1978, Chairman Ken Graveney and the Management Committee asked me to write a 'definitive' history of the Club. What follows in these pages is certainly not a definitive history, but hopefully it will give some substance to the subject and encourage others to avenues as yet unexplored.

I have called it *Gloucestershire Road* for not only is it a road I have travelled with deep affection, but also many years ago I was much attracted to the opening line of Chesterton's *The English Road* – 'Before the Roman came to Rye or out to Severn strode'. There stood the legionary as he reached the crest of Birdlip Hill, looking out over that historic landscape, towards the Severn, the Malverns, May Hill and the Forest of Dean . . . but that's another road.

I must acknowledge my appreciation for much encouragement over these last three years; to David Foot for his gentle, shrewd advice; to Ronald Seldon, one of the few cricketers to have made a century and taken all ten wickets in a day's game, for checking through the script, and to the late Chris Reichwald, both colleagues at Blundell's; to Bill Grace and May Bernard for details of the Grace family, also to the Reverend Gilbert

Jessop of his illustrious father; to Neville Weston the supreme authority on W.G.; to Stephen Green M.C.C. Curator at Lord's for his patient direction to the earliest days of cricket; to Bert Avery and John Mace for their statistics; to Jennifer Park and Susie Goscomb for their diligent typing of the manuscript; and finally to many Gloucestershire friends my totally inadequate thanks. The errors are mine.

Four hundred and ninety-six cricketers have now played for Gloucestershire leaving behind them an incomparable cricket legacy. Many of them appear in these pages, many many more have no memorial here. To every one of those who has travelled along this Gloucestershire Road, and to the generations of those who have stood on the Roadside watching ... may our labours not have been in vain.

November 1982.   GRAHAME PARKER

Cricket Comes to Gloucestershire 1

1706-1870

Gloucestershire's cricket story begins almost on the playing fields of Eton. The earliest known description of a game of cricket appeared in 1706 in the form of a Latin poem by William Goldwin. Born in 1682, the son of a Windsor baker, he won a scholarship to nearby Eton College on 23 March 1696, proceeded to King's College, Cambridge, 3 October 1700, was appointed Headmaster of Bristol Grammar School in 1707 and eventually became Vicar of St Nicholas, Bristol in 1717. He died on 6 January 1747.

The poem of ninety-six lines, Latin hexameters, paints a delightful picture of a game he had watched somewhere in rural Kent during the first years of the eighteenth century. Before it

An early cricket match.

could begin a much respected elder cricket statesman had to settle a disagreement over the 'rules' that were to apply. As the game proceeded it is described flamboyantly until concluded by a mighty blow that carried the ball away on the wind amid roars of approval. It had for long been considered a figment of the writer's lively imagination since the first edition of the Laws of Cricket did not appear until 1744, by which time the rules had advanced in the natural evolution of the game. It was not until 1949 that the Richmond Articles of Agreement of 1727 came to light to confirm that Goldwin had observed accurately what had taken place in 1706.

Legends, traditions, opinions, make up the pre-history of the game. Cricket historians cannot seem to agree over its place of origin although most would suggest it derived from the Weald borders of Kent, Sussex and Surrey. The habit, hobby, pastime, recreation, game, another rural sporting social occasion, call it what you will, spread slowly westward.

The first reference to a game of cricket in Gloucestershire is to be found in the *Gloucester Journal* of Tuesday, 16 September 1729. No doubt it would have been played under the same rules that applied to Goldwin's game. The match was to be played on the following Monday, for 'upwards of twenty guineas', on the Town Ham, that area of Olney Island between the two arms of the Severn where from time immemorial Gloucester folk had sought their amusement and settled their differences. Unfortunately there is no later report of the result. First a canal in 1797, then a railway and sidings in 1842, and much later in 1982 a bypass, have cut the area into ribbons, but occasional games of cricket, rugby and football are still played there.

The next reference in a Gloucestershire newspaper is not until 29 August 1752, in Felix Farley's *Bristol Journal*. The game was to be played on Monday, 31 August, on Durdham Down, another area where the locals practised their playful and often bloodthirsty pastimes. The match was 'for twenty guineas between XI of Bristol and XI of London, wickets to be pitched at 11 am'.

These challenge matches were an early feature of the game. The English instinct for gambling had found a new outlet. No longer was it to be bear-baiting or cock fighting, but cricket between teams often of professional cricketers sponsored by aristocrats.

There is an increasing number of reports of cricket in Gloucestershire and the surrounding counties during the early years of the nineteenth century – Bath, Bristol, Cheltenham, Cirencester, Gloucester, Hereford, Kingscote, Ledbury, Minchinhampton, Raglan, Ross, St Briavels, Stow-on-the-Wold. The challenge matches slowly gave way to club matches and soon clubs were formed with regular fixtures – Clifton 1819, Lansdown 1825, Gloucester 1829 and followed by a whole spate of others by the 1850s – Bedminster, Bitton, Cheltenham, Chipping Sodbury, Cirencester, Frenchay, Knowle, Moreton-in-Marsh, Portishead, Bristol Schoolmasters, Shirehampton, Stroud, Westbury-on-Trym. This was the core of cricket within the County but must have been only a fragment of the games played.

Two Gloucestershire cricket personalities now entered the County story. Firstly, Robert Henry Kingscote, 1802–1882 and a member of one of the oldest county families of Kingscote, 6′ 6″, a mighty batter who played for one of the earliest cricket teams in the County. Of him it was written:

> 'A fine slashing hitter as ever was found,
> He sometimes hit the ball out of the ground;
> An excellent thrower, a hundred yards clear,
> And the ladies protest he runs like a deer.'

In cricket there is always a balance between bat and ball. This is disturbed periodically when the balance is recovered by legal adjustment or some other factor. By the beginning of the last century batting had so developed that bowlers felt they were under severe handicap. Bowlers bowled what we would call underarm. The controversy was over what constituted underarm – hand below or above the elbow. The matter was settled by compromise during Kingscote's Presidency of the M.C.C. in 1828 – to the level of the elbow. Round arm bowling, hand below the level of the shoulder, became the law in 1835, overarm, hand above the shoulder, in 1864.

Robert Kingscote's nephew, Captain H. B. Kingscote, played three games for the County in 1877 and scored 4 runs. He served in India and became a Colonel.

Whilst these bowling developments were taking place the second influential character came on to the scene, Dr Henry Mills Grace. It was Dr Grace who patiently led Gloucestershire to its Road and showed it the direction it should take. The Graces are the central thread of the story into the present

Dr and Mrs Grace, the parents of E.M., W.G., and G.F.

century. His father, Henry Grace, had married Elizabeth Mills, a daughter of the chief steward at Long Ashton Court, Somerset. Cricket historians have it that he had been brought over from Ireland previously to be a footman there. A line of Irish Graces has been researched back to Norman times, but the critical link with Henry Grace has never been established. The Graces themselves see their ancestry a further generation back through William Grace, rope maker, of Charlbury, Oxfordshire, who died in 1772, with earlier connections with Hinton Underwood on the Buckinghamshire border.

Henry and Elizabeth Mills Grace had three daughters, Mary, Ann and Elizabeth, and a son Henry Mills, born 22 February 1808. It was his marriage to Martha Pocock at St Michael's, Bristol, on 3 November 1831, that led to this prodigious family of cricketing Graces. The Pococks had illustrious forebears. A Nicholas Pocock was a notable marine artist. Several of his paintings can be seen in the Merchant Venturers Hall at Bristol. Martha's father, George Pocock, was a highly successful Bristol schoolmaster proprietor of a large private school on St Michael's Hill, Bristol, and a scientific inventor of some eccentricity. He produced a caning machine for schools, but his outstanding inventions were in the Aeropleustic Art, or the navigation in the air by the use of kites or buoyant sails. He travelled the local countryside in a carriage drawn by a kite and often outpaced horse-drawn vehicles. In 1828 he caused a national stir by travelling from Bristol to the Ascot Races in his kite carriage where King George IV was much impressed. George Pocock is reputed to have flown his young daughter, Martha, across the Avon Gorge in a box kite. There may never have been any cricket Graces!

It was a delightfully happy and productive marriage. They lived first at Long Ashton, then after Henry had qualified as a doctor in 1831 (so many of the later Graces became doctors), at Downend House, Downend, at that time a long straggling village four miles from Bristol. A keen sportsman and a good and popular doctor, ably supported by Martha, he entered every aspect of village life.

They had five sons and four daughters; Henry, born 31 January 1833; Annie 1834; Fanny Hellings, 28 May 1838; Alfred, 17 May 1840; Edward Mills, 28 November 1841; Alice Rose, 21 March 1845; Elizabeth Blanche, 5 December 1846; William Gilbert, 18 July 1848 and George Frederick, 13 December 1850. They were all born at Downend House although there is

The Chesnuts, Downend.

a suggestion that William Gilbert was born at the nearby mid-wife's Clematis Cottage.

By 1850 the family had outgrown Downend House and moved across the road to the Chesnuts, spelt so by the Graces but Chestnuts locally. It was in the orchard behind this house that all the Grace boys began their cricket careers. Any spare moment of the year found Dr H.M., Uncle Alfred Pocock coaching the boys, often with mother watching, encouraging and criticising.

These two Pococks had a great influence on the successful course they were to pursue, and in a wider sense on the development of what was then little more than a rustic pastime into an international sport.

The girls, and even the dogs, were called upon to play their part. Don, Ponto and Noble fielded and retrieved the ball from the deeper recesses of the trees, their sure instincts telling them into which areas the ball was likely to be hit. The elders always demanded that the correct shots should be played. The dogs were completely confounded by that small boy Edward Mills who seemed to hit the ball into places where the others did not. No matter where the ball was bowled it always seemed to finish up amongst the trees on the leg side, or even in the pond. Only a small section of the boundary wall remains at that Downend orchard which gave birth to these incomparable Graces and in a wider sense to modern cricket.

The eldest sons, Henry and Alfred, both played cricket, but not with the distinction of their younger brothers. Both became doctors. Henry, who also married a Pocock, practised in Kingswood Hill, Bristol, and Alfred in Chipping Sodbury. The latter, known as the Hunting Doctor, was one of the best horsemen in the County and was the only Grace who smoked. He lived longer than any of the others!

Dr H.M. had considerable organising ability with a clear perception of the future of the game in the Bristol region. He was responsible for the formation of the Mangotsfield Club in 1844; its amalgamation with Coalpit Heath formed the West Gloucestershire Cricket Club in 1846. They played their cricket in the midst of the rapidly expanding Bristol coalfield. Thus the first steps towards a Gloucestershire County Cricket Club had been made. The expanding programme of fixtures and the status of the West Gloucestershire Club attracted the better club cricketers but no doubt Dr Grace saw it also as a vehicle to provide the exciting ability of all his sons with better cricket.

By the 1850s cricket had developed into a popular pastime which fitted happily into British life. One important factor in this context was the 'circus' of leading professional cricketers travelling the country to play local sides of seventeen or eighteen players. Formed and captained by William Clarke (1798-1856) of Nottingham, landlord of the old Trent Bridge Inn, cricket missionary and the first of cricket's entrepreneurs, his All England XI attracted vast crowds wherever they played.

His professional cricketers led a busy life. They also played for their own counties in the remaining challenge and single wicket games, and coached the game, and the expanding network of the railway system greatly facilitated their tours around the country. They first came westwards in 1850 to play against eighteen of Ross, Hereford, Cirencester at Hereford then extended their tour to include Lansdown and Cirencester in 1852 and 1853. No doubt this prompted Dr H.M. to arrange for them to come to Bristol in 1854 to play against XXII of his West Gloucestershire.

This historic game was played on 22, 23 and 24 June 1854 on the Back Fields behind the Full Moon at Stokes Croft, Bristol, and was to prove the first milestone along the Gloucestershire Road. Dr Grace's gardener from Downend prepared the field and the wicket, the doctor captained the West Gloucestershire XXII and his eldest son, Henry, and Uncle Alfred Pocock also played. Mr Wintle, the landlord of the Full Moon, paid £65 for the visitors' expenses. They call that sponsorship nowadays! In these 'against odds' games all twenty-two would have fielded and the field, although without a boundary, must have been a crowded place, but not crowded enough to stop West Gloucestershire from being outgunned by 149 runs. The result may have been a foregone conclusion but, for the first time, the local cricketers and the public had seen and admired the way in which the best cricketers in the land had behaved and played their game. Perhaps of deeper significance was the fact that Mrs Martha Grace had brought her six-year-old son to the game and together, in her pony carriage, they watched every ball bowled in those three days. In after years he remembered the tents around the ground but, above all, the top hats worn by some of the All England players. That boy, William Gilbert Grace, was to become the greatest cricketer in the history of the game.

The All England XI returned to Bristol on 6, 7 and 8 August 1855 and this time the West Gloucestershire XXII were beaten by 165 runs. Dr Grace, son Henry and Uncle Alfred Pocock again played but two younger Grace boys were also included, Alfred (fifteen) and Edward Mills (thirteen). The latter had been sent for hurriedly from Kempe's School at Long Ashton to make his first appearance in big time cricket at long stop. He scampered about to such good effect that William Clarke presented him with a bat at the end of the game and Mrs Grace with a book of practical hints on cricket. That year Dr Grace and Alfred Pocock were in regular combat with the All England team. They had already played against them at Neath and Cirencester earlier in the season, and the day following this second Back Fields game they were all in Cardiff.

The All England men were in Bristol the following year, 14, 15 and 16 August 1856 but this time in the better surroundings at the Clifton Cricket Club ground on Durdham Down against XXII of Bristol and District. The deficit was reduced to 12 runs.

The seasons passed. 1862 and 1863 were critical years in the history of Gloucestershire cricket. By 1862 Dr H.M. had added another dimension to his cricketing activities. His West Gloucestershire team continued to play, but he was now directing his attention to Gentlemen of Gloucestershire games and was advocating the formation of a Gloucestershire Club, no doubt with the example of Kent, Sussex, Hampshire, Cambridgeshire, Surrey, Nottinghamshire and Yorkshire in mind. There was also a personal incentive. His third son, Edward Mills, now twenty, was exciting comment around the country. Dr H.M. and Mrs Grace were regular visitors to the Canterbury Festival then as now, although not to the same degree, a cricket, social, theatrical week of carnival. In 1862 the Gentlemen of Kent were to play M.C.C. but at the last moment M.C.C. found themselves a player short. The Kent Secretary approached Dr Grace for E.M.'s assistance. He was not a member of the M.C.C. and that was to cause some later repercussions. However he played. He made 192 not out and took all ten wickets in the second innings!

It was this, no doubt, that prompted his mother to write to George Parr, the Captain and Manager of the England team, to suggest that he give him a trial, adding prophetically that she had a younger son who would be a better cricketer because he had a sounder defence.

E.M. did go on the Parr tour to Australia in 1863/64. But much else had happened in the Gloucestershire cricket world during 1862 and 1863. On 8 and 9 July 1862 Dr H.M.'s Gentlemen of Gloucestershire defeated the Gentlemen of Devon by an innings and 77 runs at the Durdham Down ground. Some cricket historians and W.G. in his much later autobiography list this as the first of the Gloucestershire games. A Bristol press report of the game comments ... 'the County has made a good beginning and we hope they will retain the laurels they have so gallantly won and, who knows, but in time they will be fit protagonists for Cambridge, Yorkshire, Kent and even Surrey itself'. Three Graces – Henry, Alfred and E.M. played in this game and a fourth was added for the return game played at Teignbridge on 25, 26 August. W.G. aged fourteen opened the innings with E.M. He later considered this to be his first 'important' match.

These two matches had tested the cricket resources of the County. Dr H.M. had fully justified the urging of the establishment of a County Club.

1863 saw a further advance in these 'County' games. The two Gentlemen of Devon games were played again, the second of these at Tiverton. In this game the senior Graces – Henry, Alfred, Uncle Alfred Pocock and E.M. grumbled terribly at the state of the wicket. On the completion of the Devon innings seeing a big roller in the corner of the field they pulled it out and rolled the pitch. E.M. then made 132. 1863 also saw the first encounter against Somerset, at the Sydenham Fields, Bath on 24, 25 August which Gloucestershire won by 87 runs. W.G. now fifteen made 52 not out in the first innings. But the highlight of the season was the visit of Parr's XI to Bristol just before their departure for Australia. The match was billed as XXII of Bristol and District *v* All England XI, and was played at the Durdham Down ground. These titles can be confusing but there can be no doubt that the core of the local side was from Dr H.M.'s West Gloucestershire. Four Graces played – Henry, Alfred, E.M., and W.G. The team also included D. Bernard who is Dr Richard Bernard's great-grandfather, Dr David Edward Bernard, who later married Alice Rose, a younger daughter of the Graces. The match, sponsored by local sportsmen,

ALL ENGLAND XI. v. XXII. OF BRISTOL & DISTRICT,

ON

DURDHAM DOWN, Aug. 31 & Sept. 1 & 2, 1863.

BRISTOL. First Innings.

E. M. Grace, Esq.	l b w, b Jackson	37
D. E. Bernard, Esq.	b Willsher	0
W. Jones, Esq.	c Willsher, b Tarrant	10
J. D. B. Trenfield, Esq.	st H. Stephenson, b Tinley	13
S. Bramhall, Esq.	c Moore, b Jackson	7
E. A. Howsin, Esq.	b Jackson	0
J. Sewell, Esq.	c and b Tarrant	38
E. T. Daubeney, Esq.	c Stephenson, b Jackson	44
J. Allen, Esq.	b Tinley	3
W. G. Grace, Esq.	b Tinley	32
W. E. Mirehouse, Esq.	c Tarrant, b Tinley	1
A. F. Davie, Esq.	c Clarke, b Tinley	4
H. Grace, Esq.	b Jackson	0
J. F. Fussell, Esq.	st Stephenson, b Tinley	1
A. Grace, Esq.	c Anderson, b Tinley	3
T. H. Hill, Esq.	b Tinley	10
W. Pillinger, Esq.	b Jackson	0
J. Mirehouse, Esq.	c Anderson, b Tinley	2
R. Bruce, Esq.	b Jackson	0
— Savage, Esq.	c Moore, b Jackson	0
— Budge, Esq.	st H. Stephenson, b Tinley	0
L. Harris, Esq.	not out	1
	B 2, 1-b 4	6
	Total	**212**

ENGLAND. First Innings. Second Innings.

	First Innings		Second Innings	
Tarrant	c Sewell, b Daubeney	7	run out	7
Willsher	b E. M. Grace	11	c and b E. M. Grace	13
E. Stephenson	c W. G. Grace, b Daubeney	7	c E.M.Grace, b W. G. Grace	11
Hayward	b Daubeney	3	c sub, b Daubeney	5
W. H. Moore, Esq.	b E. M. Grace	8	b E. M. Grace	3
Anderson	b E. M. Grace	4	b Howsin	6
Clarke	c W.Mirehouse, b E.M.Grace	4	c Budge, b E. M. Grace	8
Julius Cæsar	b E. M. Grace	0	st Pillinger, b Daubeney	5
H. H. Stephenson	not out	18	st Pillinger, b E. M. Grace	13
Jackson	c and b Daubeney	15	c Davie, b E. M. Grace	12
Tinley	c Sewell, b Daubeney	6	not out	17
	L-b 1, w 2	3	b 1, w 5	6
	Total	**86**	**Total**	**106**

Result,—The Twenty-two win by an innings and 20 runs.

---

aroused the greatest interest and the locals beat the England XI by an innings and twenty runs. E.M. made 37 and the fifteen-year-old W.G. 32 against the deadliest round arm bowlers in the country.

It was not to be a happy tour for E.M. He was ill for most of

the voyage out and did not distinguish himself on the cricket
field. He stayed on a while to recuperate but never went to
Australia again. When he did return home he found his tall, shy
young brother beginning to display his tremendous talents and
following closely in his footsteps. That season W.G. made the
first of his many centuries; 170 for the South Wales team on
their tour at Hove. Like some schoolboy report John Lillywhite's Companion for 1864 states: 'Mr W. G. Grace promises
to be a good bat. Bowls very fairly.' However, it was in July
1866 when he was just eighteen that he burst dramatically into
top-class cricket, playing for an England XI against Surrey at
the Oval. Having made 224 not out on the first day, he got
permission from his captain on the third to go up to nearby
Crystal Palace where he won a 440 yards hurdle race in the
National Olympian Association Meeting. From then on his
centuries and double centuries became commonplace and this
was to be the pattern for the rest of his long career – runs galore.
Whenever he returned to Bristol Club games he showed abso-
lutely no mercy. Martha's prophecy to George Parr that she
had a younger son who would be a better cricketer than E.M.
had certainly been fulfilled.

There was yet another Grace to come. George Frederick, the
last of the eight children, no doubt served his apprenticeship in
that Downend orchard encouraged by his father, that shrewd
mother, Uncle Alfred and his younger brothers. He promised
to be the best cricketer of them all. Two years younger than
W.G., and nine years younger than E.M., he was playing club
cricket before he was ten! In 1863, at the age of thirteen, he took
seven wickets for five runs for Stapleton against Hanham in
Bristol. Before he was fifteen he had played for a Gentlemen of
England XI against Oxford University. By sixteen he had
reached top-class cricket for England against M.C.C. at Lord's.
A young all-round cricketer of infinite potential with a gentle,
delightful personality and the image of his loving mother.

Such is the triumverate of Graces on which the future of
Gloucestershire cricket was to be built. Little wonder that
Gloucestershire will always be called the Shire of the Graces.

After the exciting events of 1862 and 1863 we have to wait
until 1868 for the next real step forward in the County's first-
class story. On 25 and 26 June 1868 Gloucestershire played and
beat M.C.C. and Ground by 134 runs on a West Country team's

An early photograph of the West Gloucestershire team taken at Knole Park on 12–13 July 1866. All five Grace brothers played in this match, the youngest G.F. was just 15 years of age. Left to right back row: *Rev. H.W. Barber, H.M. Grace (father of W.G.), H. Gruning (black beard), A. Pocock (uncle of W.G.).* Middle row: *W. G. Grace, Henry Grace, Dr E.M. Grace, Alfred Grace.* Front row: *F. Baker, W.J. Pocock, G.F. Grace, R. Brotherhood.*

first visit to Lord's. It is surprising to find that the County's first-class story does not begin here.

There is confusion over the official date of origin of Gloucestershire C.C.C. – 1870 or 1871. The problem lies in the fact that no written or reported formal declaration has ever been found. It will have been seen that Dr H. M. Grace organised Gentlemen of Gloucestershire or 'Gloucestershire' games from 1863 onwards. Rowland Bowen, that great cricket historian, caustically summed up the matter in the *Cricket Quarterly*, Vol. 1 No. 1 of January 1963 thus:

'There has been much mystery about the origins of the present club, and it is by no means entirely cleared up. Statements by apparently reputable authorities have hovered between 1870 and 1871, or indeed tried to have it both ways and perpetrated the following absurdity: In 1870 Dr H. M. Grace put the club on a sound basis, though it was not formally established until the following year. It is highly questionable whether any more meaningless sentence on a matter of cricket history has ever been written. It is curious that the precise date has been searched for by many people in the files of local newspapers without success. It is perhaps something to be able to establish the year precisely for the first time, viz. 1871.'

The source of contention is that there was already a 'County' club in 1870. At first it had been called the County of Gloucestershire and Cheltenham C.C. This was formed in 1842, but very little is to be found of its affairs and its cricket in contemporary newspapers. The *Cheltenham Free Press and Stroud Intelligencer* of 30 April 1842 reports 'the establishment of a cricket club to be called the County of Gloucestershire and Cheltenham C.C. is contemplated. Several gentlemen have already enrolled their names.' A notice in the same newspaper of 25 June 1842 to the effect that 'the County of Gloucester Archery and Cricket Club propose when their arrangements are completed having the exclusive use of the Cricket and Archery ground two days a week' indicates its lowly standing.

The *Cheltenham Looker On* of 31 August 1844 which briefly reports a game between the County of Gloucester Club and the Proprietory College which the 'young gentlemen' won by an innings and 15 runs confirms the low standard of cricket it played. The Club closed in 1846.

The second 'County' club, the Cheltenham and County of Gloucester C.C., was formed towards the end of 1863 on a not so very much sounder basis. 1863 was a critical year for 'Gloucestershire' cricket. We have already seen that the Bristol and District XXII had gained a remarkable victory over the All England XI at Bristol, that W.G. had played for the first time against the best cricketers in the country in this game, and that his father Dr H.M. was suggesting the formation of a County club to join the select band of counties calling themselves first-class.

There was a surprising number of local newspapers in Cheltenham at this time, and they indicate an increasing interest in cricket. The first suggestion that something is afoot is to be found in the *Cheltenham Examiner* of January 1863 which reports a General Meeting of the Cheltenham Cricket Club at the Royal Hotel at which it was announced that 'Mr F. P. Fenner, a gentleman formerly well-known as one of the greatest players in the country, was to become landlord of the Hotel. Mr C. H.

Jessop of Church Street was the club's secretary' and concludes, 'after business, excellent supper':

The *Cheltenham Examiner* of Wednesday, 11 November, reports that it was unanimously agreed 'that in absence of any cricket centre in the County of Gloucester an attempt be made to supply that want by the formation of a new ground and the establishment of a club to be called the Cheltenham and County of Gloucester Cricket Club. The Folly Ground has been proved unsuitable over a number of years. A new ground is needed and a meeting at the Royal Hotel suggested a move to Hales Road. It is reckoned that £200 be wanted for the first year.' The inaugural match on the new Hales Road Ground was on 11 May 1864 against Cheltenham College, which the College won on the first innings.

The *Cheltenham Free Press* of Saturday, 12 December 1863, lists Colonel Berkeley as President, Colonel Hart as Treasurer and Mr F. P. Fenner as Secretary of the Club. The *Cheltenham Examiner* of Wednesday, 16 December, under the heading Cheltenham and Gloucestershire C.C.: 'the list (of subscribers) contains some of the best cricketers in the County.' Not a Grace or a South of the County cricketer among them! In all of the local cricket reports of these years is there any mention of the exciting cricketers and the developments of the game in the South of the County? Gloucestershire's tribal divisions seem already firmly established!

Rowland Bowen writes in *Cricket Quarterly* Vol. 1 No. 1 of January 1963, 'At the time of its end, Lord Fitzhardinge was President of the Club; he became a Vice President of the New County Club, with the Duke of Beaufort as President, which was formed later, in 1871. We still do not know precisely when. It clearly cannot be before the end of the Cheltenham organisation – one can imagine Lord Fitzhardinge's answer to an invitation to become Vice President of the County Club had it occurred while he was still President of another club called the County Club.'

There can be no dispute in terms of cricket. Dr H. M.'s 'Gloucestershire' playing in the Bristol area had the better cricketers at least two of whom had reached national status.

If the existence of this North of the County 'Gloucestershire' is the sole reason for 'official' refusal to permit the origin of Gloucestershire C.C.C. in 1870 then that seems to be a weak

Ashley Grange, Bristol – W.G. Grace's home for many years.

premise. This club had little to offer except its exaggerated title and Lord Fitzhardinge (the former Colonel Berkeley) as President. If it had not been for the formidable reputation that the Graces had built in their South of the County 'Gloucestershire' then there may never have been a Gloucestershire C.C.C. It is doubtful if the necessary inspiration and cricketers could have been found in the North. If it had, then the headquarters would have been at Cheltenham. No doubt the nearby County Town of Gloucester would have had something to say in that matter!

The issues, the bitter sweet germs of friction of this North versus South confrontation apply even today in the politics and field activities of all matters relating to Gloucestershire sport, but now a new dimension has been added: Gloucestershire is the North and Avon is the South. In terms of cricket history there can be no doubt: the Gloucestershire Road begins at Downend.

2 The Years of Grace
1870-1887

There is no Bristol newspaper report of 1869 or early 1870 to indicate the official formation of Gloucestershire C.C.C. and although there may be some confusion now, there did not seem to be any at the time. In 1870 the County played two first-class games against Surrey and another game against M.C.C. at Lord's. Dr H.M. had been organising County games since 1862, and he would only see these games as a logical progression of Gloucestershire cricket. By now his sons were creating sensation after sensation and crowds were flocking in to see them play on other Counties' grounds. Nor could there be any doubt of his own established authority in the game.

When on 2 June 1870 Dr E.M. led his Gloucestershire team on to Clifton C.C.'s ground at Durdham Down they joined the Counties at the highest level of the English game – Kent, Lancashire, Middlesex, Nottinghamshire, Sussex, Surrey and Yorkshire. Gate charges were not allowed on the Down although an appeal for support was probably made to local businesses, clubs and individuals. The Centenary Booklet of the Bristol Schoolmasters C.C. states that the club contributed £2.2s.od. to help defray the costs of the game. The reciprocal arrangement with Surrey would have satisfied that Club.

The game aroused great interest. Excited crowds made their way to the Down attracted, no doubt, as much by the prospect of some free entertainment as the opportunity to see some of the best cricketers of the country in combat. A band played. Tents, carriages and spectators lined up behind the flags marking the arena. There were no boundaries. If the ball was hit into the spectators then the batsmen ran until they dropped, or the fielders had retrieved it, no doubt subjected to ribald hilarity or obstruction if they belonged to the opposition.

Gloucestershire won this first match by 51 runs and the return at the Oval by an innings and 129 runs; W.G. made 143, appropriately the first ever Gloucestershire century. Two days later he made 172 for the County against M.C.C. at Lord's. E.M. did not play in the Oval game. He was one of five changes.

GLOUCESTERSHIRE V. SURREY,

ON

DURDHAM DOWN, June 2, 3 & 4, 1870

GLO'STERSHIRE.	First Innings.	Second Innings.
E. M. Grace, Esq.	c Southerton, b Street .. 2	c and b Vince 18
W. G. Grace, Esq.	c Pooley, b Southerton .. 26	c Pooley, b Southerton .. 25
T. G. Matthews, Esq.	c Street, b Southerton .. 5	c Mayo, b Southerton .. 7
F. Townsend, Esq.	b Street 11	c Pooley, b Southerton .. 20
G. F. Grace, Esq.	hit wicket b Southerton 16	c Griffith, b Southerton 1
C. R. Filgate, Esq.	c Griffith, b Street .. 15	not out 48
J. Halford, Esq.	l b w, b Street 6	hit wicket b Southerton.. 2
J. Mills, Esq.	c Pooley, b Southerton 15	c Pooley, b Southerton .. 2
J. A. Bush, Esq.	not out 3	c T. Humphrey, b Southerton 1
R. F. Miles, Esq.	run out 0	b Southerton 8
W. D. Macpherson, Esq.	c Street, b Southerton .. 2	b Southerton 5
	B 3, l-b 2 5	b 2, l-b 1 3
	Total 106	Total 167

SURREY.	First Innings.	Second Innings.
T. Humphrey ..	c Halford, b W.G. Grace 1	b G. F. Grace 5
Jupp	c E. M. Grace, b W.G.Grace 14	not out 50
E. Pooley ..	c Filgate, b W. G. Grace 10	c and b G. F. Grace.. .. 8
Brown ..	c Filgate, b W. G. Grace 3	c E. M. Grace, b G. F. Grace 3
H. H. Stephenson ..	b G. F. Grace 4	b W. G. Grace 0
R. Humphrey ..	c and b W. G. Grace .. 5	c E. M. Grace, b W. G. Grace 1
G. Griffith ..	not out 41	c Mills, b W. G. Grace .. 5
J. Street	b G. F. Grace 4	b Miles 5
H. Mayo, Esq.	c E. M. Grace, b G. F. Grace 15	b G. F. Grace 4
Vince	b G. F. Grace 1	c G. F. Grace, b Miles .. 0
J. Southerton	st Halford, b Miles .. 26	b Miles 0
	B 7, l-b 2, w 1 10	b 3, l-b 1, w 3 7
	Total 134	Total 88

ANALYSIS OF BOWLING.

GLOUCESTERSHIRE.	1st Innings.				2nd Innings.			
	Balls.	Runs.	Maidens.	Wickets.	Balls.	Runs.	Maidens.	Wickets.
Southerton ..	163	43	16	5	202	67	20	9
Street	160	58	12	4	72	38	2	0
Vince	—	—	—	—	124	59	14	1
SURREY.	1st Innings.				2nd Innings.			
W. G. Grace ..	124	65	11	5	136	27	23	4
G. F. Grace ..	140	56	15	4	204	31	35	3
E. M. Grace ..	20	2	3	0	—	—	—	—
R. F. Miles ..	4	1	0	1	64	23	6	3

Result, Gloucestershire wins by 51 runs.

GLOUCESTERSHIRE V. M.C.C.,

AT

LORD'S, August 1 & 2, 1870.

GLO'STERSHIRE.	First Innings.
W. G. Grace, Esq.	c Wootton, b Shaw .. 172
C. S. Gordon, Esq.	b Price 55
F. Townsend, Esq.	c Biddulph, b Price .. 0
G. F. Grace, Esq.	run out 9
J. A. Bush, Esq.	l b w, b Price 4
G. Strachan, Esq.	c Biddulph, b Price .. 0
W. H. Baily, Esq.	b Shaw 7
R. F. Miles, Esq.	b Shaw 0
J. J. Cross, Esq.	b Price 5
E. S. Morris, Esq.	c and b Shaw 13
A. C. Master, Esq.	not out 0
	B 8, l-b 5 13
	Total 276

M.C.C.	First Innings.	Second Innings.
J. Jardine, Esq. ..	run out 4	c Master, b G. F. Grace .. 18
Biddulph	c G. F. Grace, b Miles .. 0	c Gordon, b Miles 1
A. Shaw	c Townsend, b Miles .. 17	c G. F. Grace, b Miles .. 13
W. Price	c Townsend, b W. G. Grace 18	c Bush, b W. G. Grace .. 25
J. Fellows, Esq.	run out 0	run out 50
W. Parnell, Esq.	b W. G. Grace 2	c Bush, b W. G. Grace .. 2
Wootton	c and b Miles 10	c Bush, b W. G. Grace .. 15
R. Forster, Esq.	c W. G. Grace, b Miles .. 0	c Bush, b Miles.. 1
E. Craigie, Esq.	c W. G. Grace, b Miles .. 0	c Bush, b W. G. Grace .. 0
W. Moore, Esq.	not out 10	c Master, b G. F. Grace .. 2
Farrands.. ..	b W. G. Grace 2	not out 5
	B 1, l-b 1 2	b 2 2
	Total 76	Total 114

ANALYSIS OF THE BOWLING.

GLOUCESTERSHIRE.—1ST INNINGS.				
	Balls.	Runs.	Maidens.	Wickets.
A. Shaw	254	107	17	4
Price	172	66	12	5
Farrands..	68	34	4	0
Wootton	80	56	5	0
M.C.C.—1ST INNINGS.				
W. G. Grace	66	38	3	3
R. F. Miles	64	34	2	5
2ND INNINGS.				
W. G. Grace	52	27	5	4
R. F. Miles	86	44	4	3
G. F. Grace	104	41	14	2

Result,—Gloucestershire wins by an innings and 88 runs.

A. C. Master who played in the M.C.C. game is Algernon Chester-Master of the Almondsbury Chester-Master family. He was educated at Marlborough College and played two games for the County. He was the father of Edgar Chester-Master who played one game and died in Durban, South Africa, in 1979.

The *Wisden* reports of the 1870 and 1871 seasons read as follows:

1870. 'The Shire played a brief but brilliant cricket season in 1870 winning every match of the eleven played. There was no County Club for Gloucestershire then in existence, the matches being arranged by, and played under, the management of W. G. Grace; however, there is very little doubt that in 1871 a County Crisket Club for Gloucestershire will be established on a firm basis . . .'

1871. 'The formation in 1871 of a County Club for Gloucestershire is a most important addition to the County Cricket Clubs which, after all is said, written and done, are the real mainstays of the popularity of the game . . .'

Gloucestershire had entered the national cricket arena with a flourish led by their strapping bearded giant, supported on the field by his brothers and off it by his father. W.G. had by now taken over E.M.'s position as the leading cricketer in the country. There were others, but they had no more than walking-on parts; the Graces held the centre of the stage. All of them were amateurs and, as we shall see later, some more than others. They had grown up together on the cricket field. After all it was now more than twenty years since Dr H.M. had shown them the Road ahead. There was Frank Townsend (better remembered perhaps as the father of an illustrious cricketing son, Charles Townsend), tall, handsome, Headmaster of a Clifton School, a popular all round sportsman who could bowl a crafty underarm; J. A. Bush, 'Frizzie' to his friends, son of Colonel Bush, the first C.O. of the Bristol Rifles; Clifton, in 1872 the first Gloucestershire Rugby international, he played locally for Clifton R.F.C., for forty years Sword Bearer of the City of Bristol, great wicket keeper, cheerful, frolicksome and as heavily whiskered as W.G.; T. G. Matthews, who made the first first-class double-century (201) against Surrey at Clifton the following season; R. Fenton Miles (of the great King's Weston House, Bristol family), slow left arm bowler who contributed greatly to the early successes, and George Strachan from Prestbury, near Cheltenham, who later became Captain of Surrey. All of them were watched over by Gloucestershire's own umpire, C. K. Pullin.

In the face of such formidable competition it is no wonder that the Cheltenham and County of Gloucester C.C. wound up its operations on 14 March 1871. The Surrey game of 1870 was the only one to be played on the Downs. By 1871 the County had obtained permission from the College Council to play on Clifton Close and spectators could now be charged admission. Gloucestershire games continued to be played there until 1932.

Two games were added to the fixture list, against Nottinghamshire at Clifton and then away at Trent Bridge where twenty-five thousand spectators crowded in attracted by the

Graces. Gloucestershire suffered their first defeat, and by ten wickets, although W.G. made 79 in the first innings and 116 in the second.

Perhaps the most significant event of the year was the death of Dr H.M. on 23 December. The godfather of Gloucestershire cricket, his vision, patience and the respect in which he was held had led it from humble beginnings in his own Mangotsfield, Coalpit Heath, Downend villages of South Gloucestershire into the national arena. He was buried in Downend Churchyard. His tombstone is inscribed: 'In fond remembrance of Henry Mills Grace, M.R.C.S. & L.S.A., Surgeon to the Royal Gloucestershire Hussars who died on December 23rd, 1871. Age 63

First recorded minutes of Gloucestershire C.C.C., 26 April 1873.

years.' No reference to cricket but he had lived to see his dreams fulfilled. A thriving Gloucestershire C.C.C. is his memorial.

Games against Sussex and Yorkshire began in 1872. Yorkshire had repeatedly requested a fixture appreciating the drawing power of the Graces, and they were not to be disappointed. In the first game at Bramall Lane, Sheffield, in the two innings W.G. made 150, took 15 wickets for 79 and Gloucestershire won by an innings and 172 runs.

There is no record of the background to the happenings off the field until 1873. By now E.M. is shown to be the Secretary and W.G. the Captain. E.M. had captained the first ever game and perhaps it had been decided that he should run the Club with W.G. as Captain. W.G. was not a great administrator and from the beginning the Minutes are in E.M.'s own handwriting and continue so until his retirement as Secretary in 1909.

They begin: 'Meeting held at the White Lion Hotel, Bristol on Saturday, 26 April at 2 o'clock.' The White Lion later became The Grand. Meetings continued to be held there until after the Second World War. The first reported meetings are taken up with a dispute with Nottinghamshire that obviously had developed during the previous winter. A Committee Meeting of 20 March is referred to although the Committee may well have been in existence in 1871, or even perhaps 1870. Dr H.M. was listed as Hon. Treasurer for 1870 and 1871, and now included were Dr E.M. and four others who had appeared on the cricket field for Gloucestershire – R. F. Miles, J. A. Bush, T. G. Matthews, F. Townsend. The issue of the row which had been brewing with Nottinghamshire was whether W.G. would play at Trent Bridge in the coming season. They refused to make the fixture on the day in question until they could be certain. He had already promised to play in Joseph Rowbottom's Benefit Match in Yorkshire. On his behalf E.M. suggested a compromise date but the Committee disagreed. When asked if he would play at Trent Bridge, E.M. icily refused. The temperature rose and E.M.'s next entry was crossed out later by the Chairman with an angry pen. It would have read: 'After more angry conversation of not too polite a nature (as the Reverend J. Greene disputed the correctness of the notes taken by the Secretary of the Committee Meeting March 20 saying that his memory was superior to the black and white testimony of the Secretary).'

The matter was then adjourned until W.G. could attend. He didn't. He had promised Rowbottom, who had been down to London to remind him that he would play. Twenty-three thousand attended the game, twelve thousand on the first day. Such was the drawing power of W.G.'s presence. Nottinghamshire refused to change the date and Yorkshire gladly took their place. Nor did Nottinghamshire 'challenge' in 1873 or 1874 but fixtures were resumed in 1875, by which time Nottinghamshire had cooled down. Perhaps it was W.G. rather than Gloucestershire who was missed since W.G. filled the grounds wherever he went. It was said much later that half the bricks of the pavilions of the County Grounds around England belonged to W.G.

The Graces may have been rumbustious, argumentative and shrewd characters, but there was always a mischievous twinkle in a Grace eye. E.M.'s derisive comment of a Committee Meeting held at the White Lion Hotel, Bristol, on Tuesday, 25 November, at 3 o'clock is as follows:

Present   E.M. Grace and that's all.

The matter does not appear to have been discussed at the next Committee Meeting!

Much more was to happen in that first exhilarating decade and 1873 was an eventful year. Gloucestershire and Nottinghamshire were bracketed as the Champion County. In those days there was no County Championship as we know it. Before 1886 the Counties more or less decided which was the Champion County by counting the number of wins, no reference being taken of the losses in first-class games. Fixtures were arranged by challenge, challenges being accepted or refused and it was not until 1891 that all the Counties were to play one another.

In 1873 the County's tally was 4–0 in wins and Nottinghamshire 5–1, so it was decided the two had shared the honours. Nottinghamshire did not play Gloucestershire because of the row. If they had, then perhaps Gloucestershire would have been the Champion County!

It was in 1873 that W.G. registered the first ever double in cricket; 2,139 runs and 106 wickets. That year he married the daughter of his first cousin, Agnes Nicholls Day, at St Matthias West Brompton, Earl's Court, on 9 October. Gloucestershire colleague, J. A. Bush, was his best man. Fifteen days later the happy couple left Southampton on the Australian tour, seen off by a party of Gloucestershire well-wishers led by his mother, Martha.

In his *Cricketing Reminiscences and Personal Recollections* of 1899 (incidentally ghost written by a cousin, William John Gordon, part-time sub-editor of *Boy's Own Paper*, and author of many books), W.G. states:

> 'As a result of overtures made to me in the spring of 1873 I agreed to form a team to visit Australia at the end of the year. The invitation came from a number of gentlemen connected with the Melbourne Cricket Club, the M.C.C. of Australia, who cabled me enquiring "Can you, will you, bring a team at the end of the year?"'

He selected and engaged a party of twelve amateurs which included G.F., W. R. Gilbert and J. A. Bush of Gloucestershire. It was a strenuous tour of cricket, travel and junketing and at the end resulted in controversy and animosity between W.G. and the Australian authorities who were in open conflict over a number of issues. It looks as if the team received a percentage of the gates which had exceeded all Australian expectations; they reckoned they had been fleeced. The tour party arrived back on 17 May 1874, just in time to start the cricket season and by the 21st W.G. and G.F. were playing for Thornbury against Clifton at Alveston. They both made centuries.

At Melbourne on 12 March 1874 the touring team had played XVIII of Victoria. Both W.G. and G.F. were bowled out by a young giant of a bowler from up state Sandhurst by the name of William Midwinter. Perhaps it was then that W.G. discovered Midwinter had been born at St Briavels in the Forest of Dean. In fact, his parents had emigrated to Australia when William was nine and settled on the Bendigo Goldfields. Midwinter joined the Melbourne Cricket Club in 1873 and played against the tourists in both their matches. In every respect he resembled a beardless W.G., 6' 2", 14 stone, a great all rounder with a strong right arm and known locally as the Bendigo Giant. After the tour he was soon playing in inter-state games and then for the All Australia XI which registered the first ever win against an England touring side on the James Lillywhite tour of 1876/77. Midwinter was now an international cricketer. There is no evidence that W.G. was involved but he came to this country immediately afterwards, landing in the Thames but was in Bristol the next day. No reference was made in the Minutes of 1877 of his arrival nor his eventual departure in 1882.

Midwinter first played for the County of his birth against England at the Oval in the game that resulted in an expenses flare-up. He took 7 for 35 in the first innings and 4 for 46 in the second and proceeded to play a great part in the success of the 1877 season.

Gloucestershire were the outright leaders of the Counties in 1876. It was an all round team performance with W.G. leading the way having made 1,278 runs in August. In ten days he had made 839 runs, 344 for M.C.C., 177 against Nottinghamshire followed by 318 not out against Yorkshire at Cheltenham, the highest ever Gloucestershire score. Before the end of the month he had added 400 not out against Grimsby XXII. As Tom Emmett, the great Yorkshire bowler and wit remarked 'It was Grace before lunch, Grace after lunch, Grace all day'.

Then came 1877, perhaps the greatest season in the County's history. That first handful of years was no doubt the most successful in the Club's history and 1877 the greatest of these. Seven games out of eight were won and Gloucestershire had not lost a game in two years. W.G. made only one century but he had a very good bowling season.

A full Australian team toured this country in 1878. They arrived with eleven players and were joined by Midwinter who played a number of games for them in the first part of the season. On 20 June, when they were to play Middlesex at Lord's, Bannerman and Midwinter were preparing to open the Australian innings when W.G. and J. A. Bush burst into the Pavilion 'and entered into conversation with Midwinter'. They 'persuaded' him to depart with them for the Oval where Gloucestershire were to begin their game against Surrey. W.G.'s parting shot 'You haven't the ghost of a show against Middlesex' stung the Australians into action. Their manager set off in pursuit. The Oval gates were shut in his face. W.G. shouted back, 'You are a damn lot of sneaks'. The Australians beat Middlesex by 98 runs and Surrey beat Gloucestershire by 14.

The Australians were rightly furious for not only had they some bitter memories of W.G.'s behaviour in the 1873 tour of Australia, but already on this tour they had complained about

Opposite;
Gloucestershire team
*1874.*Left to right –
standing: *C. K.*
Pullen (umpire), T. G.
Matthews,F. J.
Crook, J. A. Bush,
R. F. Bush, E. M.
Grace, E. M. Knapp.
Seated: *E. C. B.*
Ford, F. Townsend,
W. G., G. F. Grace,
R. F. Miles.

the three Gloucestershire professionals–amateurs playing against them for the Gentlemen of England; now here was W.G. kidnapping one of their key players from under their noses. They were further incensed because he was now playing for an English county, thus making him ineligible to play for them again on tour. The increasingly bitter letters that passed between the County and Conway, the Australian Manager, were written painstakingly into the Minute Book by Dr E.M. All, that is, except the final apology from W.G. that settled the matter. The relevant page is blank except for the heading: 'Mr W. G. Grace wrote a letter of apology to the Australians.'

The letter is to be found in the Australian account of the Tour:

> The Cottage,
> Kingswood Hill,
> Bristol.
> July 21st.

Dear Sir,

I am sorry that my former expression of regret to the Australian cricketers has not been considered satisfactory. Under the circumstances, and without going further into the matter, I wish to let bygones be bygones. I apologise again, and express my extreme regret to Mr Conway, Boyle and yourself, and through you to the Australian cricketers, that in the excitement of the moment I should have made use of unparliamentary language to Mr Conway. I can do no more but assure you that you will meet a hearty welcome and a good ground at Clifton.

> Yours truly,
> W. G. Grace.

They did and they handed out the first ever defeat to the County on a home ground with fast bowler, Spofforth, in full cry. Midwinter did not play. He had a strained thumb!

Midwinter continued to play for Gloucestershire and became the first of the inter-hemisphere cricket commuters. He commuted between England and Australia from 1880-1882 to play six successive seasons of cricket with voyages of forty to fifty days between each. He toured with English teams to Australia and later, on his permanent return home in 1883, with Australian teams to England. He holds the unique record for being the

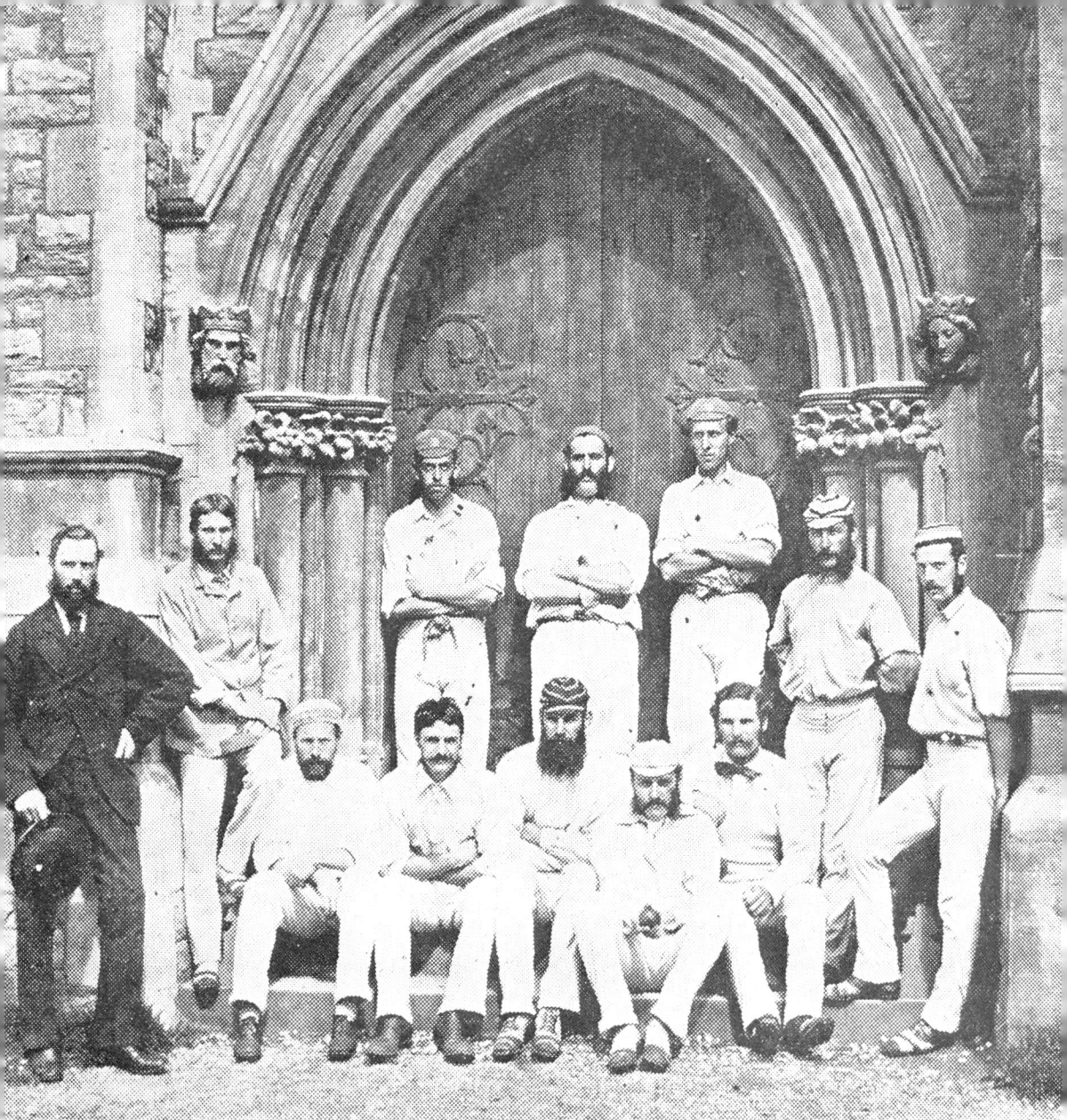

only cricketer to have played in Tests for both England and Australia against each other, four times for England and eight for Australia. He died on 3 December 1890, aged thirty-nine, saddened by the deaths of his wife and two daughters. He was buried in the Roman Catholic compound of the Melbourne Cemetery beside his wife and children. The graves and the surrounding area were cleared recently by the Melbourne Cricket Society.

The first of the County Colts games had been played in 1873 at the Gloucester Spa, but it was not until 1877 that these games became a feature of the early season, perhaps with the dual purpose of satisfying the outburst of the county-wide acclamation following the success of the 1876 season, and the need to recruit younger players into the County teams. The habit was established to play one of these games in the North of the County and the other in Bristol. In the years that followed Cirencester and Gloucester staged these games but then, as in recent years, they reverted to Bristol owing to the cost of staging the games, and then only spasmodically outside Bristol.

The part the North of the County was to play in the affairs of Gloucestershire Cricket may have suffered from the demise of the Cheltenham and County of Gloucestershire Cricket Club in 1871 but it brought the beginning of a flourishing Cheltenham C.C., and of what became, and still remains, one of the great occasions of the cricket season, The Cheltenham Cricket Festival. Gloucestershire played Surrey on the Cheltenham College Ground on 18, 19 and 20 July 1872. It would appear that James Lillywhite, the College coach and a member of one of those great Sussex cricketing families, managed the game. The first reference to him in the Minutes of 1 June 1874 reads: 'that James Lillywhite shall have the management of the Cheltenham match, the same as he had for last season, and that he shall be paid the sum of ten pounds for so doing.'

The single Cheltenham game became two in 1878 and so the Cheltenham week began. A Minute for 9 March 1878 reads: 'A letter from James Lillywhite read to the Meeting – also Mr James Lillywhite attended in order to induce this Committee to organise a week's cricket at Cheltenham instead of only one match. After a prolonged discussion it was proposed by Capt. T. S. Warren, seconded by F. Townsend, that we are obliged to decline having two matches at Cheltenham this year through the dates of the matches having already been fixed. But that it shall be taken into consideration by this Committee for next year.' It was. 'James Lillywhite was paid £120 to run it and cover all the local expenses.' The games played were against Sussex on 19, 20 and 21 August, and Yorkshire on 22, 23 and 24 August 1878.

·Both James Lillywhite and his son-in-law, Edwin W. Lawrence, appeared at later and relevant meetings. Lillywhite

NOTTINGHAMSHIRE
v.
GLOUCESTERSHIRE.

A GRAND

CRICKET MATCH

Will, by the kind permission of the Council, be played on the

COLLEGE GROUND,
CHELTENHAM,

MONDAY, TUESDAY & WEDNESDAY,
AUGUST 13th, 14th, and 15th, 1877.

The Players will be Selected from the following Names :—

NOTTINGHAMSHIRE.		GLOUCESTERSHIRE.	
Mr A. W. Cursham	J. Hind	Mr W. G. Grace	Mr W. O. Moberly
Mr R. Tolley	F. Morley	Dr E. M. Grace	Mr C. R. Filgate
R. Daft	W. Oscroft	Mr G. F. Grace	Mr W. Fairbanks
F. Wild	A. Shrewsbury	Mr F. Townsend	Mr F. G. Monkland
J. Selby	F. Tye	Mr J. Bush	Mr W. G. Gilbert
W. Barnes	W. Flowers	Mr R. E. Bush	Mr C. Haynes
M. Sherwin	A. J. Brooks	Mr R. F. Miles	W. Midwinter

Admission Each Day, One Shilling.

Tickets for the Three Days, 2s.; Colleges and Schools, Sixpence each; if taken on or before Saturday, August 11th. Reserved Enclosure Sixpence each.

TO BE HAD OF MR. JAMES LILLYWHITE, 3, QUEEN'S CIRCUS.

N.B.—*Should the Match terminate early, a Second Match, namely,*

GLOUCESTERSHIRE *VERSUS* CHELTENHAM
(WITH BROOMSTICKS) (WITH BATS)
Will be Played.

Refreshments supplied by Mr George, 367, High Street. Luncheon at 2-30, 3s. per head.

Cards of the Match will be Printed on the Ground, Price Twopence.

S. H. BROOKES, PRINTER, 370, HIGH STREET, CHELTENHAM.

died on 24 November 1882 but the Minutes of 27 October 1882 stated: 'Resolved that in the event of the death of James Lilly-white before the matches at Cheltenham in 1883, his son-in-law, Mr Lawrence, or the representatives of the family, shall

1877 team that beat England at the Oval by 5 wickets. Left to right – back row – *W. O. Moberley, W. Fairbanks, G. F. Grace, F. G. Monkland, W. R. Gilbert, W. Midwinter.* Front row: *Capt. Kingscote, F. Townsend, R. F. Miles, W. G. Grace, E. M. Grace.*

have the management of the week, the same as he has hitherto done the same.'

Midwinter was the first of the Gloucestershire professional cricketers. W. H. Hall had played for the Gloucestershire team that had so soundly beaten the M.C.C. and Ground team at Lord's in 1868 but that is the only reference to him and, as was the custom in those days, he was probably a bowler. He had little opportunity to display his talents; W.G. and E.M. shared all the wickets.

William Alfred Woof, the second full-time professional, born in Gloucester on 9 July 1858, appeared in the second of the Colts matches to be played at Cirencester in 1878. A slow left arm bowler he took four wickets, including W.G.'s, in the Gloucestershire innings. His first County game was against Surrey at the Oval on 19 June 1880, and he and Midwinter were great friends. He played regularly from 1881 following G. F. Grace's death at the end of the previous season. Midwinter did not return for the 1883 season. His place was taken by Jack

Painter, a batsman who could bowl. (W.G. was once loudly barracked by the locals for not bowling him during a Cheltenham week game.) Both these players appeared from Colts matches and were North of the County players from Gloucester and Bourton-on-the-Water respectively, as was the third, Fred Roberts from Mickleton. He first appeared in 1887 and, in a career that continued until 1905, took 963 wickets for Gloucestershire. The first professionals were generally bowler work horses, and amateurs the batsmen. Alec Bedser has recently commented that batsmen alone seemed eligible for knighthoods; the only bowler thus honoured was Sir Francis Drake! Few of the amateurs became established players; they were mostly university students and schoolmasters who played during their summer vacations. It was also the custom to play a number of local players for home games outside Bristol.

Rule book 1879.

After the tremendous achievements of the first decade, the County's fortunes gradually slipped. Perhaps the exhilarating excitement of success had been overtaken by dull routine. Gradually the professionals became the permanent backbone of the team whereas, originally, and until the arrival of Midwinter in 1877, the teams consisted of amateurs. The number of professionals on the staff gradually increased from one in 1877, two by 1878, to seven in 1901 and then nine in 1907. Nine professionals played in the Warwickshire game of 1912.

The amateurs came and went and W.G. alone seemed to go on for ever. Only those with the ability or private means survived. As the seventies passed into the eighties most of the early heroes, Frank Townsend, T. G. Matthews, J. A. Bush and W. R. Gilbert, had left the field. Even E.M. played less for the County, no doubt tied up with his increasing secretarial duties and his official and recreational activities. Only a few had distinguished themselves until the arrival of C. L. Townsend and G. L. Jessop in the early nineties. James Cranston, a left hand batsman, first played for the County in 1876 but left Bristol in 1883 to play a few games for Warwickshire, the County of his birth. He returned to Gloucestershire in 1889 with great success and played for England in the 1890 Test against Australia at the Oval. Others were William Octavius Moberly, William Wade Fitzherbert Pullen, who had made his Gloucestershire debut just before his sixteenth birthday, William H. Brain, Cliftonian, born in Wales, wicket keeper who took over from J. A. Bush

ENGLAND v AUSTRALIA 1880 (Only Test)

Played at Kennington Oval, London, on 6, 7, 8 September.
Toss: England.   Result: ENGLAND won by five wickets.
Debuts: England – W. Barnes, E.M. Grace, G.F. Grace, W.G. Grace, Hon. A. Lyttelton, F. Morley, F. Penn, A.G. Steel; Australia – G. Alexander, G.J. Bonnor, T.U. Groube, P.S. McDonnell, W.H. Moule, G.E. Palmer, J. Slight.

William Gilbert Grace, who scored England's first Test century, and his two brothers, Edward Mills and George Frederick, provided the first instance of three brothers playing in the same Test. 'W.G.' and Lucas shared the first hundred partnership in Test cricket – 120 for the second wicket.

ENGLAND

E.M. Grace	c Alexander b Bannerman	36	(6) b Boyle	0
W.G. Grace	b Palmer	152	(7) not out	9
A.P. Lucas	b Bannerman	55	c Blackham b Palmer	2
W. Barnes*	b Alexander	28	(5) c Moule b Boyle	5
Lord Harris*	c Bonnor b Alexander	52		
F. Penn	b Bannerman	23	(4) not out	27
A.G. Steel	c Boyle b Moule	42		
Hon. A. Lyttelton†	not out	11	(1) b Palmer	13
G.F. Grace	c Bannerman b Moule	0	(2) b Palmer	0
A. Shaw	b Moule	0		
F. Morley	run out	2		
Extras	(B 8, LB 11)	19	(NB 1)	1
Total		**420**	(5 wickets)	**57**

AUSTRALIA

A.C. Bannerman	b Morley	32	c Lucas b Shaw	8
W.L. Murdoch*	c Barnes b Steel	0	(3) not out	153
T.U. Groube	b Steel	11	(4) c Shaw b Morley	0
P.S. McDonnell	c Barnes b Morley	27	(5) lbw b W.G. Grace	43
J. Slight	c G.F. Grace b Morley	11	(6) c Harris b W.G. Grace	0
J.M. Blackham†	c and b Morley	0	(7) c E.M. Grace b Morley	19
G.J. Bonnor	c G.F. Grace b Shaw	2	(8) b Steel	16
H.F. Boyle	not out	36	(2) run out	3
G.E. Palmer	b Morley	6	c and b Steel	4
G. Alexander	c W.G. Grace b Steel	6	c Shaw b Morley	33
W.H. Moule	c Morley b W.G. Grace	6	b Barnes	34
Extras	(B 9, LB 3)	12	(B 7, LB 7)	14
Total		**149**		**327**

AUSTRALIA	O	M	R	W	O	M	R	W
Boyle	44	17	71	0	17	7	21	2
Palmer	70	27	116	1	16·3	5	35	3
Alexander	32	10	69	2				
Bannerman	50	12	111	3				
McDonnell	2	0	11	0				
Moule	12·3	4	23	3				
ENGLAND								
Morley	32	9	56	5	61	30	90	3
Steel	29	9	58	3	31	6	73	2
Shaw	13	5	21	1	33	18	42	1
W.G. Grace	1·1	0	2	1	28	10	66	2
Barnes					8·3	3	17	1
Lucas					12	7	23	0
Penn					3	1	2	0

FALL OF WICKETS

Wkt	E 1st	A 1st	A 2nd	E 2nd
1st	91	28	8	2
2nd	211	39	13	10
3rd	269	59	14	22
4th	281	84	97	31
5th	322	84	101	31
6th	404	89	143	–
7th	410	97	181	–
8th	410	113	187	–
9th	413	126	239	–
10th	420	149	327	–

Umpires: H.H. Stephenson and R. Thoms.

with a hat trick of stumpings off C. L. Townsend 1893; H. V. Page, Cheltonian, O.U.C.C., who returned to the College as schoolmaster and became father of a future captain, D. A. C. Page, and finally, J. J. Ferris, Australian, left arm bowler who played for Australia before joining G.C.C.C. in 1890, but who did not reproduce his Australian bowling performances and returned home in 1895. With W. W. Read's England team he toured South Africa where he seemed to relish his return to the Southern Hemisphere for he had a highly successful tour. He went back to Australia in 1895 but then joined the Imperial Light Horse. He died in Durban on 17 November 1900. He will best be remembered as one of the few cricketers to play for both England and Australia.

It is impossible to keep the Graces out of the story during these years. The success, or otherwise, of the County depended upon their performances. The ebullient E.M. – The Little Doctor, The Coroner – spent less time on the cricket field, but his extravagant behaviour enlivened every game in which he played. A brilliantly eccentric batsman, his range of shots varied from the off to the outrageous 'draw' shot playing the ball to the leg from behind his legs or beneath a cocked up left leg! He was rated the best point of all time. He once snapped up a catch so near to the bat that he passed the ball to the wicket keeper without moving. Once whilst batting at the County Ground against Somerset, he was hit on the hand. He threw down his bat, tore off his gloves and hopped around rubbing his fingers. A wag shouted 'What's wrong Doctor, holding an inquest on it?' E.M. flared like a blow lamp, ripped out a stump and set off across the ground. The barracker saw him coming and made for the Ashley Down Road gate. E.M. climbed the pailings and charged in pursuit. He lost the chase. He returned to the crowd's applause. At the wicket he was asked if he had caught him. 'No, he's still running.' It was said that the only thing E.M. could not do on a cricket field was to keep wicket to his own bowling!

When the Graces arrived on the scene bowlers were changing from round arm to overarm and reaping the benefit of bad wickets. Cricket jargon was full of terms like 'undertakers', 'rib roasters', 'nose enders', and 'shooters'. Batting against fast bowlers was a much more dangerous occupation than it is today. The ball often flew high and wide over a wicket-keeper's head and long stop was a very important position in the field – sometimes a wicket-keeper needed two long stops. W.G. always stood his ground against the fastest bowling and hit black and blue he never retreated and never complained. None of this headgear nonsense for W.G. Crossland the Lancashire fast bowler caused a near riot at the Oval in 1883 when he bowled what would later be called body-line. His next game was against Gloucestershire at Clifton College and he soon had the ball whistling through W.G.'s beard. When a section of the crowd began barracking loudly W.G. went over to them and

G. F. Grace 1850–1880.

threatened to close the ground if they did not stop. They did and he went on to make a century.

W.G. first attended the Bristol Medical School in 1868, but did not qualify until 1879. He rarely gave a thought to anything outside his cricket. His marriage and his increasing family responsibilities no doubt inspired him to take his studies more seriously. These were completed at St Bartholomew's and Westminster Hospitals. He received his diploma in Edinburgh and returned as Dr W. G. Grace, L.R.C.P. (Edinburgh), M.R.C.S. (London), overnight to play at Lord's. His bedside manner suited the occasion. No doubt he was held in great respect and awe but his kind, gentle spirit shone through his medical work, particularly if children were involved.

There are several well documented occasions when Dr W.G.'s medical skill was called for on the cricket field. The Kent amateur, C. J. M. Fox, put his shoulder out when playing at Gloucester in 1890, and then again at Bristol in 1892. On both occasions two Gloucestershire cricket doctors were soon in attendance. E.M. held the head and W.G. pulled the shoulder back into position. Free of charge no doubt!

The fuss caused by the Midwinter kidnapping in 1878 continued during Lord Harris's tour of Australia the following winter. It was a tour of 'much unpleasantness'. The Australians, who were not expected in this country for 1880, appeared without a fixture list. A 'Test' was arranged during the course of the season and began at the Oval late in the season on 6 August. All three Graces, E.M., W.G. and G.F. played for England. It was to be the only Test in which three Gloucestershire players appeared together until 1937 when Wally Hammond, Charles Barnett and Tom Goddard played against New Zealand at Old Trafford, and proved to be the only appearance E.M. and G.F. made for England. G.F. distinguished himself, collecting a pair but bringing off one of the great catches in cricket history. He was a brilliant outfielder. G. J. Bonnor, the mighty Australian hitter, hit a ball so high and far that the batsmen were starting their third run before G.F., sprinting along the leg boundary, caught it reputedly 115 yards from the wicket. A fortnight later, on 22 September 1880, following a game at Stroud, George Frederick died of pneumonia in the Red Lion Inn, Basingstoke and was buried beside his father in Downend Churchyard. At the time of his death he was training to be a doctor. A bachelor,

of cts.	Total No. of No Balls.	Total No. of Wide Balls.	Bowlers.	Total No. of Balls.	Total No. of Runs.	No. of Maiden Overs.	No. of Wickets.	Bowlers.	Total No. of Balls.	Total No. of Runs.	No. of Maiden Overs.	No. of Wickets.

OBSERVATIONS.

Drawn owing to the death of Mrs Grace — The Mother of the famous Cricket...

he was engaged to Anne Louise Robinson who, in 1885, became E.M.'s second wife.

Martha, mother of the Graces, died on 25 July 1884 during the second day's play of the Gloucestershire/Lancashire game at Old Trafford and the game was abandoned immediately when the news reached the ground. The result of the game: 'Drawn, owing to the death of Mrs Grace'. Such was the respect in which she was held in cricket that hers is the only lady's name in *Wisden*'s Cricket Index. She was buried in the Downend Churchyard beside Dr H.M. and son G.F.

The salaries and expenses paid to players provide much interest, not least on the matter of inflation over the years but it is difficult to arrive at a sensible figure, say between 1880 and 1980. There are many factors to be considered but a sensible, analysed opinion suggests that it might conservatively be twenty times. £1 then would be worth £20 now. In those early years there had been numerous scuffles over expenses to be paid to the amateurs, the Secretary and later the professionals.

A few examples reflect the point. The first references to E.M.'s salary are: 'The Secretary be paid a salary as heretofore'. The specific detail comes in 1878, when it was raised to £50 per annum. In 1875 W.G. and G.F. were allowed expenses of £80 and £65 for the season. It was the custom for the Champion County to play an England XI at the Oval during the following season. Gloucestershire played two such games in 1877 and 1878, the expenses to be borne by the Surrey Club. Gloucestershire claimed £102 10s., the main items of which were E.M.

1884 membership card.

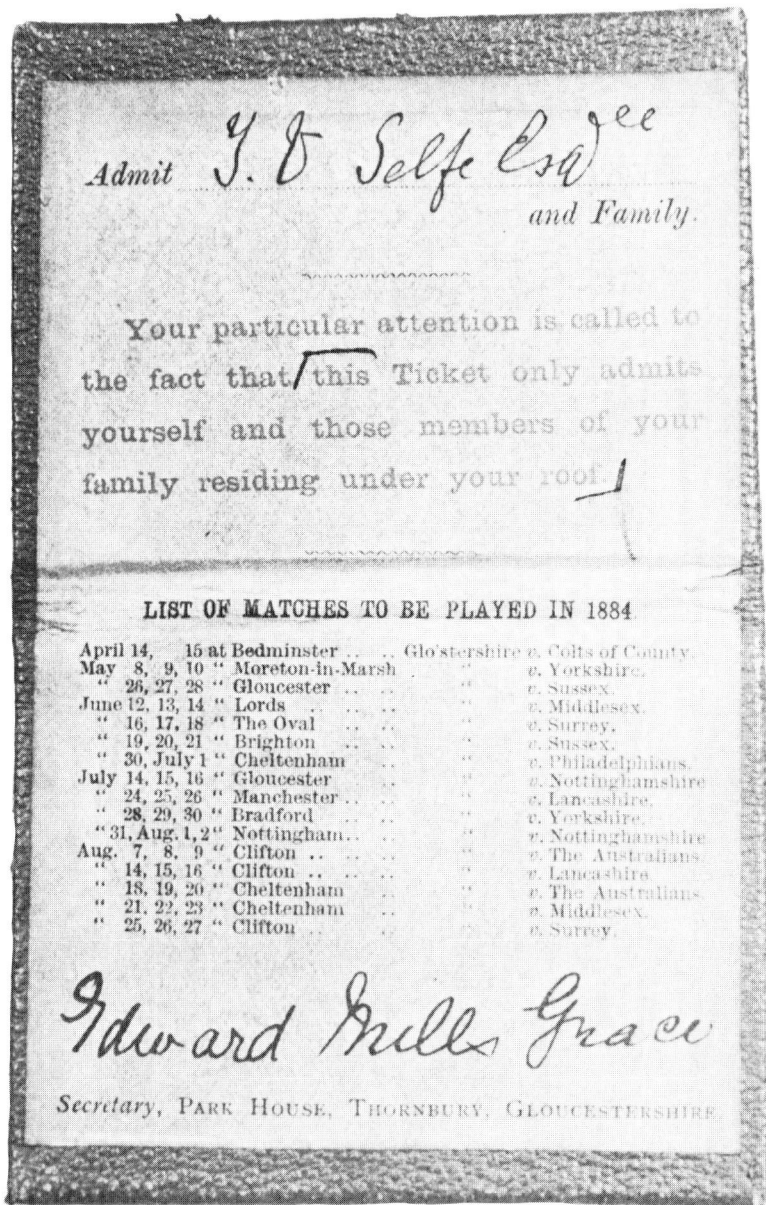

LIST OF MATCHES TO BE PLAYED IN 1884

April 14, 15 at Bedminster	Glo'stershire	*v.* Colts of County.
May 8, 9, 10 " Moreton-in-Marsh	"	*v.* Yorkshire.
" 26, 27, 28 " Gloucester	"	*v.* Sussex.
June 12, 13, 14 " Lords	"	*v.* Middlesex.
" 16, 17, 18 " The Oval	"	*v.* Surrey.
" 19, 20, 21 " Brighton	"	*v.* Sussex.
" 30, July 1 " Cheltenham	"	*v.* Philadelphians.
July 14, 15, 16 " Gloucester	"	*v.* Nottinghamshire
" 24, 25, 26 " Manchester	"	*v.* Lancashire.
" 28, 29, 30 " Bradford	"	*v.* Yorkshire.
" 31, Aug. 1, 2 " Nottingham	"	*v.* Nottinghamshire
Aug. 7, 8, 9 " Clifton	"	*v.* The Australians.
" 14, 15, 16 " Clifton	"	*v.* Lancashire
" 18, 19, 20 " Cheltenham	"	*v.* The Australians.
" 21, 22, 23 " Cheltenham	"	*v.* Middlesex.
" 25, 26, 27 " Clifton	"	*v.* Surrey.

Secretary, PARK HOUSE, THORNBURY, GLOUCESTERSHIRE

£20, W.G. £15 and Midwinter £10. Surrey strongly objected and the figure was reduced to £80 10s., E.M. £10, W.G. £10, Midwinter £10 and G.F. £7 10s. A proposal that the Club should pay the difference of £22 was only defeated by the Chairman's casting vote.

The gate charge for spectators was 6d (2½p) and Members' Subscriptions 10 guineas but there was a full-scale row in Committee over the gate charge for the W.G. Testimonial game against Yorkshire at Clifton College. The game took place at the time of W.G.'s qualification as a Doctor and there was some suggestion that he would give up much of his cricket. A National Testimonial was set up to acknowledge his great contribution to the game and it was decided he was to be given 'the net receipts' of the Clifton game. Without any reference to the Committee, E.M. advertised that the gate charge for the game would be 1/-d. (5p)! A series of bitter Committee Meetings ensued which resulted in one immediate Committee resignation from the first meeting and four more from the next (these later withdrew their resignations and were reinstated) before the matter was resolved 'that the price of admission be the same as altered by the Secretary'. The National Testimonial brought W.G. £1,485, a marble clock and two large ornaments.

A. H. Grace 1866–1929.

E.M. did lose a battle at the Committee Meeting on 6 December 1878. The issue was: 'Is the Secretary, who is a paid member of the Club, qualified to vote at a Meeting?' It was proposed by W.G., seconded by Dr H. Grace that he should. This motion was defeated by the casting vote of the Chairman.

The Grace family picnic which was an annual event and in this picture there are 45 members of the family.

Club accounts 1886–1889.

Items	1886	1887	1888	1889
Credit Balance	953- 8- 8	1320- 7- 3	1496-13	881- 1-10
County Ground Matches				339-10
Clifton "	500-14	630- 9- 6	881- 9- 3	279- 6- 6
Cheltenham "	335-13- 6	240- 9- 6	593- 3- 6	344-18- 6
Gloucester "	163- 8- 6	106- 1- 6	39- 0- 6	98- 3- 9
Other Grounds	48- 2- 9	120	120	72-11- 3
Priv:towell Refrsts	125	145- 5	135	113-10
Test Matches				
Gate Money from Counties	36-10- 6			
Members Subscriptions	413-12- 8	417-19	456-13	546-11
Sundries				28
Interest	24- 5- 6	24-19- 8	22- 6- 1	13- 8-10
Donations				
Intt on County Ground Shares				
Guarantors				
	2600- 4-11	2905-11- 5	3743-10- 4	2717- 1- 8

Items	1886	1887	1888	1889
First Class Matches Played	— 18 —	— 18 —	— 18 —	— 18 —
Preparing Grounds	85- 8- 8	77- 7- 8	99-10-11	91- 8- 3
Umpires	70	80	80	37- 7
Scoring & Telegraph	53- 4	55- 7- 6	57- 2- 6	63-18
Material Tenthire &c	172-19- 8	188- 1	164- 4- 2	163- 7- 8
Money & Check Takers	55-17- 6	56-14- 6	63-18- 6	74- 4- 6
Printing Advts Postage &c	89- 8- 9	79- 0- 3	88-13- 5	86-18- 9
Luncheons				89-11-11
Ground Staff				72-10
Police	31-16- 1	24-19- 8	36-14- 6	39- 4- 5
Sec's Salary & Auditor	88- 3	88- 3	88- 3	103- 3
Sundries & Bank Charges	31- 7- 6	54-18- 4	54- 8- 8	9- 0- 6
County Ground Rent			1000	
Gate to Foreigners			363-18- 1	13- 9- 9
" " Counties				14-13
Amateurs Expenses				
Pros "	701-15- 6	704- 8- 6	765-13- 9	774-12- 6
Cash in hand	1320- 7- 3	1496-13	881- 1-10	1033- 4- 5
Contributions Benefits &c				
	2600- 4-11	2905-11- 5	3743-10 4	2717- 1- 8

Obviously the Graces did not intend the matter to rest there. A Special General Meeting was called on 10 January 1879 to ratify the first formulated Rules of the Club. The one source of contention centred on a proposal by W.G. that the phrase 'ineligible to vote' should read 'eligible to vote'. This was defeated by twenty-three votes to twelve but immediately brought a substantive motion that as this was not a two-thirds majority of the voting, the rule should remain as proposed, i.e. that the Secretary did have a vote. This was carried. The next Meeting shows that ten members had resigned on the issue. E.M. backed down, 'he did not intend to exercise his right to vote in future!' The lost members came in from the cold and the Graces had won on a technical knock-out.

From 1883 G.C.C.C. paid Dr W.G. £36 for a locum during the summer months.

48

The first full Australian tour to this country was in 1878. In one of their lesser matches they played against a Gentlemen of England side at Princes. Six Gloucestershire players were included: W.G., E.M., G.F., W. R. Gilbert, J. A. Bush and G. Strachan. The Australian Manager objected to the 'Gentlemen' label when he discovered that W.G. and Gilbert (a cousin of the Graces) received £60 for playing. It was asserted that W.G., G.F. and W.R.G. 'were invariably paid for playing'.

The Last of the Grace Years
1888-1899

The 1880s passed into the 1890s but before they did a momentous event had occurred. The Club had purchased an area on Ashley Down that was to become its headquarters. The first reference to the need for a County Ground occurs in the Minutes of 31 October 1884: 'That the following members of the Committee form themselves into a sub-committee to make enquiries, and to find out whether there is any field to be had for a County Cricket Ground.' The Sub-Committee, H. W. Beloe (soon to become the first regular Chairman of the Club and to serve in this capacity until 1914), J. A. Bush, F. Townsend, W. G. Grace and T. G. Matthews. Mr E. G. Clarke, one of the sporting figures in Bristol, was added to this Committee and he took a leading part in the eventual acquisition of the County Ground. Many areas were under examination, a level area on the Redland Estate, land at Westbury on Trym and Ashley Down. It would seem that there was a wider interest in Bristol sporting circles advocating the provision of a Sports Ground.

The next Committee Meeting held on 5 December 1884 shows that they had visited some land in Eastville that was 'most advantageous and desirable'. This was in W.G. country. He was living at Thrissell House, Stapleton, at the time. The Committee had seen Mr T. Dyke, who was probably the agent for Sir Greville Smyth who owned the land but there was the problem of a footpath that ran across it. The Committee went out to see it and it was reported in the Minutes that: 'the Secretary order a carriage to convey members of the Committee from the Grand Hotel on Friday next (i.e. 15 January 1886) to view the proposed ground at Eastville.' Sir Greville had offered to lease them the land for fourteen years at an annual rental of £120 (later reduced to £100). The Club 'had now to decide whether to buy the ground or not'.

The matter dragged on through 1886 into 1887, perhaps giving a clue to the protracted negotiations. Thanks were expressed to the Sub-Committee 'for the great trouble they have taken about the proposed grounds'. In fact the renting of the

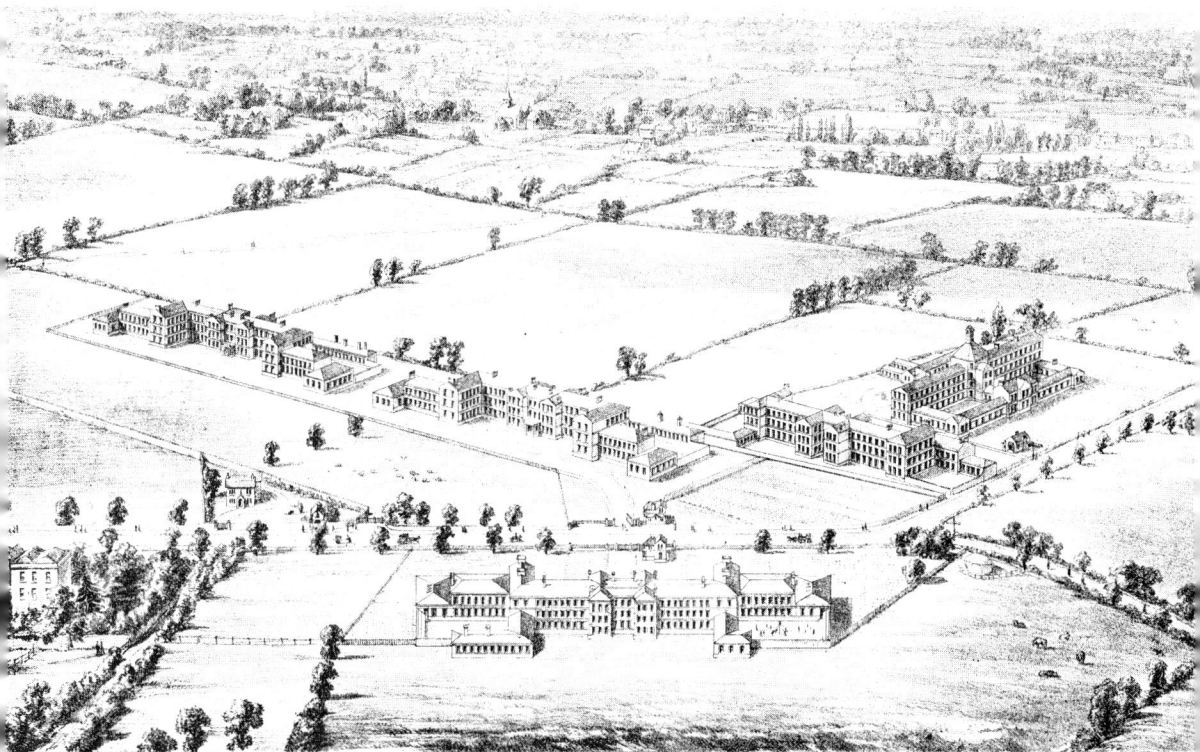

Ashley Down. The boundary wall of the present County Ground is around the two big square-shaped fields, behind the Muller orphanage buildings, circa 1880.

land at Eastville had been concluded legally and only the approval of the A.G.M. was needed. Before the next Annual General Meeting on 2 March 1888 the matter had been settled.

Twenty-five acres of agricultural land were for sale on Ashley Down, an enclave of Gloucestershire within the boundary of the City of Bristol. The Committee had entered into the purchase of all, or a part of 12 to 13 acres of the land . . . 'the County Club should have the sole and exclusive use of the portion to be set apart for cricket and athletic purposes'. A Gloucestershire County Ground Company Limited was set up 'to manage the entire undertaking', and the County Cricket Club was to have the use of a cricket ground, about 14 acres, for an annual rent of £300. The County Cricket Club would have the exclusive use of '100 yards square to be marked around and retained solely for the use of the County Cricket Club all the year round'. The remainder of the area was at the disposal of the Ground Company for cricket, football, cycling, athletics, bowls and tennis;

51

Letter from E. M. Grace to J. W. Arrowsmith (committee member) indicating the first move in the purchase of land at Ashley Down for the future county ground.

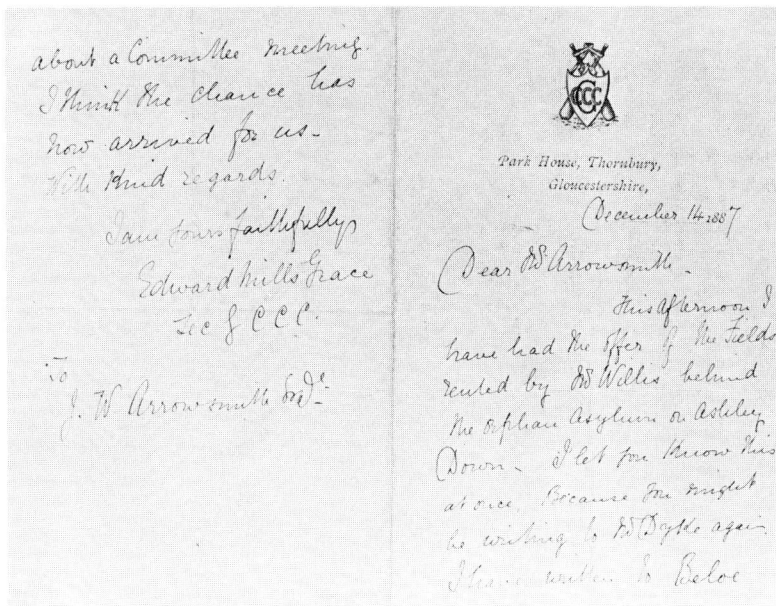

in fact what a century later would be called a sports centre.

W.G. had been actively engaged in the matter for three years and it is not surprising to find him immediately appointed a director of the Ground Company and for the next year he was almost a daily visitor to the area to watch over the Club's interests. It was not long before he and the foreman were in open conflict. Two big, like-minded men bristled at the other's interference. W.G. may have intimidated an umpire or two in his time but he had met his match here. In spite of this running battle of words the ground was completed.

W.G. also met his match in the appointment of the groundsman. He had promised the job to Tom Gregg, who had played for the County and was cricket coach to Clifton College, but no doubt persuaded by Mr E. G. Clarke, the Ground Company appointed his gardener and fellow Cornishman, John Spry. John Spry had come from Cornwall to join the Bristol Police but as he was $\frac{1}{2}''$ too short, he had taken the job as gardener to Mr Clarke. John Spry's son, Ted, who was to play for the County and follow his father as head groundsman, recounts how as a young boy he went into the unfinished Pavilion, climbed the stairs and was met by a huge bearded figure. In the wash room he told young Ted to look up at the hole in the ceiling where the plumber was fixing the showers: 'You'll see the monkey'. The boy bent over and looked up. W.G. pulled the lever and he got showered before he could jump out of the way.

One early morning W.G. arrived at the ground and found something amiss. John Spry was sacked on the spot but refused to go and told W.G. that only the Ground Company could sack him. The matter was never referred to again!

The ground was first used for a game on 22 and 23 April 1889, a Gloucestershire XI versus XXII Colts and the first County match played was against Warwickshire on 23, 24 and 25 May when the County won by 63 runs.

It was also used by various sporting organisations, cycling, athletics, the Wheelers, Bristol South, Post Office, Police and by Bristol R.F.C. before moving to the Memorial Ground, and Clifton A.F.C. In the early years many cricket clubs,

The County Ground 1890.

including Bohemians, Banks, Y.M.C.A., Commercials, United Press, United Services, St Annes, Rugbyeans, J. S. Fry and Sons, Cotham as well as the Arrows Bowling and Quoits Club of the great Bristol publishing firm of Arrowsmith also rented an area.

Urban development followed and within a few years the nearby roads constructed were named after cricket counties – Surrey, Lancashire, Derby, Kent, Nottingham, Warwick, Worcester, Somerset, Sussex Place and Kennington Avenue.

The present day habit of searching for alliterative catch phrases would have labelled the 1890s the 'Nervous Nineties'. Not for the first time in the Gloucestershire story the lack of success on the cricket field led to a rapidly declining confidence off it. The eighties ended with the County sinking to the bottom of the list of Counties. They reached there in 1891, bounced away from it in 1892 only to thump back again in 1893 and 1894.

Success depended so much on good performances from W.G. but all cricketers must expect bad seasons and W.G. was no exception. In his long career he was rarely incapacitated physically but during this period he could not rid himself of a strained knee. He was in universal demand and rarely refused a game when Gloucestershire were not playing, but even his insatiable appetite must have grown dull at times. He always opened the batting and the bowling. Once when he had bowled for a long time without any success, a fielder, with some trepidation, suggested that he should make a change in the bowling. 'Yes', retorted W.G., 'I will change to the other end.'

The County had never recovered from G.F.'s death consequently the bowling rested so much on W.G. and Woof. The arrival in 1887 of Frederick George Roberts of Mickleton, a fast left arm bowler, brought them some relief. His debut against Yorkshire at Dewsbury was sensational – 14 wickets for 171 runs in the match. He continued to bowl well into the new century forming a formidable partnership with Woof. In the same season they bowled out Kent at Moreton-in-Marsh for 28 in the first innings, Woof taking 5 for 18, Robert 5 for 8. When the County Ground opened in 1889 the Club followed a Lord's habit by employing bowlers to bowl to members in the nets. The first of these were Bill Murch, Jack Stinchecombe and Tom Gregg who were each paid 30/- (£1.50) a week.

Billy Woof did not play regularly once he had taken up his appointment as cricket coach at Cheltenham College and he was replaced by another slow left arm bowler, Arthur Paish, who continued the spin bowling tradition. Fred Roberts played on until 1905. His 963 wickets eloquently reflect his mighty labours. He took the Old English at Bath Buildings off Gloucester Road in Bristol. A room with bar was set aside for sportsmen with conversation restricted to Bristol City A.F.C. in winter and G.C.C.C. in summer. He died in Bristol on 7 April 1936.

In its history Gloucestershire has had five great wicket keepers, the greatest of these being John Henry Board. He came out of Bristol club cricket to take over from J. A. Bush in 1890 and carried on until 1914. He played in six Test Matches against South Africa and toured Australia in 1897/98 although he did not play in a Test Match. He was an amusing character who whistled at his work. Once, when he had not seen Woof's signal for an inswinger, he missed the ball. W.G. shouted, 'Stop 'im Jack'. Jack shouted back, 'I couldn't stop 'e, 'er went t'other way that 'er did'. E.M. chipped in ''ark at 'e'.

Jack Board played 430 times for Gloucestershire compared with W.G.'s 360, in a career that lasted until 1914. From 1909 to 1915 he played during the winter for Hawks Bay, New Zealand, and after the War he became a first-class umpire. He died at sea on the *Kenilworth Castle* on 16 April 1924 while returning from one of his annual coaching trips to South Africa.

1891 and 1892 were not good seasons for W.G., but he did make another visit to Australia eighteen years after his first. Lord Sheffield, originator of the Australian Inter-State tournament, the Sheffield Shield, who financed the tour, persuaded him to go for £3,000 with all expenses paid and passages for his wife and son. He played in twenty-six out of the twenty-seven games, sufficient proof that his knee had recovered!

He returned from the tour rejuvenated; the runs came again and Gloucestershire fortunes recovered, if only temporarily, in the 1892 season. The season that was to follow was momentous. The success, and survival, of any sporting organisation must depend upon luck as well as good management. So it was to be for Gloucestershire in 1893. Firstly a Clifton College schoolboy, and afterwards a Cheltenham schoolmaster, stepped on to their Road. Charles Lucas Townsend, Frank Townsend's

W. G.'s bat with which he scored 1,016 runs in May 1895. For security reasons this bat is now kept in a bank vault.

son, was just seventeen when he made his debut against Middlesex on 10, 11 and 12 August on his College Close having already taken a stack of wickets at school and in Bristol Club games. The County had continued intermittently with their early season Colts games. However, in addition this year a game was played at the end of the season on the County Ground, XII University and Public School versus XII others of the County. Charles Townsend and W.G.'s son, who was his contemporary at Clifton, played in this game, and also a Cheltenham schoolmaster, G. L. Jessop. W.G. (Junior) was not in their class although he got a Blue at Cambridge and later played for the County. He was a Mathematics Scholar, became an assistant master at Oundle and moved on to the R.N. College at Osborne as a Science Instructor where he died of peritonitis on 2 March 1905.

Charles Townsend became one of the County's greatest cricketers. He was a tall, slim, gentle person who bowled leg breaks with an occasional off-break. His first major contributions were as a bowler, but later he became an outstanding left hand bat. Towards the end of his first season he got a stumping hat trick against Middlesex with W. H. Brain as the wicket keeper standing in for Jack Board. W. H. Brain had the ball mounted and presented it to Charles Townsend. It is still treasured by the family reminding them of their illustrious forebear.

He took 124 wickets in his first full season in 1895. He gained the cricketer's double in 1898, 1,270 runs and 145 wickets, to become a Wisden Cricketer of the Year. The following year came another double, 2,440 runs and 101 wickets. After 1901 he played less cricket in order to concentrate on a legal career and later practised in Stockton-on-Tees; he continued to act as W.G.'s solicitor. His son, D. C. H. Townsend, distinguished himself by making 193 for Oxford in the 1934 Varsity Match. This was a unique record for one family; four generations of first-class cricketers, Frank Townsend, Charles Townsend, D.C.H. and J.R.A. who played for Oxford University. Two other sons of Frank, A.F.M. and F.N., played for the County.

W. H. Brain's brother, J.H., also an Old Cliftonian, played for the County. They were members of the great South Wales brewing family and together were closely associated with Glamorgan's acceptance as the seventeenth member of the County Championship in 1921.

A problem came to a head during the winter of 1892/93. The first indication appears in a Committee Minute of 9 December 1892: 'Re selection of players. Seven Committee Members spoke – but no resolution was put to the Meeting.' The fuse had been lit. From the very beginning W.G. had, with lofty indifference, picked the teams himself. He ran everything to do with the cricket. He had a leaning towards amateurs from public schools, Clifton, Cheltenham and Marlborough, both boys and masters, to the exclusion of local club cricketers. Many of these only played on a regional basis. If a game was played at Cheltenham or Gloucester, one or two would be included but very rarely was one of these good enough to establish his place in the side. A look at the statistics shows that from 1870 to 1914, 245 amateurs played for the County but only 78 played more than ten games.

By the time of the next Committee Meeting on 26 January 1893, W.G. had written a letter resigning from the Committee and the Captaincy. 'The Committee have heard with much

Charles Lucas Townsend who first played for the county in 1893 aged 16 and whilst a pupil at Clifton College. His rise to fame was meteoric. A leg break with off break bowler, and a left hand bat, he achieved the double in 1898 and 1899. In his Gloucestershire career he made 7,754 runs and took 656 wickets.

Business letter concerning the ground from W. G. Grace to J. W. Arrowsmith.

regret of the resignation of Dr W. G. Grace from the Committee and the Captaincy of the County XI believing he has taken this course in consequence of what took place at the last meeting on 9 December. They beg to remind him of the assurance then given him, that the Committee did not wish to take any action distasteful or antagonistic to him as they still have the same confidence in his captaincy now, as previously to the Meeting on 9 December, they request him in the interest of the County XI and of cricket generally to reconsider his determination and withdraw his resignation.' There was not a word directly relating to the selection of the team.

W.G. played 14 out of 16 games in 1893. The next Committee reference is on 5 September 1893: 'Dr W. G. Grace's letter withdrawing his resignation read' but 'that an endeavour be made to ascertain whether it was the general wish of the Committee Dr Grace would be prepared to concur in the appointment of a Selection Committee.' His reply reached them by the

Meeting of 31 October 1893, '. . . with regard to the Selection Committee I will have nothing to do with it.' The Graces did not deal in compromises.

The matter rested there. He carried on as before.

At the same meeting the Committee had to deal with another cricketer complaint. Billy Murch, Jack Board, Fred Roberts and Jack Painter were not happy with the precarious nature of their employment by the Club. They were interviewed separately following which it was decided that the first three were still 'not quite satisfied' but Painter was 'quite satisfied, but no guarantee could be given that they should play in all matches next year'.

E. M. Grace towards the end of his career.

In the early 1920s a young Gloucester boy of the Crypt School, himself destined one day to play for Cambridge University and Gloucestershire was shown the mark high up on one of the Beaufort Terrace houses outside the Spa Ground where a Jessop rocket had landed. There seemed to be plenty of cracks in the masonry. Such was the power of the Jessop saga that many such legends of mighty hitting persist around the grounds where he played.

Gilbert Laird Jessop, born on 19 May 1874 at 30 Cambray, Cheltenham, the eleventh child of a local doctor, Henry Edward Jessop, was named after another doctor, William Gilbert Grace. There was nothing about his family background to suggest their paths would one day meet on the world's cricket fields. As an energetic young boy he spent every spare moment of his day playing cricket and was a self taught cricketer with a remarkable natural ability for the game. He went to Cheltenham Grammar School when he was eleven and was in the School team at thirteen. At fifteen, on the death of his father, he left school to join the teaching staff of Alvechurch Grammar School, Worcestershire, where he was able to continue playing cricket. He moved to other schools, South Woodford, Essex, Burford Grammar School and finally to Beccles College (Hockey's) Suffolk. In the vacations he played wherever he could find a game of cricket. His introduction to Gloucestershire came in the trial match towards the end of the 1893 season between the Universities and Public Schools XI and the Rest of the County. Charles Townsend, aged seventeen, who had already played for the County was in the opposition. It proved an eventful game for Jessop. He began by running out W.G.'s son. If that did not exactly impress the Old Man who was watching, he must have noticed Jessop's 53 runs and his 4 wickets for 39 and admired the lightning fielding and throwing that was soon to electrify the cricket world.

The following year he made his debut for the County at Old Trafford on 31 July 1894. He arrived at the wicket to stop a hat trick and significantly he hit the first ball to the boundary. He went on to make 29, the top scorer in the Gloucestershire innings of 99. W.G. was heard to remark, 'Well, we've found something this time'. A Lancashire newspaper report the following day did not agree with him. 'If Mr Jessop's batting is no better than his bowling or fielding, he is scarcely likely to become an acquisition to the Western shire.' *Wisden* was slightly more optimistic at the end of the season: 'Mr Jessop did uncommonly well for a first season and with increased experience should do well in the future. He certainly displayed considerable natural aptitude for the game, but in view of so many disappointments there is no inducement to indulge in many great hopes.'

It is wrongly assumed that Jessop must have been a big man; in fact he was slightly built and in his prime was 5′ 7″ and 11 stone. Nor was he a slogger who favoured the leg side. The critics considered the late cut was his best shot. Fearlessly, not recklessly, he attacked even the fastest of bowlers and destroyed any bowler who could not control his length and line. He was nicknamed 'The Croucher' because of the way he crouched menacingly over his bat to catapult himself at the next ball. At first he was generally considered a fast bowler, batting in the lower middle order, a bit of a slogger, but gradually he brought a discipline to his batting. He did make a century in each innings of a match four times, in his career. He was picked for his first Test Match in 1899, for his bowling (and was over-bowled) but he had neither the build nor the stamina to match the demands of that breed of hard men.

There was menace in the air when Jessop went in to bat. The fielders retreated towards the boundary, spectators looked for cover, members sought a safe refuge for their drinks, householders around a ground stood by to defend their properties, all prepared for some explosive action. He was also a brilliant cover point; 'miraculous' was the word most commonly used to describe his fielding. He threw out many a batsman at either end.

In 1894 and 1895 he could only play for the County on the completion of schoolmaster duties. Yorkshire received the first of his many onslaughts on 22 August 1895 at Cheltenham when he scored 51 out of 53 in 18 minutes. In 1896 at the age of twenty-two he went up to Christ's College, Cambridge. His arrival was awaited eagerly and although he won a Blue as a Freshman he was not at all successful that season. However, he certainly was in 1897 when Cambridge won the Varsity Match by 179 runs. He took 6 wickets for 64 runs in the first innings and made 42 in 15 balls in the second. Previously he had made 140 against the American touring side, the Philadelphians, at Cambridge. In his first game on returning to the County he blasted 126 out of 176 in 90 minutes. A few days later an onslaught on the Yorkshire bowling at Harrogate brought him 101 out of 118 in 40 minutes. By the season's end he had completed the cricketer's double, 1,219 runs and 116 wickets. *Wisden* named him as one of their five cricketers of the year. He played four seasons for Cambridge and was captain in 1899. He left Cambridge, having completed only seven terms out of a possible twelve, without a degree. He was a very good all-round games player, playing football and hockey at Cambridge and on returning home for the vacation occasionally turned out as a nippy wing three-quarters for Gloucester R.F.C.

There was more excitement to be found in Gloucestershire cricket during those first years of Jessop. Gradually W.G. had been piling up his centuries. The rate quickened on his return from Australia after the 1891/92 tour. By 1892 the total was 92, by 1893 it was 95 and at the end of 1894 it had reached 97. 1895 was to be his greatest season. He had been playing first-class cricket for thirty-two years and was almost forty-eight years old. In early May he scored two more centuries to make it 99.

The sixteenth of May found Gloucestershire playing Somerset at the County Ground where Somerset batted first and made 303. At the end of the day W.G. was 38 not out. The next day was bitterly cold, with flurries of snow in the air. The crowds poured in. Mrs Grace and her daughter, Bessie, watched from the Ladies' Stand. No doubt the prospect of W.G.'s hundredth century kept everyone warm. They might have had to wait for another day if that young Clifton schoolboy, Charles Townsend had not held fast at the other end. With two runs to go Sammy Woods bowled the great man a full toss outside the leg stump.

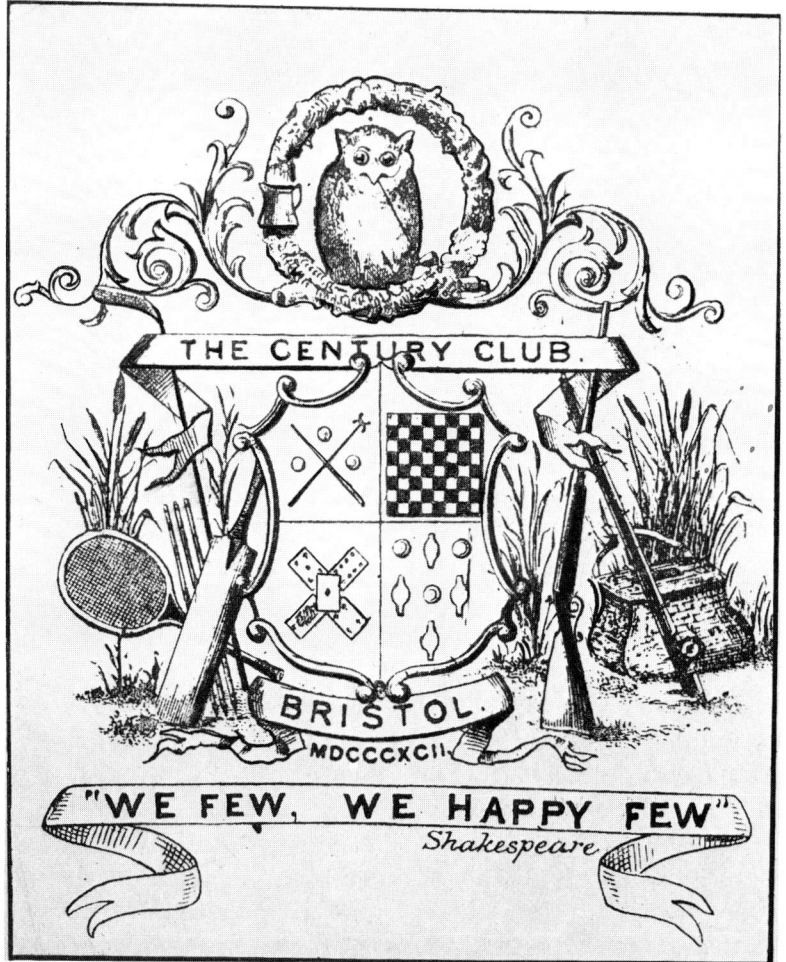

He hit it for four. The ground erupted. E.M. came down the steps of the pavilion, towel over his arm waiter fashion, carrying a magnum of champagne and some glasses. Play was held up for five minutes as toasts were drunk in celebration. W.G. with relentless application went on to make 288. Somerset could think of better ways to thank them for that full toss. Charles Townsend was lbw for 95.

A few days later, playing for the County against Kent at Gravesend, he made 257 runs in the first innings and was 73 not out in the second. He had bowled the first ball of the game and hit the winning shot off the last. He had been on the field for every ball of the three days.

Letter from W.G. to J.W. Arrowsmith concerning the proposed testimonial in recognition of his hundred hundreds.

In twenty-two days of that memorable May of 1895 he had scored 1,016 runs. Twice before, in August 1871 and August 1876, he had scored over 1,000 runs in a month but this was the first time the feat had ever been achieved in May. Throughout the season runs flowed from his bat like the Severn Bore on a spring tide and by the end of it he had made 2,346 runs. The *Daily Telegraph* launched a National Cricket Shilling Testimonial which brought him £4,281 9s. 1d. There were others. G.C.C.C. added £100, £1 for each century perhaps, but a scant reward for his formidable contribution to their affairs. The Club was in the throes of a financial crisis. However, they did give him a Century of Centuries Dinner at the Victoria Rooms, Bristol, on 24 June. The total of all the donations came to £9,073 8s. 3d. Some amateur!

The County came away from the bottom during those disastrous years, 1893 and 1894, to become fourth in W.G.'s Indian Summer year of 1895. The Old Man had become a bit of a liability in the field and spent most of his time standing ponderously at slip directing operations. He was lucky to have three fine amateur outfielders at his bidding, Charles Townsend, Gilbert Jessop and Cyril Sewell, and also a professional Harry

63

Wrathall of Cheltenham, who developed into a first-class batsman. He and William Henry Hale of Birmingham joined their
seniors, Jack Painter, Fred Roberts and Bill Murch to add
substance to the performance. The amateurs ebbed and flowed
around this hard core; Reginald William Rice of Tewkesbury
and Oxford, who batted 217 times for the County; the four sons
of Lady Bateman Champain, C.E., H.F., J.N. and most promi-
nently Francis Henry, who had all been to Cheltenham College;
and finally, William Stanley Alston Brown of Clifton, who was
to bring distinction to the County on and off the field until after
the First World War.

1898 and 1899 brought the final chapter in W.G.'s long Gloucestershire career. The fuse that had been lit over the Selection
issue in 1893 had smouldered on. W.G. ran all Gloucestershire
cricket and took his teams on to the field. The explosion came

when the rumours that had been voiced towards the end of the 1898 season came to the notice of the Committee. They wrote to him asking him to state 'exactly' which games he intended to play in 1899. W.G. considered this an ultimatum. Unbeknown to them on 13 November 1898 he had already signed a contract to be Captain and Manager of London Counties Cricket Club. He was to live in the immediate neighbourhood of Crystal Palace, his son, Charles Butler, was allowed to attend the Engineering School there free of charge, and he was to be paid £600 per annum plus 1/-d. (5p) of every guinea collected in membership fees and at the gate. W.G. replied to the Committee's letter resigning the Captaincy with a blistering last sentence: 'I have the greatest affection for the County of my birth but for the Committee as a body the greatest contempt.' He had slammed the door in their faces. They asked him to withdraw this remark. He refused. After four games at the beginning of 1899, he was gone from Gloucestershire for ever.

His place as Captain was taken by Walter Troup who had an Indian Army background and whose father was General Colin Troup, C.B. Born in India, Walter came to a preparatory school in Bristol before moving on to Cheltenham College. He then joined the Indian Police Service. His first County game was in 1887 and he also played Rugby and Hockey for Gloucestershire. If he had resided in Gloucestershire permanently he would have been one of the County's greatest cricketers. He did the next

Congratulatory letter from the Prince of Wales to W.G. on the occasion of his scoring 1,000 runs during the first month of the cricket season.

best thing. He became a specialist in wangling sick leave for himself. In 1893 on one of these leaves, and as the time of his return to India approached, he went to W.G. to seek his advice. 'Fetch me a pen, ink and paper. I'll soon settle it.' Dr W. G. Grace then wrote a letter saying Troup was in a very low state of health and he strongly recommended outdoor exercise, cricket in preference. Troup played for the County for the remainder of the season!

Troup had also heard rumours of W.G.'s impending departure at the beginning of the 1899 season. One morning as they were leaving Lord's, W.G. turned to him and said, 'I'm not playing against Yorkshire on Monday. You Captain the side,

C. L. Townsend and W. G. Grace.

play the same eleven as today, and put Roberts in my place.'
There had already been some trouble about the composition of
the team and when they heard this, the Committee hastily called
a Meeting, no doubt convinced that the W.G. problem had to
be settled at once and for all time. Troup and J. A. Bush stayed
up long into the night drinking and talking with W.G. He was

67

adamant. He would not remove that deeply wounding last sentence.

Later W.G. deeply regretted what he had done. In his favour it should be said that he had hoped to combine the captaincy of both sides since the L.C.C.C. was of no great consequence. Troup again overstayed his leave. At the end of it his fellow amateurs gave him a clock, and the professionals a silver flask. Jack Board presented it and jokingly remarked 'that they knew it would be useful!' Troup continued to return periodically to this country and played an occasional game until 1911.

1899 also saw the end of W.G.'s Test career. He captained the first Test of the series against the Australians at Trent Bridge. It is of passing interest that from 1870 he had been by far the greatest cricketer in the world but he had not captained England in this country until 1888. Much younger and perhaps more aristocratic cricketers had been appointed over him. An elitist society, no doubt. He was booed from the field at the end. His fielding, he was fifty and over eighteen stone, had become a liability and his huge frame was by now suffering from the metal fatigue which affects all cricketers. As one critic put it 'the ground is now too far away.' His authority over the international cricket scene had evaporated at last.

1899 was indeed an unhappy year for W.G. His young daughter, Bessie, died of scarlet fever on 6 February 1899 at the house he had bought to be near his work at Crystal Palace, 7 Lawrie Park Road, Sydenham now rebuilt and called 'Grace Lodge', a hostel for the National Westminster Bank. A tall vivacious girl with the 'Grace' ability for sport, she had previously attended Clifton High School.

The London Counties Cricket Club was part of the great Crystal Palace Exhibition complex of 1851 and even today the ground on which the cricket was played has not yet been swallowed up by the National Sports Centre. The L.C.C.C. was to lose its first-class status in 1904 but not before W.G.'s breach with Gloucestershire had been closed. His bark had always been worse than his bite; if this time he had bitten the hand that had fed him for so long, he soon regretted it. On 29 May 1902 he brought the L.C.C.C. team to Bristol to play a Charles Townsend XI at the County ground in aid of an N.S.P.C.C. Appeal, that raised £76 16s. 4d. He was made a Life Member of the Club in 1902. He must have relished the occasion in 1903 when

Testimonial Match at the County Ground for John Spry (groundsman). J. W. Arrowsmith is seated between E. M. Grace and W. G. John Spry is behind J. W. Arrowsmith and Ted Spry is in the back row behind his father. 4–5 September 1908.

L.C.C.C. beat his old County with his help of 150 runs. This was the match in which Charlie Parker made his debut for Gloucestershire.

Ben Travers, the famous playwright, recalled an occasion during this period at a Crystal Palace London Counties game when W.G. (not for the first time in his life!) disputed an umpire's decision. 'I well remember that umpire's almost petrified attitude intimidated by the awe-inspiring majesty of the supreme dictator. The intimidation prevailed. Grace was given not out, which was a tremendous stroke of luck for me, for W.G. proceeded in his masterful way and I have always been able to boast that I saw the great man make a century.'

W.G. now played much less cricket. In 1906, forty-one years after his first appearance in the Gentlemen *v.* Players game he made his last. After scoring 74 he came back into the dressing-room, threw his bat on to the table and declared, 'I shan't play any more'. He played his last first-class game in 1908, his very

This is reputed to be the last picture of W.G. and was taken in his garden at Fairmount, Mottingham.

last game of cricket on 25 July, 1914, aged sixty-six. His extraordinary cricket career had reached its end; his score significantly 69 not out. He had played in 869 games in his first-class career, 360 of them for Gloucestershire. His restless energy was to be satisfied by golf, curling and bowls. He played bowls for England and in 1903 became the first President of the English Bowling Association.

G. Neville Weston, the acknowledged leading authority on W.G., has spent a lifetime tracing every run, wicket, catch and stumping of his Champion. At the beginning of 1981 they read as follows:

	Runs	Wickets	Catches	Stumpings
First-class matches	54,904	2,879	871	5
Minor matches	45,283	4,578	656	52
Grand Totals	100,187	7,457	1,527	57

W.G. made 126 centuries in first-class cricket, 51 of them for Gloucestershire, and 95 in minor matches for a total of 221. His last century was in a London County C.C. game against Whitgift Wanderers at Crystal Palace on 26 June 1908. He made 111 not out and took 7 wickets. His youngest son, Charles Butler (who died on 6 June 1938 at the wicket hitting the boundary to record his Club's highest ever score) made 68 runs and took 3 wickets.

The coming of the War in 1914 greatly disturbed him. He thought all cricket should stop when it began. He moved from Sydenham to Fairmount in Mottingham Lane, Mottingham (now Fairmount Ladies Rest Home). Early in October 1915 he suffered a stroke while working in his garden. He managed to return to the house, was put to bed in a room overlooking the garden but he never recovered. He died during the morning of 23 October following a Zeppelin raid on nearby Croydon. The Country and the Empire were dismayed at the news and the Germans sensing its great propoganda value claimed that he had been killed in the raid. Many of his friends from Gloucestershire and around the country attended the funeral at the Elmers End Cemetery. He was buried beside his son W.G. (Junior), and his daughter Bessie. His wife Agnes was buried beside them in 1930.

So passed a National hero: Dr William Gilbert Grace,

L.R.C.P. (Edin.), M.R.C.S. (London) – Gilly to his family and close associates. W.G., the Doctor, the Champion, the Old Man to the cricket world. The first of the superstars and an amateur who relatively made as much money from cricket as modern tennis players and golfers make out of theirs, variously described as the warmest, the kindest and the greatest of all cricketers.

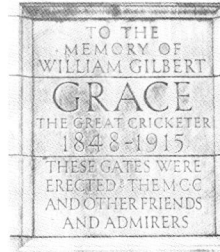

Inscription on the Grace Memorial Gates at Lord's.

As is the case in too many of these pre 1914–18 cemeteries, the area slowly reverted to English-type wilderness. For a time following World War II, the grave was tended by W.G.'s grandson, John Grace of Exmouth, and E.M.'s son, Dr Edgar Grace of Thornbury, when they visited London. In 1948 Don Bradman is reported to have accompanied some Australian cricketers to the site to commemorate W.G.'s birth, but cricket pilgrims had the greatest difficulty in finding the grave. In 1965 the Rev. A. N. B. Sugden drew attention to the neglected state of the grave and Mr R. G. Ingelse, a Dutch pilgrim, was so shocked at its dilapidated state that he wrote a letter to the *Daily Telegraph* on 23 October 1965. The outcome was the W.G. Memorial Fund. The grave was put in order. Eventually the XL Club, 40 Club of old cricketers, took over and it is now in excellent order, but still amid a surrounding wilderness. Cricket pilgrims can rest awhile before continuing their journey at the nearby Dr W. G. Grace hostelry, opened in 1966.

GRACE. William Gilbert. 1870-1899
Captain 1873-1899 inclusive. 361 matches

BATTING AND FIELDING

b. Downend, Bristol 18 July 1848 22 Tests v. Australia	Innings	Not Out	Runs	Highest Innings	Average	50's	Centuries	Stumpings	Catches
DERBYSHIRE	2	–	22	20	11.00	–	–	–	1
ESSEX	3	–	195	126	65.00	–	1	–	2
GLAMORGAN									
HAMPSHIRE									
KENT	40	6	1634	257	48.05	6	4	–	22
LANCASHIRE	75	8	2154	112	32.14	9	3	–	56
LEICESTER									
MIDDLESEX	68	7	2848	221*	46.68	21	5	–	30
NORTHANTS									
NOTTS	84	5	3276	182	41.46	14	11	–	50
SOMERSET	30	–	1248	288	41.60	2	4	–	27
SURREY	97	7	2815	160*	31.27	14	4	3	55
SUSSEX	73	6	3172	301	47.34	17	6	–	48
WARWICKS	15	1	392	70	28.00	1	–	–	10
WORCESTER									
YORKSHIRE	87	4	3801	318*	45.79	20	9	1	47
CAMBRIDGE									
OXFORD									
AUSTRALIANS	31	4	902	116*	33.40	4	2	–	17
M.C.C.	3	1	255	172	127.50	–	1	–	4
ENGLAND	4	–	94	31	23.50	–	–	–	4
PHILADELPHIANS	1	–	113	113	113.00	–	1	–	2
S. AFRICA									
W. INDIES									
TOTAL	613	49	22921	318*	40.64	108	51	4	375

GRACE. William Gilbert. 1870–1899

BOWLING

1.69 R.P.O.	Overs	Maidens	Runs	Wickets	Average	Best Bowling	5 Wickets in Innings	10 Wickets in Match
DERBYSHIRE	51.2	25	76	7	10.85	6-34	1	–
ESSEX	42.1	15	77	7	11.00	7-44	1	–
GLAMORGAN								
HAMPSHIRE								
KENT	716.3	274	1177	50	23.54	7-55	4	1
LANCASHIRE	1284.1	454	2409	117	20.58	7-37	9	1
LEICESTER								
MIDDLESEX	1443.1	474	3000	133	22.55	7-30	12	2
NORTHANTS								
NOTTS	2233	1022	3163	189	16.73	9-55	15	4
SOMERSET	662.4	226	1330	92	14.45	8-31	12	5
SURREY	2788.3	1168	4198	284	14.78	8-81	26	4
SUSSEX	1986.4	742	3441	166	20.72	7-46	13	4
WARWICKS	215	71	386	11	35.09	4-46	–	–
WORCESTER								
YORKSHIRE	2259	903	3790	198	19.14	8-33	17	4
AUSTRALIANS	753.1	280	1446	67	21.58	8-93	4	2
M.C.C	53.3	19	98	12	8.16	4-27	–	–
ENGLAND	152	75	189	13	14.53	4-46	–	–
PHILADELPHIANS	42	16	91	7	13.00	4-47	–	–
N. ZEALAND								
PAKISTAN								
S. AFRICA								
W. INDIES								
TOTAL	14683.3	5764	24871	1349	18.43	9-55	115	29

4

The Jessop Era
1900-1914

We must retrace our steps. A Committee Minute of the A.G.M. of 29 April 1897 reads: 'That it be an earnest request to the Committee to review their efforts to introduce some young rising professionals into the County team and that this General Meeting pledges itself to support the Committee in any expenditure that may be necessary in this direction' and of 27 April 1899: 'That the Committee be requested to advertise for five additional professionals to be employed in Gloucestershire.' Each shows the urgency for additions to the permanent staff.

The outcome may have been responsible for the arrival of Arthur Paish from Gloucester and of Ted Spry, the son of John Spry, groundsman at the County Ground, both spin bowlers of the whirling action. They were followed quickly by Harry Huggins and Percy Mills, of Stroud and Cheltenham, in 1901 and 1902. Arthur Paish returned to Gloucester as groundsman for the Wagon Works. He had one very good year but his action was ruled suspect. However he had seen the arrival of two of the greatest left arm spin bowlers in 1903 – George Dennett and Charlie Parker. Edward George Dennett from Upway in Dorset was found by Gilbert Jessop playing in Bristol club cricket, although he had played as professional for the Grange Club in Edinburgh.

George Dennett 1880-1937.

Charlie Parker was born at Prestbury near Cheltenham on 14 October 1882 into a farming family of six boys and girls. His eldest sister became a gifted musician and Charlie himself could discourse most knowledgeably on music and on the cricket field conducted his own brand of Enigma Variations. He attended Cheltenham Grammar School a few years after Gilbert Jessop. During his schooldays he was no doubt a studious boy with his sporting inclinations towards golf rather than cricket. He became a near scratch golfer and some say he could have been better than his brother, Arthur, who was the professional at the Cotswold Hills Golf Club at Cleeve Hill. He joined the Tewkesbury C.C. where he met up with Alf Dipper. F. H. Healing and Dr Adair Dighton, prominent members of the

Gloucestershire XI v Somerset 1901. Back row left to right: *H. Wrathall, F. Roberts, T. Langdon, A. Paish, J. Board, H. Huggins.* Front row: *W. S. A. Brown, T. H. Fowler, G. L. Jessop, C. O. H. Sewell, R. W. Rice.*

Club, also served on the County Committee.

Charlie Parker made his debut against London Counties where W.G. was enthroned, and no doubt W.G. would have assessed the lithe, easy action of this tall young seam bowler with the serious, studious face. This was to be the only game he played in 1903 and 1904. He began his first-class cricket career against Lancashire at Old Trafford in 1905 where he claimed his first victim, the notable amateur Test batsman, R. H. Spooner. Such was the competition he faced from George Dennett that he did not play in 1906 either and when he started to play more regularly in 1907 he had played only two games and taken one wicket in four seasons. Not an auspicious beginning to a remarkable career. He was just another very ordinary left arm slinger.

Alfred Ernest Dipper, born at Deerhurst on 9 November

1885, also came from farming stock and was one of John and Emma Dipper's ten children. There had been Dippers farming in the area since the 1700s and many of their graves are to be found in the Deerhurst churchyard. He too joined the nearby Tewkesbury C.C. and played his first County game as a hurried replacement against Kent at Tonbridge in 1908. He batted No. 9 but significantly was 56 not out at the end of the innings. He was moved up the order and in a few matches had made 56 and 64 against Sussex at the Gloucester Spa. As is so often the case, a new batsman or bowler does not immediately establish his place in the side. It was not until 1911 that he could command his. He made 1,101 runs in that season and the captain, Gilbert Jessop, was so pleased that he sent a letter to the father and bet him a brace of partridge he would make even more runs the following season. The letter also advised him that his winter allowance had been reduced to 10/-d (50p) weekly. He did not claim his bet for Alf missed much of the next season through appendicitis.

Alf Dipper scored many of his runs on the leg side. The story goes that the Deerhurst boys, with their one end pitch, played in a field where there was a bed of nettles under the hedge on the leg side and the young Alf soon learnt the value of hitting the ball in that direction. Many a future County captain would be driven to distraction trying to close the gaps on the legside, but it was like trying to keep water in a colander.

Great spin bowlers demand a great wicket keeper. They had to wait a few years for the arrival of Harry Smith in 1912. Born at Fishponds on 21 May 1891 he came into the County side via nearby Frenchay C.C. where at first he had bowled leg spinners before developing a natural ability behind the stumps. Gloucestershire cricket will be for ever in the debt of these five great professionals, Percy Mills, George Dennett, Charlie Parker, Alf Dipper and Harry Smith who, with their skill, their industry and their loyalty were to serve their County into the 1930s.

Cricket often rears in families and generations. Sussex is the County of the Parks, the Langridges, Cornfords; Worcestershire the Fosters; Norfolk the Edriches; but Gloucestershire too commands a truly formidable list, the Graces, the Townsends, Brownlees, Roberts, Barnetts. Then there were the four sons of Lady Bateman Champain who played for the County during this period to the First War. A distinguished quartet, one became an admiral, another a bishop and Francis Henry, known as Frank, was an outstanding all-round athlete of Corinthian stature. He won cricket and rugby Blues for Oxford, was a most stylish, forcing batsman and brilliant fielder who fitted completely into the exciting pattern of Jessop cricket. He played 84 times for the County making four centuries, became a schoolmaster, first at Sedbergh and finally at Blundell's, Tiverton, Devon. He suffered a heart attack just before Christmas 1942. When the ambulance arrived to take him to hospital he looked up at the two white coated attendants and remarked, 'Ah, I see the umpires are going out'. He died that evening of 29 December 1942.

The Robinsons are another great Gloucestershire cricket family. They sprang from Elias Arthur Robinson who founded

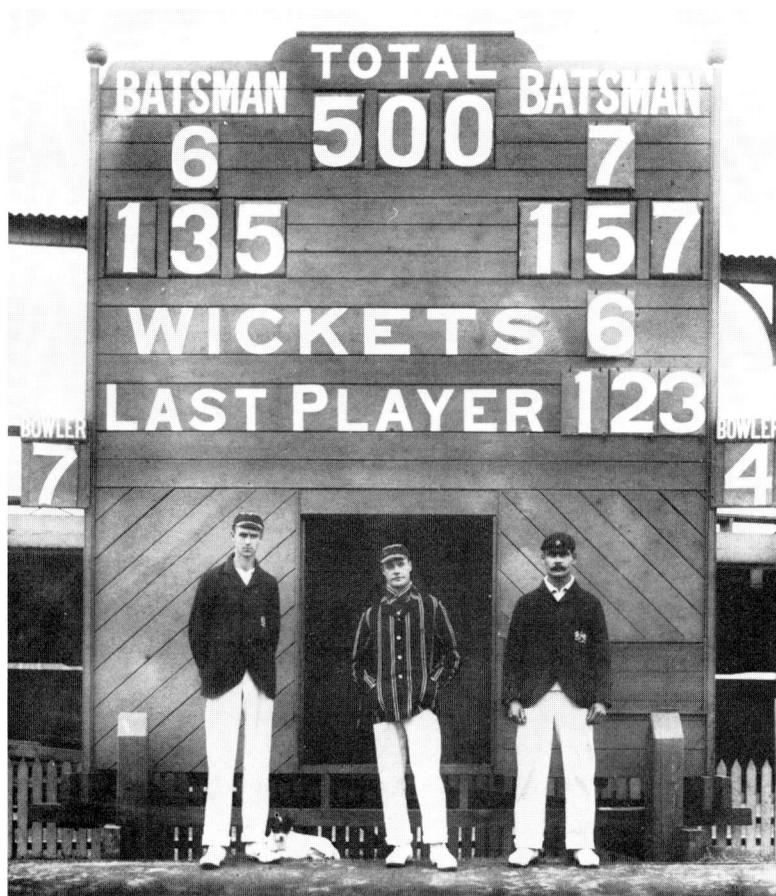

Gloucestershire v West Indies, Bristol, 28–30 June 1900, C. L. Townsend, G. L. Jessop and H. Wrathall stand in front of the scoreboard showing details at the fall of Jessop's wicket.

77

GLOUCESTERSHIRE V. WEST INDIANS,

AT

COUNTY GROUND, BRISTOL, June 28, 29 & 30, 1900.

GLO'STERSHIRE. First Innings.

W. S. A. Brown, Esq. ...	c Mignon, b Burton ...	60
N. O. Tacart, Esq. ...	c Burton, b Mignon ...	9
Board	c Goodman, b Burton ...	3
H. J. Hodgkins, Esq. ...	b Burton	0
Wrathall	c Constantine, b Mignon	123
C. L. Townsend, Esq. ...	b Mignon	140
G. L. Jessop, Esq. ...	c Hinds, b Mignon ...	157
O. Wreford-Brown, Esq.	not out	44
Langdon	c Sproston, b Burton ...	50
Paish	b Burton	0
Roberts	b Mignon	11
	Byes 15, l-b 6, n-b 1	22
	Total	619

WEST INDIANS. First Innings. Second Innings.

	First Innings		Second Innings	
S. W. Sproston, Esq. ...	c Paish, b Townsend ..	1	c Townsend, b Paish ...	36
C. A. Ollivierre, Esq. .	c Paish, b Roberts ...	15	run out	42
G. C. Learmond, Esq. ...	c Langdon, b Townsend	0	c Board, b Langdon ...	17
P. A. Goodman, Esq. ...	run out	38	c Paish, b Roberts... ...	34
F. Hinds, Esq.	l b w, b Roberts	8	c Board, b Townsend ...	34
L. Constantine, Esq. ...	b Roberts	21	c sub., b Brown	65
Burton	b Roberts	0	c sub., b Townsend ...	11
W. Bowring, Esq.	not out	5	c Townsend, b Langdon	21
A. Warner, Esq.	b Roberts	3	l b w, b Langdon	24
W. H. Mignon, Esq. ...	b Townsend	1	c Board, b Townsend ...	10
Woods	b Townsend	0	not out	5
	Bye 1, l-b 2, n-b 1 ...	4	Byes 7, n-b 1	8
	Total	96	Total	307

ANALYSIS OF THE BOWLING.

GLOUCESTERSHIRE. 1st Innings.

	Overs.	Mdns.	Runs.	Wkts.
C. A. Ollivierre	23	1	138	0
Burton	25	4	71	5
Woods	33	5	147	0
W. H. Mignon...	33.3	4	148	5
F. Hinds	8	0	76	0
P. A. Goodman	7	1	17	0

Woods bowled 1 no-ball.

WEST INDIANS.

	1st Innings.				2nd Innings.			
	Overs.	Mdns.	Runs.	Wkts.	Overs.	Mdns.	Runs.	Wkts.
C. L. Townsend	16.5	1	53	4	17.1	1	62	3
Roberts	16	8	39	5	18	4	50	1
Paish	—	—	—	—	15	2	63	1
W. S. A. Brown	—	—	—	—	27	10	67	1
Langdon	—	—	—	—	13	3	57	3

Roberts bowled 1 no-ball.   Roberts bowled 1 no-ball.

Result—Gloucestershire won by an innings and 216 runs.

the great Bristol paper organisation in the 1840s. There was a Family Robinson team with regular fixtures from 1878 to 1914, but as the pressures of the daily round increased, these were restricted to August Bank Holiday games as the Second War approached, but a few occasional games were played in the 1950s. In the earlier period one of the most sharply contested games was against the Grace family XI. There was an occasion at the County Ground when the Graces found themselves short of a wicket keeper. Dr E.M. took the gloves but in a few overs he was called away on an urgent case and Jack Board, the County keeper, took over. The patient must have made a quick recovery for a little later E.M. was spotted amongst the spectators in the Stand. Foster Gotch Robinson, born in Bristol on 19 September 1880, who took over the family business and in 1936 received a knighthood, and his cousin, Douglas Charles Robinson, who chose the Army as his career and won an M.C. in the First War, both played first during this Jessop period.

Two other future captains began their Gloucestershire careers in those years leading to the First War, William Henry Rowlands and Michael Arthur Green.

Such was the material at hand for Gilbert Jessop when he left the London Stock Exchange and took over his captaincy of the County in 1900 following the departure of W.G. for Crystal Palace and Troup for India. The portents seemed good but distance in time will always simplify the issues. By then he was the most exciting batsman in the game and in 1899 had already played his first Test Match, but as a fast bowler, batting well down the order. The County was indeed lucky to have his quiet authority, example and leadership at this difficult time.

There also began a continuing, happy relationship with the Committee; no longer were they subjected to a cricket field dictatorship, and it is not surprising that the County's fortunes turned for the better. Jessop's contribution in 1900 was phenomenal: 179 in 105 minutes against Sussex and 104 in 70 minutes and 139 in 85 minutes (ten of which had been lost retrieving the ball from outside the ground) against Yorkshire; by the season's end he had completed a remarkable first-class double, 2,210 runs and 104 wickets.

Charles Townsend did not play regularly after 1901. He was only twenty-four but he turned his attention to his legal career. That season Jessop made 2,323 runs in first-class cricket but had taken only 25 wickets for Gloucestershire. The back strain, first experienced in that Test Match in 1890 where he had been overbowled never left him and he rarely bowled flat out again. He played four more Tests against Australia in 1902 and in the match at the Oval on Wednesday, 13 August, he played what C. B. Fry has described 'as the greatest innings in cricket'.

Surrey County Cricket Club.

KENNINGTON OVAL, AUGUST 11, 12 & 13, 1902.

ENGLAND v. AUSTRALIA.

AUSTRALIA.	First Innings		Second Innings	
1 Mr. V. Trumper	b Hirst	42	run out	2
2 Mr. R. A. Duff	c Lilley, b Hirst	23	b Lockwood	6
3 Mr. C. Hill	b Hirst	11	c MacLaren, b Hirst	34
4 Mr. J. Darling	c Lilley, b Hirst	3	c MacLaren, b Lockwood	15
5 Mr. M. A. Noble	c & b Jackson	52	b Braund	13
6 Mr. S. E. Gregory	b Hirst	23	b Braund	9
7 Mr. W. W. Armstrong	b Jackson	17	b Lockwood	21
8 Mr. A. Hopkins	c MacLaren b Lockwood	40	c Lilley, b Lockwood	3
9 Mr. H. Trumble	not out	64	not out	7
10 Mr. J. Kelly	c Rhodes, b Braund	39	l-b-w, b Lockwood	0
11 Mr. J. V. Saunders	l-b-w, b Braund	0	c Tyldesley, b Rhodes	2
	B 5, l b 3, w , n-b 2	10	B 7, l b 2, w , n-b ,	9
	Total	324	Total	121

1st Innings ... 1 for 47 2·63 3·69 4·82 5·126 6·174 7·175 8·256 9·324

2nd Innings 1 for 6 2·9 3·31 4·71 5·75 6·91 7·99 8·114 9·115

ENGLAND.	First Innings		Second Innings	
1 Mr. A. C. MacLaren	c Armstrong, b Trumble	10	b Saunders	2
2 Mr. L. C. H. Palairet	b Trumble	20	b Saunders	6
3 Tyldesley	b Trumble	33	b Saunders	0
4 Hayward	b Trumble	0	c Kelly, b Saunders	7
5 Hon. F. S. Jackson	c Armstrong, b Saunders	2	c & b Trumble	49
6 Braund	c Hill, b Trumble	22	c Kelly b Trumble	2
7 Mr. G. L. Jessop	b Trumble	13	c Noble, b Armstrong	104
8 Hirst	c & b Trumble	43	not out	58
9 Lockwood	c Noble, b Saunders	25	l-b-w, Trumble	2
10 Lilley	c Trumper, b Trumble	0	c Darling, b Trumble	16
11 Rhodes	not out	0	not out	6
	B 13, l b 2, w , n-b	15	B 5 l-b 6, w , n-b	11
	Total	183	Total (9 wkts)	263

1st Innings ... 1 for 31 2·36 3·62 4·67 5·67 6·83 7·137 8·179 9·183

2nd Innings ... 1 for 5 2·5 3·10 4·31 5·48 6·157 7·187 8·214 9·248

BOWLING ANALYSIS.

AUSTRALIA.—First Innings.

	Overs.	Maidens.	Runs.	Wickets.
Lockwood	24	2	85	1
Rhodes	28	9	46	0
Hirst	29	5	77	5
Braund	16·5	5	29	2
Jackson	20	4	66	2
Jessop	6	2	11	0

Lockwood and Rhodes each bowled one no-ball.

Second Innings.

Rhodes	22	7	38	1
Lockwood	20	6	45	5
Jackson	4	3	7	0
Hirst	5	1	7	1
Braund	9	1	15	2

ENGLAND.—First Innings.

Trumble	31	13	65	8
Saunders	23	7	79	2
Noble	7	3	24	0

Second Innings.

Trumble	33·5	4	108	4
Saunders	24	3	105	4
Armstrong	4	0	28	1
Noble	5	0	11	0

Umpires—C. E. Richardson & A. A. White.   Stumps drawn 6.30 p.m.

RESULT. ENGLAND WON BY ONE WICKET.

MERRITT & HATCHER, Ltd., "Cricket" Office, 168, Upper Thames Street, E.C.

England had been set 263 runs to win on a difficult wicket. Jessop went in with the score at 48 for 5 and for the next hour and a quarter he savaged the Australian bowling. When he was out he had scored 104 out of the 139 runs added. Fifteen runs were still required with the last man on his way to the wicket. That was the occasion when George Hirst of Yorkshire went to meet fellow Yorkshireman, Wilfred Rhodes, and spoke those immortal words, 'Wilfred, we'll get 'em in singles'. They did! England had won by one wicket.

In the meantime Jack Board had become a thoroughly reliable batsman and had already made a double century when in 1903 he and Jessop added 320 runs for the sixth wicket against Sussex at Brighton. Jessop went on to 200 in two hours and finally 286 in two hours and a quarter. His back gave out in the Test against the Australians in July 1909 and although he never bowled fast afterwards he continued to take wickets, bowling at a medium pace and at times switching to off breaks and leg cutters.

Gloucestershire results began to deteriorate again as early as 1901 and one sure proof was the loss of the Townsend/Jessop partnership to Gloucestershire and to England, for both of them would have been great Test players. There was one other cricketer, Cyril Octavius Hudson Sewell, born in Pietermaritsburg on 17 December 1874, who unfortunately could not give his full time to the game and who eventually took over the captaincy from Jessop. He was the son of J. J. Sewell, an early contemporary of W.G. and one of the founder members of the Club. He was a native of Cirencester, had been to school at Marlborough, but later emigrated to South Africa. Cyril returned to this country in 1894 with the first South African team to tour this country. He remained behind to study law, and played for the County from 1895 until the First War. He was a brilliant batsman and fielder.

1909 has often been labelled the worst season in the history of the Club. There was a complaint at the A.G.M. of 27 January 1910 that 'Gloucestershire had become "a chopping block", year after year, for the stronger Counties.' Some of the more

C. O. H. Sewell.

Gloucestershire C.C.C. 1905.
Standing: H. J. Huggins, E. J. Dennett, J. H. Board, T. Langdon, D. T. Mills, W. H. Hale.
Seated: F. E. Thomas, R. T. Godsell, G. L. Jessop, L. D. Brownlee, H. Wrathall.

81

Lord's Ground.

ENGLAND v. SOUTH AFRICA.

MONDAY & TUESDAY, JULY 1, 2, 1907, (Three-Day Match.)

ENGLAND.	First Innings		Second Innings
1 C. B. Fry	b Vogler	33	
2 Hayward	st Sherwell, b Vogler	21	
3 Tyldesley	b Vogler	52	
4 R. E. Foster	st Sherwell, b Vogler	8	
5 Braund	c Kotze, b Faulkner	104	
6 Hirst	b Vogler	7	
7 G. L. Jessop	c Faulkner, b Vogler	93	
8 J. N. Crawford	c Sherwell, b Schwarz	22	
9 Arnold	b Schwarz	4	
10 Lilley	c Nourse, b Vogler	48	
11 Blythe	not out	4	
	B 24, l-b 6, w 2, n-b	32	B , l-b , w n-b .
	Total	428	Total

FALL OF THE WICKETS.

1 54	2 55	3 79	4 140	5 152	6 363	7 335	8 347	9 401	10 428
1	2	3	4	5	6	7	8	9	10

ANALYSIS OF BOWLING.

Name.	O.	M.	R.	W.	Wd.	N-b.	O.	M.	R.	W.	Wd.	N-b.
Kotze	12	2	43	0								
Schwarz	34	7	98	2	2							
Vogler	47.2	12	128	7								
White	15	2	52	0								
Nourse	1	0	2	0								
Faulkner	12	1	53	1								
Sinclair	6	1	22	0								

SOUTH AFRICA.	First Innings		Second Innings	
2 W. A. Shalders	c Lilley, b Arnold	2	b Hirst	0
10 P. W. Sherwell	run out	6	b Blythe	115
3 M. Hathorn	c Foster b Hirst	6	c Fry b Blythe	50
5 A. D. Nourse	b Blythe	43	not out	11
6 G. A. Faulkner	c Jessop b Braund	44	not out	12
1 S. J. Snooke	lbw, b Blythe	5		
4 G. C. White	b Arnold	0		
7 J. H. Sinclair	b Arnold	0		
9 R. O. Schwarz	not out	0		
8 A. E. Vogler	c Lilley, b Arnold	3		
11 J. J. Kotze	b Arnold	0		
	B 9, l-b 2, w 1, n-b	12	B 15, l-b 2, w , n-b 17	
	Total	140	Total	185

FALL OF THE WICKETS.

1	2	3	4	5	6	7	8	9	10.
1	2	3	4	5	6	7	8	9	10.

ANALYSIS OF BOWLING.

Name.	O.	M.	R.	W.	Wd.	N-b.	O.	M.	R.	W.	Wd.	N-b.
Hirst	18	7	35	1			16	8	24	1		
Arnold	22	7	37	5			13	2	41	0		
Jessop	2	0	6	0								
Crawford	5	1	20	0			4	0	19	0		
Blythe	8	3	18	2			21	5	58	2		
Braund	7	4	10	1			4	0	26	0		

Umpires—Millward and West. Scorers—G. G. Hearne and Martin.

Play commences 1st day at 11.30, 2nd and 3rd day at 11.
Luncheon at 1.30 p.m.   Stumps drawn at 6.30 p.m.

ONE PENNY.

South Africans, 1907.

TEST MATCH ENGLAND'S TEAM v SOUTH AFRICA

England v South Africa at Lord's 1907.

difficult games had been dropped already and easier ones introduced. One of these was Northamptonshire who had just joined the First Class Counties and were bowled out for 12 at Gloucester Spa. George Dennett took 8 wickets for 9 in the first innings and 7 for 12 in the second. Gloucestershire did not win. It rained all the third day! That season George Dennett became the first Gloucestershire bowler to take 200 wickets. Not all was gloom; the County beat Yorkshire in a memorable game at Bristol in 1906. Gloucestershire scored 164, to which Yorkshire replied with 159; George Dennett took 8 for 85. Yorkshire looked to be winning until the last few overs of the game when Jessop had the last wicket lbw with one run to go. That run cost Yorkshire the Championship.

There must have been much euphoric and wishful thinking as the bells greeted the new century. The portents that had looked so bright for G.C.C.C. in 1900 gradually clouded over as the first few years passed. Not a thought would have been given to fields where cricket was to be no more than a happy memory. Besides the loss of Charles Townsend and Jessop's bowling incapacity and increasing ill health, the performances of the older professionals began to show the inevitable diminishing returns against the advance of the younger. George Dennett was the one exception. These years were the golden years of English County cricket which the West Country could not match.

From the very beginning the finances of the Club had maintained a small annual balance, but the upkeep of the County Ground imposed a demand that could not be sustained. Membership of a Club is the barometer of its success and the first indication of the storms ahead can be seen in the Minutes of a Special General Meeting held on 20 February 1902, attended by 104 members of the Club. It had been called to ratify a new set of rules, one of which was to increase the membership fees, and to impose others. This was actually carried, only to be rescinded at the A.G.M. that followed on 24 April 1902 attended by 153 members. Over 200 proxy votes were also recorded.

Another Special General Meeting of 28 January 1904 dealt exclusively with the financial position of the Club and gave warning of the greater problems ahead. It concluded with a motion proposed by the Chairman, H. W. Beloe, seconded by J. A. Bush and carried unanimously: 'That this meeting approved of the circular (copy of which has been sent to each member of G.C.C.C.) asking for guarantees to the amount of £2,000 to enable the Committee to carry on the work in connection with the Club.'

A credit balance of £2,726 2s. 4d. in 1879, reduced to £295 19s. 2d. in 1904 had decreased to £87 19s. 2d. in 1911. W. S. A. Brown organised a Carnival which produced £115 and saved the Club from further embarrassment, and in 1912 another took place at the Clifton Zoo. Over the winter of 1911–12 the professionals' pay was reduced by half. At the beginning of the next season they were distributed around the County to help defray some of their wages, but 'it was agreed there would be no saving of expenses, but it would be more advantage to the County cricket in general'.

England v *South Africa 1907 – diagram showing Jessop's score of 93 in 70 minutes.*

Chairman Henry Beloe, sugar broker, who had sustained the club so steadfastly since he became the first permanent Chairman in 1888, greeted members to the A.G.M. of 30 January 1913 with the sombre words that 'he had never before had to meet them with such a disastrous balance sheet'. C. O. H. Sewell, who was now the Secretary and Captain of the Club prophetically 'asked Members to support the Club better by

G. L. Jessop arriving at the ground.

saying kind instead of unkind things of the team and the Club generally'.

A few years before in 1909 Gloucestershire left behind another milestone along their Road. E.M. retired as Secretary. He wrote up the Minutes of the A.G.M. of 28 January 1909. He did not complete them, neither were they signed by the Chairman at the beginning of the next A.G.M. of 27 January 1910. Unhappily there is no reference to his departure in those written, incidentally, by Gilbert Jessop, the next Secretary. Unrecorded went a lifetime of tireless endeavour on behalf of the County Club. His memorial from Gloucestershire County

W. S. A. Brown.

Cricket Club lies in those minutes so meticulously written since the first recorded Committee Meeting of 20 March 1873. So the last and the most interesting of the Graces had left their Gloucestershire cricket.

An appeal for donations towards a Dr E. M. Grace Testimonial was begun on 27 February 1909. It raised £600.

E.M. died on 20 May 1911 at his Thornbury home, Park House. His memory is commemorated with a glass window in Downend Church and a plaque in Thornbury Church. His grave is in the Downend Churchyard in company with so many of the Graces.

Gilbert Jessop relinquished the Secretaryship of the Club as reported at the A.G.M. of 25 January 1912: 'They also congratulated the County on having obtained the services of Mr C. O. H. Sewell as Secretary,' who duly 'thanked the Committee for having elected him to the post and giving him the opportunity promoting the welfare of the County Cricket Club to the best of his ability'.

Although the handwriting of the Minutes was to change again, the problems remained. Gilbert Jessop gave up the Captaincy at the end of the following season. He continued to play but did not bowl again. His hurricane batting and quick-silver fielding continued to thrill whenever he played. There can be no doubt that he was not in the best of health. For too long and too often alone he had borne the formidable load, nobly with captivating charm and modesty. He had indeed made his exciting contribution to Gloucestershire cricket in those twenty years. He moved house from London to Shire-hampton the more to enjoy his golf.

The final tribute to this great cricketer must remain with C. B. Fry's memorable comment that 'No man has ever driven a ball so hard, so high and so often in so many different directions. No man has ever made cricket so dramatic an entertainment.'

To complete the Jessop story. He met his future wife on the boat bringing back McLaren's team from the 1901–02 Australian Tour. He was playing a game of catch with two children on the deck when the rubber tobacco pouch they were using hit one of the two ladies passing. The one gave them a frosty look the other smiled. She was Millicent Osborne of Hamilton, New South Wales. They became engaged three weeks later and were married at Christ Church, Lancaster Gate, on 8 October, 1902,

86

with Charles Townsend acting as best man. He was forty at the outbreak of the War, volunteered immediately but was soon invalided out of the Army. After the hostilities he devoted his attention to writing his book *A Cricketer's Log*, and various articles. In 1922 he became Secretary to Edgware Golf Club until his continuing ill health in 1936 forced him to retire. He and his wife then went to live in his son's vicarage at Fordingham St George in Dorchester. Millicent died in June 1953 but Gilbert, in delicate health, lived on until 11 May 1955, a week short of his eighty-first birthday.

Such was Gilbert Jessop. But there is a delightful postscript to add. In 1966 a Gilbert Jessop Society was founded in Australia. Messrs J. D. J. Beatty and M. J. Detmold at the Faculty of Law in the University of Adelaide, South Australia 'thought that cricket generally was in the doldrums and we wanted a Society that could represent the real spirit of the game'. The University lies near to the Torrens River and Jessop is the only cricketer ever to hit a ball from the Adelaide Oval into the river. A Jessop collection is now housed in the University Law Library. The Rev. Gilbert Jessop donated some family items in memory of his illustrious father.

F. E. Thomas.

It is interesting to note that with Gilbert Jessop, 1910, and Cyril Sewell, 1912, Gloucestershire had operated the Captain/Secretary appointment before the First War that was adopted by many of the Counties after the Second. Sewell's batting and fielding and his flair for Captaincy gave the cricket some confidence. The results for 1913 improved. George Dennett was now one of the most feared bowlers in the country – he never did play in a Test Match, and the younger professionals, Alf Dipper, Charlie Parker and wicket keeper Harry Smith, had established their positions in the side.

So to that fateful year. The 1914 A.G.M. was held on 29 January at the Town Hall, Cheltenham, with Canon R. Waterfield in the chair. This was the first time that a Club A.G.M. had been held outside Bristol. The significance can be seen in the long-serving Harry Beloe's opening speech, 'It must be remembered that the financial position of the Club was worse than last year chiefly due to the very bad receipts at Bristol. The support given by the public at Cheltenham was gratifying and so long as this continued Cheltenham would receive its proper share of matches.' These were to be the last reported Minutes

G. L. Jessop was commissioned into the Manchester Regiment at the start of the First World War. He's seen here making a recruiting speech in Manchester and it is reported that approximately 600 men marched behind the band to the recruiting depot.

of the 1914 season. Gloucestershire won only one game and, as in 1909, finished at the bottom of the Championship Table. The support was negligible and 'the good people of Bristol studiously kept away from the matches at Ashley Down'. There was little hope for the future, either on or off the field.

War was declared on 4 August 1914. The last game played was against Surrey at the Oval on 31 August and Gloucestershire lost by an innings and 36 runs in two days. This was also the last game for Surrey. The Oval had already been requisitioned by the War Office but Surrey were given permission to play that one game. Gloucestershire had the greatest difficulty raising a team and took the field with ten men. George Dennett and Alf Dipper had already joined up and Captain Mike Green obtained special leave from the Gloucestershire Regiment. The one bright spot of that unhappy game was provided by Cyril Sewell, who made a flashing 165 out of 230 runs in two hours. A young opening batsman named Jack Hobbs made a chanceless 141 for Surrey.

The Minutes of the Cheltenham A.G.M., held before the season began, were signed by Chairman Harry Beloe on 27 October 1914, but there is no other record of the Meeting. *Wisden* reports that the professionals had been given permission to join another County; Gloucestershire would not go on paying them. It was decided to continue the Club for another year but 'no fixtures should be arranged for 1915'.

Gloucestershire cricket had collapsed and it is doubtful if the Club could have appeared for another season. They were on the road to nowhere. They had stumbled to the cross-roads and were looking into the gathering storm for the way ahead.

JESSOP. Gilbert Laird. 1894–1914
Captain 1900–1912 inclusive. 345 matches

BATTING AND FIELDING

b. Cheltenham 19 May 1874 18 Tests for England 13 Australia 5 South Africa	Innings	Not Out	Runs	Highest Innings	Average	50's	Centuries	Stumpings	Catches
DERBYSHIRE	3	–	150	93	50.00	2	–	–	4
ESSEX	24	1	749	86	32.56	6	–	–	17
GLAMORGAN									
HAMPSHIRE	20	1	1016	161	53.47	2	5	–	10
KENT	64	–	1357	87	21.20	8	–	–	34
LANCASHIRE	45	2	1381	168	32.11	10	1	–	25
LEICESTER									
MIDDLESEX	52	2	1537	124	30.74	6	2	–	17
NORTHANTS	15	–	515	162	34.33	2	1	–	10
NOTTS	59	2	2136	206	37.47	16	4	–	45
SOMERSET	57	5	1903	234	36.59	10	4	–	40
SURREY	57	4	1559	139	29.41	7	3	–	39
SUSSEX	47	2	2052	286	45.60	10	5	–	26
WARWICKS	39	1	1233	126	32.44	4	3	–	19
WORCESTER	42	1	1405	165	34.26	5	4	–	21
YORKSHIRE	51	1	1285	139	25.70	5	3	–	32
CAMBRIDGE	6	–	8.	48	13.50	–	–	–	5
OXFORD									
AUSTRALIANS	14	1	274	57	21.07	1	–	–	5
INDIANS	2	–	103	79	51.50	1	–	–	2
N. ZEALAND									
PAKISTAN									
S. AFRICA	6	–	93	26	15.50	–	–	–	2
W. INDIES									
PHILADELPHIANS	1	–	101	101	101.00	–	1	–	1
LONDON COUNTY	1	–	6	6	6.00	–	–	–	–
TOTAL	605	23	18936	286	32.53	95	36	–	354

JESSOP. Gilbert Laird. 1894–1914

BOWLING

	Overs	Maidens	Runs	Wickets	Average	Best Bowling	5 Wickets in Innings	10 Wickets in Match
DERBYSHIRE	46	7	166	4	41.50	2-70	–	–
ESSEX	265.5	66	627	27	23.22	8-29	1	–
GLAMORGAN								
HAMPSHIRE	60	11	135	8	16.87	3-23	–	–
KENT	632.3	171	1581	78	20.26	8-82	3	–
LANCASHIRE	452.5	119	1287	53	24.28	8-54	3	–
LEICESTER								
MIDDLESEX	696.5	219	1679	70	23.98	8-58	4	1
NORTHANTS	38.3	15	65	4	16.25	2-3	–	–
NOTTS	353.3	128	772	31	24.90	4-15	–	–
SOMERSET	423.5	101	1176	44	26.72	5-79	2	–
SURREY	521.2	167	1299	69	18.82	6-72	6	2
SUSSEX	443.4	150	1096	47	23.31	6-33	2	–
WARWICKS	439.3	146	956	49	19.51	7-92	3	–
WORCESTER	311	80	973	47	20.70	7-77	1	–
YORKSHIRE	511.4	126	1357	60	22.61	7-61	4	–
CAMBRIDGE	46	7	169	5	33.80	4-111	–	–
OXFORD								
AUSTRALIANS	137.3	24	386	14	27.57	7-91	1	–
INDIANS	14.5	2	47	3	15.66	3-47	–	–
N. ZEALAND								
PAKISTAN								
S. AFRICA	15.5	7	39	4	9.75	4-33	–	–
W. INDIES								
PHILADELPHIANS	23.1	5	49	3	16.33	3-26	–	–
TOTAL	5434.2	1551	13864	620	22.36	8-29	30	3

5

Gloucestershire C.C.C. Resuscitated
1918-1923

Four muddy, bloody years were to pass before the storms cleared and the cricket sun came out again. History remained indifferent. Gloucestershire gathered themselves together, found their Road, took one wistful look back at the mirage of those golden years now fading into the distance and then set off into their future.

Sixty-four of their cricketers had joined the services; fourteen had died and many others had been seriously wounded.

The Club was 'entirely suspended' following the unhappy conclusion of the 1914 season. It remained so until 1918 when *Wisden* reports:

> 'Immediately following the Armistice, many great efforts were at once made to put the Club on its feet again. A Committee was formed and meetings held for the purpose of getting support were engaged all over the County.'

However, the most significant event of those First War years was the sale of the County Ground in 1915 to Messrs J. S. Fry & Sons, Ltd. 'as a recreation ground for their employees, but it will be available for Gloucestershire C.C.C. Matches after the War.'

After prolonged deliberations and with commendable foresight the Committee members, some of them from before the War, some old cricketers, some business men, some lawyers, all of them devoted to the cause of Gloucestershire cricket, gradually thrashed out a constitution and a set of rules that in general have persisted to the present day. The Minutes of those years after that War reflect an air of confidence and industry that was not often matched by results. Their brief was 'the resuscitation of the Club', and the task of restoring life to an almost lifeless corpse was achieved. Their Chairman was J. A. Bush's younger brother, R. E., who had also played in the W.G. era; the members were Harry Beloe, Chairman during the difficult years, his brother G.H., W. S. A. Brown, Major C. Troup and H. V. Page, all of them cricketers. But now new and younger members appeared who served the County with distinction in the years ahead. They included the Reverend J. H. Seabrook, A. E. Stanley Hill, W. T. Pearce, E. W. Leonard Olive, H. Walker, F. O. Wills, H. G. Roslyn, F. G. Robinson, D. C. Robinson and W. H. Rowlands.

In his opening remarks at the 1920 A.G.M. of 30 March, held in the Grand Hotel, Bristol, Lord Beauchamp reflected that he was delighted to be the Club's President in its Jubilee Year. So much for the critics who would have 1871 the year of the Club's formation.

It is found that the Club was run by the General Executive Committee, with Finance, Match and Selection Sub-Committees. The Council of the Club was first so called in the Minutes of the 1921 A.G.M. but there is an implication that it had come into being during 1920. The main committee had been enlarged as far back as 1910 to give a wider representation of members across the County, when specific details of this representation appeared for the first time: from Gloucester four members; Cheltenham four; Stroud two; Forest of Dean North and South two; the Cotswolds one; Tewkesbury one; Thornbury and District one; Wootton-under-Edge one; Berkeley, Sharpness, Dursley one; Cirencester and District one and Bristol eighteen. Eighteen from the North of the County and eighteen from Bristol with the addition of one representative from J. S. Fry & Sons. The composition of the Council has changed only slightly through the years, but its function has remained. It is the corner-stone of the Club, the buffer between the members and the Committee. They met quarterly, elected the Chairman, the Captain and the other Officers of the Club and agreed to the composition of the Sub-Committees.

Other information is to be found in those first Minutes after the War. George Dennett had joined the Somerset Light Infantry and had been commissioned from the ranks. When the 1919 season commenced he was still serving in India. He did not play again until 1920 when he received his long postponed benefit. Gilbert Jessop was in ill health and had retired. Cyril Sewell was serving in Italy.

Success had to be earned and came only slowly. A Special Appeal raised £4,203. There were annual losses of £1,680, £1,339 and £1,030 in 1920, 1922 and 1923. The only profitable year was 1921 (£1,552) when a fine summer coincided with

F. G. Robinson's
Gloucester XI v
H. J. Packer's XI 18
May 1921. Front
row: *C. W. L.*
Parker, P. Mills,
W. H. Rowlands, Miss
Robinson, F. G.
Robinson, Mrs
Walker, A. E.
Dipper, P. F. C.
Williams, E. G.
Dennett, Wally
Hammond is behind
Mills and Rowlands.

games against the Australians at Bristol and Cheltenham.

The County played at all the home grounds free of charge, thanks to Messrs J. S. Fry & Sons, Ltd. (for reference purposes the County ground in these years and until 1933 is known as Fry's), H. J. Packer & Co. Ltd whose ground was known as Packer's or Greenbank, the Gloucester C.C. known as the Spa, Messrs the Gloucester Wagon Works Co. Ltd., known as Wagon Works, the Councils of Cheltenham and Clifton Colleges and eventually the Cheltenham C.C., the Victoria Ground.

In the history of the County there have been very few years when membership of the Club has not been a major problem. Chairman R. E. Bush, at the 1920 A.G.M., summed it up for all time: '... with a population of about a million, they ought certainly to reach a membership of 2,000 . . . Bristol has done magnificently in resuscitating the old Club, and it was rather a matter of regret they had not received a greater measure of help from those in other parts of the County.' However, in 1921 the membership reached a target of 3,000; the books were closed but reopened almost at once.

Soon the Minutes mentioned 'achievements' and reflected a growing confidence and authority that was offering help to others. 'The Bristol and District Cricket Association said their application for the preparation of cricket pitches on the Downs had been most favourably received.' A similar application to the Sanitary Committee of the Corporation of Bristol with regard to the Parks, had met with a reply 'that it could not be entertained', but the Committee 'would gladly confer with the Cricket Association because it was the smaller clubs who supplied the County with players.' Also in 1921 came the interesting comment, 'Mr Bush and Mr Foster Robinson both pleaded the cause of the new Bristol Rugby Memorial Ground which deserved the enthusiastic support of local cricketers and sportsmen.'

W. G. Tunnicliffe (son of the great Yorkshire cricketer, John Tunnicliffe who came to Bristol in 1908) became the Club's Secretary in 1922 and was the first full time non-playing Secretary. Walter Pearce had filled the position in an honorary capacity. In a sense E.M. had been a playing Secretary, amongst his many other interests, while Gilbert Jessop and Cyril Sewell were Secretary/Captains. For the first time Gloucestershire cricket became comprehensively objective and businesslike with a cohesion that had been lacking before the war.

Gloucestershire played sixteen championship games in 1919. Fifteen counties restarted their first-class fixtures. Worcestershire were not able to do so, but played 'friendlies', whilst Glamorgan did not join the Championship until 1921. Before the season began there had been much controversy over the issue whether the games should be of two or three days' duration. Eventually the former was accepted. The counter proposals that it would prove an expensive experiment, that some counties would experience difficulty in getting together a satisfactory team (Gloucestershire certainly did so) and that the counties should play either two or three day games as they wished, was defeated. At the end of that season the County finished in the middle of the table. They held that position in 1920 and 1921 but slumped to thirteenth in 1922.

So first-class cricket restarted. The Gloucestershire teams of the 1920s still contained some of the pre-war names. In 1919 there were some significant absentees; Gilbert Jessop's health had finally broken down; Cyril Sewell was still serving in Italy and George Dennett in India; Jack Board and Tom Langdon did not play after the War. Foster Robinson captained the side from 1919 to 1923, then followed Harry Rowlands of Cheltenham and occasionally Michael Arthur Green, Bristol born, who became a Regular Officer of the Gloucestershire Regiment and after the Second War, Secretary of Worcestershire C.C.C. The Barnetts of Cheltenham and Wycliffe College were another great Gloucestershire cricket family; Charles Sherborne, father of the renowned Charles, and his brothers Edgar and Percival, also played during these years as did the old professionals, Harry Huggins and Tom Gange – fast right arm bowler born in Pietermaritzburg, South Africa, who played in 37 matches and took 103 wickets.

The Gloucestershire team of the Grace days was at first all amateur, and remained so for many years, with only the addition of an occasional professional. As the years passed gradually the professional staff was increased, but the basis of the team remained amateur. There were to be some notable exceptions, but the roles would soon be reversed.

When George Dennett returned after six years service in India he took his well-deserved but long postponed Benefit in 1920. For a few more years he continued to wheel away with his bewitchingly enticing slow left arm spinners aimed at the off stump. Where George Dennett teased out batsmen Charlie Parker bristled with aggression. Only once again, in 1921, did he take over 100 wickets in the season. His first-class career ended in 1926 when he succeeded Billy Woof's son (also Billy), as cricket coach at Cheltenham College. He had taken 2,082 wickets for his County yet had not played in a Test Match. He died at Cheltenham on 15 September 1937 of Parkinson's Disease.

Charlie Parker 1882–1959.

Unrelieved season-long toil was now the lot of Alf Dipper, Charlie Parker, Percy Mills and Harry Smith. They shouldered their heavy responsibility with a deep sense of loyalty and duty with only an occasional wry smile of complaint.

Twice rejected by the Army during the War, Charlie Parker eventually joined the newly formed R.A.F. When George Dennett returned in 1920 he found he was facing some formidable opposition in the Gloucestershire bowling department. Charlie

Parker was a highly intelligent person with many an academic interest who could out talk all but the most knowledgeable. Len Hopwood told a story many years later that well illustrates this side of his character. Gloucestershire were playing Lancashire at Old Trafford and Charlie was batting with a rather pompous amateur whose call 'Yes' or 'Run' could be heard all over the ground. Inevitably there arose an occasion when he had mis-judged the run. This time when he shouted 'Run', Charlie duly ran, but could see he had no chance of reaching the other end. Waving his bat above his head like a Dervish war dancer, he shouted 'I'm out, I'm out'. George Duckworth at the target end was so convulsed with laughter that he missed the return and Charlie was saved. Charlie considered it was time to deliver his verdict. He turned on the culprit at the other end, and in a voice that could also be heard in the Pavilion demanded like a snap-ping guillotine 'Who the hell do you think I am, . . . Pegasus?'

He had started his career in 1903 as just another seam bowler, but his astute mind had seen the harvest of wickets to be reaped from George Dennett's bowling. He would also have appre-ciated that it presented a more subtle and less physically de-manding way of earning a living.

It is hearsay, without any official confirmation, that before the 1919 season began he stated his case to the Committee. Delivered an ultimatum is probably nearer the mark! 'I will bowl spinners from now on and if you don't like it I will find another County that does.' So began a quite remarkable bowling career. Where before the War he was bowling a few hundred overs a season he now bowled thousands. He was thirty-six. His life's work had only just begun.

His long fingers spun the ball like a top. On a difficult wicket he was unplayable; on a good one he would bowl out even the best of batsmen. No-one took him lightly; he bowled with the precision of a machine and was rarely collared. Lithe and over six feet tall he would glide through a day's bowling with unbut-toned shirt sleeves flapping about his wrists always with a cap pulled down at a rakish angle over his right eye and a smooth effortless rhythm that did not change as the overs passed. His was a classic action – left arm hidden behind the body as he approached the wicket, brought over fully extended at the moment of delivery in a lazy circular arc that defied analysis from the other end. To the end of his days he would talk unceasingly about his search for that mystery of flight which would lead him to the left arm spinner's Eldorado. Perhaps he never did find it, but his 3,278 wickets in first-class cricket shows he came nearer to it than any other bowler in the history of the Club.

He was not immediately successful in 1919, although by the season's end he had taken 92 wickets, but every year from 1920 to 1935 he took many more than a 100 wickets in a season.

Very soon a pattern was established when he and Percy Mills would bowl all through an innings. There was many an occasion in the coming years when he would bowl seamers with a new ball and then switch to spinners. Some batsmen declared that there seemed to be only a slight change in pace. There was surely many an occasion when he must have wished he had joined another County with some reliable batsmen to provide him with a decent total at which to bowl. Nor would he have relished the opportunity it gave him to improve his batting through two or his own side's innings whilst restricting to one innings of bowling against the enemy. No doubt it was those early years, and during his short visits to the peace and quiet of the dressing-room, that inspired the fatalist in him which accepted that it was man's destiny to suffer.

Charlie spoke his thoughts. There are as many legendary stories about him still echoing around Gloucestershire as there are about W.G. It must have been a few years later, during W.H. Rowland's captaincy, to which one of them refers. It was after the tea interval and he had toiled all day and spun almost nothing. Every bowler had been tried. His fingers cried out for a rest. The captain came up to him and asked, 'Who shall I put on next, Charlie?' Back came the quick fire retort 'If I were you, I should put the ... clock on.'

In 1920 he and Percy Mills bowled through both innings of the Hampshire game at Clifton, except for one over in which George Dennett was allowed to steal the twentieth wicket. Between them they bowled out Glamorgan at Swansea in the first ever innings between the two Counties. They went one better in 1925 when they bowled every ball in both innings against Worcestershire at the Gloucester Wagon Works. He and Alf Dipper (7 for 87) between them bowled out Kent at Gloucester, but still the County lost by nine wickets. That was another pattern. Dipper made the runs and Parker took the wickets. The first basic principle of cricket is to make runs and Gloucester-shire were mighty short in this department during those years.

The 1921 season was one of those memorable long, hot rain-less summers when even the trees gave up the unequal struggle and the grass burned to dust. Charlie with his matchless control of flight and spin was now in his element. That gentle flowing action brought him 164 wickets and his only Test Match, the fourth of the series against Australia at Old Trafford. Perversely it was spoilt by rain. England had already lost the first Test at Trent Bridge by 10 wickets, the second at Lord's (the only Test in which Alf Dipper was to play), by 8 wickets, and the third at Leeds by 219 runs. At Old Trafford England had declared at 362 for 4 wickets. They then bowled out Australia for 175. C. W. L. Parker bowled 28 overs for 32 runs and 2 wickets which included C. G. Macartney who had destroyed the English bowlers in the previous Tests. From the start the pitch was wet and lifeless, but there were other reasons why Charlie Parker did not play again for England. The Establishment did not appreciate that articulate bowling geniuses are not easy to live with. No doubt they had received the message!

T. W. J. Goddard 1900–1966.

He returned to Bristol for the Somerset game. For the first and only time he took all ten wickets in an innings, for 79. He followed this up with three more wickets in the second innings and the County won an exciting game by a single wicket.

The game of that Cheltenham Festival was against the Australians. In the first game against them at Bristol earlier in the season the result had been a draw, but the Australians had scored 533 for 8 wickets, Macartney 149, Parker 28.4 overs, 109 for 1. Now the County were to lose by an innings and 136, the Australians 438, Macartney 121, Parker 50.2 overs and 5 wickets for 148. There was some recompense for the County. Thanks to these two games, and the matchless summer weather, the only profit of the five years following the War was reported.

In true fictional style Charlie Parker left his most sensational bowling for his Benefit match against Yorkshire in 1922. The game was one of the two at first scheduled to be played at Clifton but could not be fitted into the College vacation so the Fry's Athletic Ground took the games. The first was against Sussex and the second, the Benefit game, on 9, 10 and 11 August. Gloucestershire batted first and made 172. Yorkshire followed and were all out for 66. Such are the bare facts. It was remarkable that the County should bowl out the premier county for so small a total, but Charlie Parker had been engaged in one of the greatest bowling performances in the history of the game. By his seventh over he had taken four wickets. With the last ball of that over he clean bowled Norman Kilner. Unfortunately, the first ball of his eighth over had also hit the batsman's wicket, but had been called a no-ball. With each of his next three balls he clean bowled the incoming batsmen, Macaulay, Dolphin and Waddington, to claim his first hat-trick. He had hit the stumps five times in succession. His analysis at the end of the innings was 9 for 36 in 10.2 overs. The sublime and the ridiculous are never far apart in cricket. Gloucestershire were then bowled out for 58, leaving Yorkshire 167 to win. They easily passed that total with four wickets. His Benefit brought Charlie Parker £1,075.

If in the period 1919 to 1923 Charlie Parker carried the Gloucestershire bowling, Alf Dipper dominated the batting. He alone could be relied upon to stay at the wicket all day; the rest of the batting was just a matter of small bits and pieces. In his career he carried his bat eleven times, two more than W.G. ever did, through a complete Gloucestershire innings. Dip, as he was known to the cricket world, had already made over 1,000 runs in 1911, 1913 and 1914 and he continued to do so every season from 1919 through to 1930. There were five years in that period when it totalled more than 2,000. In all he played in 361 matches for the County and made 27,948 runs, which included 53 centuries. By comparison, W.G. played in 360 Gloucestershire matches, made 5,000 less runs and 51 centuries.

A. E. Dipper 1885–1945. He scored 27,948 runs for Gloucestershire in 860 innings; only Wally Hammond has scored more runs for the County.

A workmanlike rather than a spectacular opening bat, he is best remembered for his addiction to playing to the on side, which defied any field placing, and also for his batting stance; slightly angled to leg, he shuffled ponderously around in his crease like an arthritic penguin, never played a ball he did not have to, had a negligible backlift and a bat that seemed to get wider as the years passed. He played in only one Test Match. Phlegmatic, shy, almost wordless, he was a thoughtful character of great worth who lived in Gloucester for most of his cricket life.

Percy Mills was another bowler who chose a more gentle yet profitable way of earning a living on the cricket field. As the years passed he reverted from his medium paced right arm seam bowling to off spinners and cutters and took an armful of wickets to show the possibilities of such a change to a colleague who was to be one of the greatest exponents of the art. He was a kindly, lovable person who played on until 1929 when he became cricket coach to Radley College.

Wicket keeping to great spin bowlers is a demanding occupation. Jack Board did not play again after the War. He had played 430 games for the County, taken 699 catches, made 317 stumpings, scored 13,092 runs, including 8 centuries, and played in six Tests. Before Jack Board was 'Frizzie' Bush and after came Harry Smith, the third of the great Gloucestershire wicket keepers. Small, compact, courageous to a degree, he had played football for Bristol Rovers, and later Bolton Wanderers. He became a most valuable batsman and in those early years, Dip's one reliable partner. In 1919 he made a century in each innings against Hampshire at Southampton. He was a wicket keeper whose hands with their double thumb nails bore testimony to his bruising duties which he accepted with modesty and wry humour. Although he played on until 1935 his health began to deteriorate as early as 1925. It was only when others took over that his real worth was recognised. He was never ranked the best wicket keeper in the country, that position belonged to George Duckworth, but he did play in one Test. He played in 393 matches for his county, took 443 catches, made 263 stumpings and 13,330 runs; a great contribution to the Gloucestershire story. He died of tubercular meningitis – his brother and two sisters died of the same ailment – on 12 November 1937.

These were the old guard of professionals who had all started their careers before the War and who were expected to shoulder the burden and the blame. There grew up a new generation of cricketers, most of whom did not make a great impact. There was Bernard Sydney Bloodworth (Bernie to everyone), of Cheltenham who was engaged as a left arm spin bowler/batsman. He was pressed into service as reserve wicket keeper to Harry Smith, and later scorer, baggage man, cricket valet to Wally Hammond and finally groundsman at the County Ground. He was a much respected and lovable character who bore his many duties with an unruffled humour that defied any imposition upon his gentle way of life.

He was followed by Jack Bessant, a right arm, fastish bowler of cheerful disposition, and William Robert Gouldsworthy, who both joined the staff in 1921; their main claim to fame was that they set up a record last wicket partnership of 131 runs against Somerset at Bristol in 1923 – W.R.G. 65 not out and Jack Bessant 50.

Two other great cricketers joined the Club in the three years immediately after the First War, Walter Reginald Hammond and Thomas William John Goddard.

'There will never come another W. G. Grace,' proclaimed *Wisden* in their report of the Gloucestershire season for 1921. Little did they know that a young Cirencester Grammar School boy (who was to out-Grace W.G.), had already stepped briefly on to the Gloucestershire Road in 1920.

Reginald Walter Hammond was born at Dover on 19 June 1903. At the time his father was a Warrant Officer at the Duke of York's Military School. He died in France during the First War. His military duties had taken the family to China and Malta. The boy was sent to Cirencester Grammar School as a boarder and from his earliest days there he had shown an outstanding natural ability for any ball game. Mr Fraser, the headmaster, wrote to Foster Robinson bringing his remarkable cricket scores – he made 365 not out in a house match – to the attention of the County. His first introduction to Gloucestershire cricket was in an early season game for a County XI against Old Cliftonians in 1920. He made an attractive sixty and then took two wickets and a catch. He was sixteen. He made his first-class debut as an amateur at the Cheltenham Festival against Lancashire on 18, 19 and 20 August and recorded a duck. He played in the second Festival game against Leicestershire, and the following game against Worcestershire at Worcester. In his four innings of 27 runs in those games, or in his fielding (he did not bowl), there was little to suggest his future greatness, nor indeed that any other County would be interested. He had spent much of his holidays at friend Billy Neale's parents' farm at Berkeley and had ideas of taking up farming. His mother had her misgivings about a career in cricket but she and Wally signed a contract with Gloucestershire. However, the news of his immense potential had not been lost on Kent, the county of his birth. They registered a complaint that he was not qualified to play for Gloucestershire. This was upheld and meant that he had to serve a two years' qualification period for the County. Thus, in 1921, he was not allowed to

play in any championship games. However, he did play, again as an amateur, against the Australians in their two games. At Bristol he made 1, at Cheltenham 0 and 1; little indication here for the Australians of some formidable future problems. It was in the second innings of the Festival game that Arthur Mailey took all ten Gloucestershire wickets.

He was bowled first ball by fast bowler Gregory in the Cheltenham game. Wally told one of the few stories against himself of that ball. 'I had a long backlift in those days. I recognised it as a half volley, but I heard the ominous rattle behind me before I had finished my backlift.'

Wally had that rare natural ball game ability that made coaching quite unnecessary. He could have made a career in soccer – at golf – he was for many years a scratch golfer; indeed at any sport. In 1921 he went to live in Bristol, played for Bristol Rovers that season, could have played for the City in 1922, but he didn't much care for the soccer scene. He may have been

Gloucestershire v Sussex 1922. Third row: *T. Crawford, Brownrigg, Stannard, Bessant, Cornford, Bowley, H. Reed.* Second row: *Cox, Dipper, Roberts, Smith, Street, Dennett, Parker, Mills, Hammond.* Front row: *Capt. M. A. Green, W. H. Rowlands, W. J. Malden, P. F. C. Williams, A. E. Gilligan, F. C. Robinson, A. H. Gilligan, K. A. Higgs, Tate.*

grateful for the assistance and encouragement of Mr Fraser, his Headmaster; he did, however, acknowledge the advice he had received from George Dennett whose patience and quiet, easy manner did much to build his confidence. It is interesting how often bowlers become very good coaches of batting. Much later Tom Graveney was to have the same respect for Charlie Parker's words of wisdom.

There seems to have been some confusion over the two-year period of qualification. He played in the first five games of the 1922 season. Perhaps Gloucestershire had taken into account the time he had spent at Cirencester and Berkeley; maybe there were deeper motives at work. In any case, Kent objected and he did not play again in 1922.

During the season he acted as a sort of assistant coach to John Tunnicliffe at Clifton College. 'Long John' of Pudsey, a tall, hard hitting batsman, one of the greatest slip fielders in the history of the game and a member of Lord Hawke's Yorkshire XI which won seven County Championships in successive years, became cricket coach to Clifton in 1908. There is little to suggest that Wally Hammond was ever coached seriously but perhaps he did learn something about the art of slip fielding from the famous 'Long John'. He played for clubs around the County particularly Gloucester C.C.

1923 was his first full season. He was now a professional. In his very first game against Surrey at Fry's, he made 110 and 92 in the two innings. By the season's end he had made 1,421 runs and taken 18 wickets. At first he was a quite brilliant cover field. It was to be a few years yet before that thrilling combination of Parker bowling and Hammond at slip or gully developed. From the very beginning his every movement on the cricket field bore the hallmark of epic quality.

Another legendary Gloucestershire cricketer began his career in those years. Thomas William John Goddard of Gloucester was almost three years older than Hammond. A tall, lissome youth with a crop of curly black hair, he developed as a medium fast bowler with the Gloucester Wagon Works Club where Arthur Paish was both groundsman and coach. In those days the County was desperately short of opening bowlers. He took a wicket in his debut game against Middlesex at Gloucester Spa in 1922 and joined the staff the following season. His performance of 5 for 19 in 11 overs against Surrey at Fry's promised much, but he was not destined to become a fast bowler. He laboured on for a few years and was dropped from the regular staff in 1927 to serve as an apprentice at Lord's, but that is for later.

Most of the amateurs were batsmen in the traditional pattern. Some elder statesmen played a few games; Charles Barnett's father, C.S., and his uncle, E.P.; Cyril Sewell, who retired to his Cotswolds in 1919; Charles Townsend completed his illustrious career in 1922 but not before he had saved the day in another of those sublime to the ridiculous Gloucestershire days. In 1920 at the Fry's Ground, Somerset had bowled out the County for 22. Gloucestershire went on to win by 4 wickets, thanks to his fine innings of 84. He returned to his law practice in Stockton-on-Tees. All of these had seen their County find its Road again. The younger statesmen, F. G. Robinson who completed his captaincy in 1923, and D.C., took over from 1925 to 1927; in between came one year, 1924, with Philip Francis Cunningham Williams, Old Etonian of Dorset landed gentry stock, in charge, but business would no longer wait for them to spend their summer days on a cricket field. There were still to be young amateurs of exceptional ability; Frederick James Seabrook of Gloucester, Haileybury and C.U.C.C.; Reginald Prescott Keigwin, of Clifton, C.U.C.C., who played for Cambridge at hockey, soccer and racquets, became an authority on Hans Christian Andersen, was made a Knight of the Danish Order of Danneborg and played nine games for Gloucestershire C.C.C. after playing for Essex; finally, and with great significance, Beverley Hamilton Lyon.

6 Wally Hammond – Greater than Grace?
1924-1930

*W. R. Hammond
1903–1965.*

Gloucestershire had made another beginning.

Wisden in 1920 had reported their cricket as: 'A modest and humble thing.' They had seen nothing over the next few years that was to suggest otherwise. They gave little respect to the fact that the Club had risen out of the almost dead ashes of the past; had brought some organisation and administrative order to its affairs; had remained solvent – just; and above all had maintained a position in the middle of the cricket Championship. If the Fates had not exactly smiled on their efforts, they had certainly not laughed derisively at them. Slowly, through much frustration and no doubt criticism, they had set a pattern for the future.

From 1924 to 1930 there were to be only small changes in the constitution and the rules of the club. The Council continued to be the corner stone around which the decisions were made and, indeed, so has it continued to the present day.

Membership had been set at 3,000 but from the almost annual appeals by the Chairman for new members, it is doubtful if the target was ever reached. Each Year Book of this period contains a list of members with their addresses. As always, the numbers varied with the performance of the team and, in addition, a vast following of interested supporters who attended the games.

Four of the first five years following the War showed a loss and it is doubtful if the Club could have survived without the Special Appeal Fund of 1919. A reserve, a Sustentation Fund, of £4,000 was set up in 1925, a season of very good gates and membership, which showed a substantial profit. With no ground of their own and therefore with no overheads and depreciations, the Club was living in a financial world protected against the harsher winds that blew outside. As the finances began to come on to a firmer base, no doubt some of the more perceptive committee members were thinking in terms of buying a ground of their own.

By the very nature of the complexity of the game, the captain of a first-class county cricket team has a greater influence on what happens on the field than in any other sport. Those were the days of the amateur captains. Perhaps they had a greater freedom of action, a greater opportunity to express their own personality within the limits of the job, but the greater were their responsibilities for the success, or failure, of the Club as a whole. So often does a new captain bring success where his predecessor has failed with the same set of individuals. In distant retrospect conclusions can only be drawn from statistics. During the Foster Robinson captaincy from 1919 to 1922, the championship positions were eighth, eighth and seventh, and then an ominous thirteenth when four captains had been pressed into service. Philip Williams's contribution was tenth in 1923. Then began the Douglas Robinson regime. As befitted a retired Regular Army Officer no doubt he brought some discipline to the cricket. At once, in 1924, the position improved to sixth but in the two following years, 1925 and 1926, slipped to tenth and fifteenth. He, too, was drawn into his business world to permit Harry Rowlands the doubtful privilege. To all intents and purposes he had retired from first-class cricket in 1922 but since then he had been listed as a deputy captain and perhaps by the urgency of the situation would have been persuaded to accept the full responsibility. As a batsman his two centuries for the county were as far apart as 1902 and 1921. He devoted himself to the bowling end of the batting order, but his experience (he had been around the cricket world as long as the older members of the side), his pleasant management of affairs and the great respect with which he was held within the Club showed the wisdom of the appointment. The positions improved to twelfth in 1927 and fifth in 1928, but there were other factors at work. By then some great Gloucestershire cricketers had served their apprenticeships and had established their places in the side.

The Minutes of the A.G.M. of 1925 held at the Royal Midland Hotel, Gloucester, highlight one of the problems. 'The Committee over the winter has been giving serious attention to the lack of bowlers. No-one of any real ability has arrived since the War.'

Age was also beginning to tell in the field. It was only when the young amateurs came into the side for the latter part of the season that any real mobility returned to the outfield. There is a wildly apochryphal Charlie Parker story which probably belongs to the Douglas Robinson era of captaincy. Charlie was bowling at the College end during a Cheltenham Festival game. By a sad lapse of the Captain's memory, three of the older members of the team, Alf Dipper, Percy Mills and George Dennett, found themselves the sole occupants of the leg side field. The moment of truth came when a ball was hit towards the square leg boundary. Their great experience told each of them that the ball was probably going to finish up nearer the other chap or, as they hoped, over the boundary. They watched it trickle to a standstill a few feet short. They had not yet moved. The batsmen were running. Charlie, hands on hips and blowing fuses, surveyed the scene with rueful disbelief. It took a shouted plaintive command from the captain at mid-off to get them into motion. Heads down they all set off in a hurrying walk towards the ball. Charlie flared 'There go my ... greyhounds'. The batsmen are reported to have run five!

We have already seen that Wally Hammond had served his qualifying period by the end of 1922. By the season's end he had made 1,421 runs. *Wisden* reported, 'Here we have in all likelihood one of the best professional batsmen of the future.' The whole country was becoming excited over his batting and his superb fielding in the covers.

Others of less dramatic potential were also maturing.

William Legge Neale, a young member of one of those great farming/hunting families, the Neales, the Prouts, the Culli-mores, of the Berkeley Vale. Born in Berkeley on 3 March 1904, a contemporary of Wally Hammond at Cirencester Grammar School, he first played for the county as an amateur in 1923. It was not until 1929 that he turned professional. He had become an established middle order batsman by 1927 when he made his highest score, 145 not out against Hampshire at Southampton, and followed it up with exactly 100 in his very next innings, at the Fry's ground against Essex. It was nine years before he made another century. He may not have fulfilled his early prom-ise, but there was an invaluable adhesive quality about his batting that held many a Gloucestershire innings together on a spinner's wicket when all around him was chaos. He was no more than a fun bowler, but he did just once have his great day. In the home Somerset game of 1937, Frank Lee and J. H. 'Monkey' Cameron had held up the Gloucestershire progress for too long. At 159 for 3 Bev Lyon brought on Bill Neale with his leg spinners. Astonishment replaced the fielders' amuse-ment as the next six wickets fell for sixteen runs, to give him an innings' analysis of 4.1 overs, 1 maiden, 9 runs and 6 wickets.

Billy invariably fielded at deep square leg to Tom Goddard's bowling and most of his 228 catches were caught in that area. If the ball was hit in the air in his direction the inclination of the fielders was to pick the spot for a rest rather than to worry about the result.

Reginald Albert Sinfield came from a completely different background. Born at Bennington near Stevenage, Hertford-shire, on 24 December 1900, he came to Gloucestershire by way of *The Mercury* Nautical Training Ship for Boys, the Signals staff of the battleship *King George V* at sixteen-and-a-half, the Lord's Ground Staff and Hertfordshire C.C.C. Like Wally Hammond, before him, he had to serve the stipulated two year

W. L. Neale.

qualification period. He first played for the County against the South Africans at Fry's and his first Championship game was against Worcestershire at Cheltenham in July 1925. He made a pair. He was in good company – so had the captain, Douglas Robinson. Fred Root, with his prodigious inswingers, had taken all four wickets. Nor was he immediately successful although he became a regular member of the side. Gradually he emerged from the lower reaches of the batting order to open the innings, first with Alf Dipper, and later Charles Barnett. He made his first thousand runs in a season in 1927.

Equally slowly he became a top line bowler. On the slower side of a medium pace, he was generally brought on to bowl after the real openers had used up what was left of the new ball, and then do a containment job before handing over to the real spinners. His intelligent perception of the game led him to direct his attention to off spin bowling. His haul of wickets increased. It was not until 1934 that he took over one hundred wickets in a season. By then he had become a main force member of the side and only partly eclipsed by the greater stars around him. His best bowling performances were reserved for the Cheltenham Festival games. Where Charlie Parker and Tom Goddard spun the ball down the slope from their respective ends, Reg Sinfield would go on at either, and with his less pronounced spinners finish off what the others had started. As Charlie Parker approached the end of his long and illustrious career, Reg Sinfield began to occupy the prime spinning berth thus vacated. He bowled much more. His control was remarkable. He could bowl at a batsman's off stump all day. Almost apologetically he would mix in his devastating leg cutter or arm ball. If it was snicked into the slips Wally Hammond caught it; if the bemused batsman missed it, Reg Sinfield turned as he stood and head uplifted bemoaned his fate to the heavens.

R. E. Sinfield.

Such was Reg Sinfield, upright of stature and character, a softly spoken, kind person with a friendly word for friend and foe, but with a wry humour that often left the recipient wondering if he was having his leg pulled – he probably was. He played on until the Second War. He became cricket coach at Clifton College and later at Colston's School.

Altogether he played in 423 games for Gloucestershire, made 16 centuries in his 15,561 runs, took 1,165 wickets and 176 catches. He performed the cricketer's double twice, in 1934 and

1937. His only Test Match was against Australia in 1938 when he was 37.

This exciting Gloucestershire talent only needed a catalyst to transform its fortunes. There was one at hand.

Beverley Hamilton Lyon was born at Caterham, Surrey, on 19 January 1902. His first experience of cricket was on the lawn of the family home with his brother, Malcolm Douglas, four years his senior. No doubt these were brotherly, argumentative affairs, for although they both went to Rugby School, their paths remained far apart; M.D. was a wicket-keeper/batsman, captain of Somerset; B.H. a batsman/bowler, captain of Gloucestershire; M.D. played for Cambridge University, B.H. for Oxford; M.D. became a lawyer; B.H., with a highly developed business acumen, was involved in the birth of Rediffusion. Perhaps M.D. had the last word in this family cricket field contest. In the Somerset/Gloucestershire game of 1930 at Taunton, he made his highest score of 210; B.H. could only make his point with exactly 100.

Bev Lyon first played for the County in 1921, a year before he gained his Cricket Blue at Oxford. He made a pair in the first of his two Varsity matches. He was one of three young amateurs brought into the side later in the season during the captaincy of the Robinsons and P. F. C. Williams but his flashing stroke play too often led to his downfall. He missed the 1925 season when he was in India on business and it was not until 1928, by which time he had played 170 innings, that he made his first century, 131, during a sixth wicket partnership of 285 in three-and-a-half hours with Wally Hammond against Surrey at the Oval. He took over the captaincy of the team towards the end of that season when Harry Rowlands dropped out. By the season's end Gloucestershire had moved up to eighth in the County Championship. The complexities of cricket excited his shrewd, restless mind and he seemed to be bubbling permanently with ideas. He had that rare ability which makes a team greater than the sum of its parts. His clinical analysis of the game had long since reduced it to its simplest form; batting meant hitting the ball, bowling hitting the wicket; each game was to be won, but above all it was to be enjoyed by cricketers and spectators alike. With him on the field cricket was fun.

There was nothing in the statistics of his long apprenticeship to suggest that in the years of his captaincy Gloucestershire was to live through its second Golden Era. But that is the end of the story. His clever use of the material available to him, his infectious cavalier approach to the game, transmitted his own supreme self-confidence to the team and their cricket. No doubt some of the professionals would have their misgivings and, no doubt, Charlie Parker would have stated his in most forceful terms, but Bev Lyon had the style that could charm the larks from the sky. The players held him in the greatest respect and the rapport that existed in his teams was remarkable.

His captaincy brought a sense of responsibility to his own batting. He made three centuries in 1929 and then five in 1930 including a century in each innings against Essex at Bristol, 115 and 101 not out. He gave up playing a few of his lashing, slashing shots as if he was in a squash court, but anything pitched up to him had to be hit out of the ground. He often claimed that if he bowled straight half volleys for a full season he would take a hundred wickets. He will be remembered as a fearless, close wicket fielder. His long sight was poor and he wore glasses. He always wore a watch fielding. Some grounds in those days did not have a clock! The professionals said it helped him time his shots!

To Tom Goddard's off spinners he took the suicidal short square leg position (Wally Hammond was in the safer leg slip position), and he caught many an impossible catch that would have satisfied even Dr E.M. In many respects they were similar characters; both were great talkers on the field, both had a mischievous sense of humour that hid the shrewdest of cricket brains and both were completely fearless and inventive in their batting and their fielding. Bev Lyon and Charlie had the greatest respect for each other. They had their 'battles' on the field which each reckoned he had never lost. The argument was always the same, which came down to the fine point, 'Who's going to set my ... field, skip, you or me?'

Often he fielded silly point to Charlie Parker's bowling. Once when Charlie complained he didn't need a silly point, he replied, 'All right, Charlie, I'm going there,' pointing to a spot nearer to the batsman. 'You put the others where you want them.' The old man just shrugged his shoulders and returned to his mark muttering to himself 'He's crucifying my ... bowling.'

When he stopped a hard shot at silly point he had the habit, disconcerting to the backing up batsman, of propelling the ball backwards at the wicket behind him, without turning. Cricket was certainly a different game when Bev Lyon was on the field.

There was an occasion at the County Ground on the most placid of wickets and with a Midland County snailing towards lunch still well short of a hundred runs. Neither the crowd's voiced disapproval, nor his own freely offered advice had moved the batsmen into any sort of action. To his nearby fielders he expounded his proposed course of action. 'I'll bowl an over of grubbers, or perhaps it'll be an E.M. over.' This refers to an over that Dr E. M. Grace bowled against Surrey at the Oval in 1865 that caused a near riot. The ball, delivered underhand, is lofted to a great height on a howitzer-like trajectory which ends with it landing vertically on to the batsman's wicket. The last over before lunch arrived. He announced to the umpires, the batsmen, the fielders, that he was going to bowl an over of grubbers. His intention was to bowl the ball bowls-like so that it just reached the block hole. The look on the batsmen's faces showed he had made his point. Apparently that was not the only occasion when he had made a similar protest.

He was on excellent terms with the Gloucestershire Committee who allowed him plenty of elbow room and, for that matter, with other captains and cricketers throughout the game. Those were the days when amateurs and professionals changed in different dressing rooms and were likely to go out on to the field through different gates. He had a respect for the Establishment but it did not extend to stuffy traditionalism; Gloucestershire would go on to the field together. There is a story of the occasion at Lord's when he told the professionals to meet the amateurs in the Long Room, and they would go out on to the field through the hallowed gate. They were turned back at the door into the Long Room. He was waiting inside, and when told of it his reply was, 'Well, if they can't go out this way we will go out through their gate.' They did. An official compromise was later worked out that the professionals should skirt the boundary fence and meet the amateurs on the outside of the gate and all proceed from there.

He was famous for his declarations. He was never afraid of declaring behind an opponent's score if he saw an opportunity to force a victory. He rarely misjudged the issue. The first successful outcome of his thinking occurred in the Middlesex game at the Gloucester Wagon Works in 1929. To all intents the game had been ruined by rain during the first two days. It was not until just before lunch on the third day that Gloucestershire passed the Middlesex score of 184. One run ahead Lyon declared. Charlie Parker then bowled out Middlesex for 121 and Gloucestershire knocked off the required runs for two wickets in less than the one-and-a-half hours remaining. Lyon's only comment was 'Got to let the dog see the rabbit'.

There are two other well documented Lyon declarations.

In 1930 Gloucestershire rose to second place in the Championship with 152 points against the winners, Lancashire, with 155 points. Over the years there have been various allocations of points, or percentages, all designed to encourage a more positive approach to the game. In 1930 eight points were awarded for an outright win, and five for a first innings lead. Gloucestershire's fifteen wins had brought them 152 points and Lancashire's ten, 155. For the following season the authorities changed the system yet again. A win would now gain fifteen points and a first innings lead was reduced to five, only for a drawn game.

Bev Lyon and the County had made their point. They went into the 1931 season with an additional incentive, but it did not help them materially. They again finished second, but this time 66 points behind Yorkshire. Unfortunately Bev Lyon missed much of the season through his increasing business commitments.

In the very first game of the season against Surrey at the Oval, once again rain seemed to have ruled out a decision. Gloucestershire began the third day with the score of 69 for one wicket. He declared the innings at 175 for seven, 83 short of the Surrey total of 258. Percy Fender, the Surrey captain, who was no slouch when it came to enterprising cricket, followed suit by declaring at 60 for 6 wickets. This left Gloucestershire with 145 runs to get in the ninety minutes remaining. They gained their win in the last over of the day by three wickets. This is how Lyon wanted cricket to be.

He followed this with his best remembered escapade. At the beginning of June Gloucestershire were playing Yorkshire at Sheffield, but again the weather prohibited a ball being bowled during the first two days. Bev Lyon proposed to the Yorkshire captain, Frank Greenwood, before play began on the third day, that one way to arrive at a decision would be for each side to bowl one ball which would go for four byes and would represent the first innings. This was accepted. Then in the second innings both sides should play for the 15 points.

Other captains had carried out various ploys to make up for play lost because of bad weather, but this was to prove to be the ultimate. Lyon won the toss. Emott Robinson bowled the first ball of the Gloucestershire first innings. It was allowed to pass safely through the field for four byes. Wally Hammond bowled the one ball of the Yorkshire first innings with the same result. Both captains had declared the innings closed at 4 for 0. Now there was everything to play for.

Gloucestershire made 171 runs in their second innings. They then bowled out Yorkshire for 124 to win by 47 runs and gained their 15 points. Unfortunately Gloucestershire were not to see Lyon again until late in the season. By then the momentum had

Wally Hammond in action.

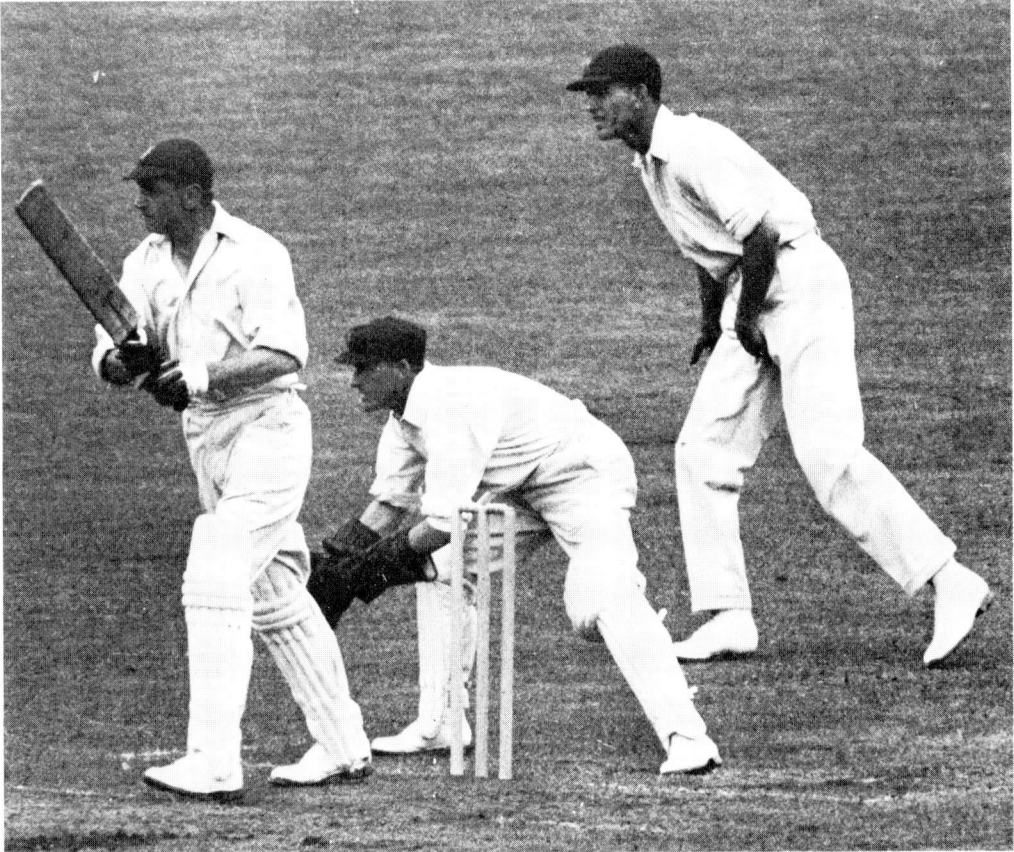

The Gloucestershire team 1929. Back row: A. E. Dipper, C. J. Barnett, W. L. Neale, T. W. J. Goddard, R. A. Sinfield, E. J. Stephens, H. Smith. Front row: W. R. Hammond, C. W. L. Parker, B. L. Lyon, L. P. Hedges, F. J. Seabrook.

been lost. They retained their second position but Yorkshire won the Championship.

The rules were changed again to prohibit such goings on before the next season began. But this is over running the order of events.

1928 and 1929 were heady years for Gloucestershire supporters. Besides this exhilarating Bev Lyon cricket, Wally Hammond's batting and Charlie Parker's bowling, was now augmented by Tom Goddard's. Tom had two bowling careers. Now had come the rebirth of the second. The first from 1922 to 1927 had been as a 'fast' bowler. He had had his moments of glory, a hat trick against Sussex in 1924, but as the seasons passed it was plain that his days were numbered. He took only 26 wickets in 1927 and was not re-engaged for 1928, but Bev Lyon's cricket brain had seen a solution. Tom Goddard, 6' 2", with a strong but not particularly athletic frame, had big hands and fingers as long as bananas. A ball in those fingers looked as if it would be more at home on a billiard table than on a cricket field. Occasionally during those years in a more relaxed period at the nets he sometimes shortened his run and bowled a few off breaks. Bev Lyon had experienced the difficulty they caused. He persuaded the Committee to send him to Lord's to concentrate on his off breaks and learn his new trade. He was so amply rewarded. Goddard returned to Gloucestershire for the 1929 season and took 184 wickets in that season, more than he had taken in all his six seasons of fast bowling. An unsubtle type of bowler, he wrapped those long fingers around the ball and spun it like a top. On a helpful wicket it bit the turf and lifted often shoulder high. Bev Lyon developed his legendary leg trap. Any mishit was snapped up by himself at short square leg or by Wally Hammond at leg slip. A desperate slog was covered by Billy Neale on the boundary at square leg. There was also a deep long on. The only avenue of escape seemed to be through the slip area. The very best of batsmen, like Bob Wyatt, were inclined to take guard outside the leg stump and snick the ball purposefully into that area.

It was in 1929 that the raucous Goddard appeal was heard for the first time. If a ball from him hit the batsman's pad anywhere near the line of the wicket a mighty 'HOW WAS 'E' would boom off like a fog horn in the Cathedral Close. If wicket-keeping to his bowling was a nightmare, then umpiring was only one degree better.

He followed his 184 wickets in 1929 with 144 in 1930.

So there came into being that perfect spin combination of left arm leg spinner and right arm off spinner. He and Charlie Parker were to take many more than a hundred wickets apiece in each season between 1929 and 1935. The sloping Cheltenham College ground seemed to have been made for them. The one sad aspect was that they were in opposite parts of their respective careers in 1929. Tom Goddard was twenty-eight, many years before his prime, but at forty-seven Charlie Parker was past his. It was too late to reap the full benefit of such a wonderful combination of bowlers.

Another perfect combination had evolved over these years. Wally Hammond's formidable talents became concentrated on his batting. He bowled less and he came in from the covers to the slips or gully to Charlie Parker. It was Dr E. M. Grace again. Nothing passed him in the deeper position. When the ball was turning he came in closer and closer at gully. At times he caught the ball in front of the bat from a defensive shot. He literally pouched the ball. At times he, or Bev Lyon at slip, would make the catch then slip the ball into a trouser pocket and often turn as if to see where it had gone. The sleight of hand was so complete that at a distance it was often difficult to see what had happened.

Bev Lyon's place in County cricket captaincy will always serve as the strongest recommendation for the amateur captain. No professional captain then, or now, would have approached the game as he did. He belonged to a different period, but his way of playing the game demanded the greatest courage, both individually and collectively. He took no credit for himself, but attributed everything to the fine professionals he led. The sporting world has stifled his like and turned itself into a negative mediocrity. He would have revelled in limited-over cricket.

He was the poker player with the nerve to play even a poor hand. At his best he held three aces, Charlie Parker, Wally Hammond and Tom Goddard. He was never dealt the fourth. A Mike Procter, or even a pre-war Colin Scott, to open the bowling and who knows what Gloucestershire might not have achieved in those golden years.

Wally Hammond was the prime ace in Bev Lyon's Gloucestershire pack. He was edging 6' with a superbly coordinated lissome frame that generated the most elegant effortless movement. He was a cricketer without any limitation and of epic performances. It was during this period from 1923 to 1930 that his genius flourished to maturity. He will be best remembered for his memorable batting, but he could just as easily have been a great fast medium paced seam bowler, and there never was a better slip fielder.

During Douglas Robinson's reign a decision was made (perhaps it was Charlie Parker's) to bring him in from the covers to slip. The County's fielding, in desperate need at times for greater mobility in the out country, no doubt suffered but with him coming into the slips the door shut on one avenue of escape for a batsman. His movement before, at, or after a slip catch was minimal. Firmly poised on both feet he caught or stopped everything within reach; no spectacular diving about, no grass marks to stain his immaculate clothing.

Good looking and with a physical presence, he was every part the classic sporting hero. He would never have admitted he had

Wally Hammond cover driving at the Oval during his innings of 199, Gloucestershire v Surrey 1930.

his own hero, but if imitation is to be the sincerest form of flattery then that hero must have been his captain. He admired his inborn style. Bev Lyon always wore a trilby and a suit. Many team and other cricket pictures of the day show Wally Hammond so dressed. On the field Lyon always carried a dark blue silk handkerchief in his right side trouser pocket. For the practical man this is a sensible arrangement. Right handed batsmen can easily get at it if it is allowed to flap outside. Pictures of

Hammond's beautiful off drive, and other shots of him on the field, show that he too had cultivated the habit.

It is very difficult to assess his precise motivation; perhaps at its root lurked an element of inferiority. Computer-like run machines are not much fun. It was not the acquisition of his cricket statistics that will be remembered; these were to far outstrip W.G.'s, but the sheer physical chemistry of their composition. Just to see him walk to the wicket was to appreciate that here was majesty. Gloucestershire cricket enthusiasts watched him bat with the same exhilaration and admiration as their predecessors had done for W.G.

Those were the days of midday newspapers which gave the latest cricket scores in the stop press. If they showed that Wally Hammond was batting, many offices and factories and not a few schools suddenly found that some of their members had urgent business elsewhere!

Like all great batsmen he learned the value of each of his repertoire of shots; he reduced the margin of error in those he used most to nil. He never hooked anything but the rankest long hop, and that was despatched to some distant roof. His front foot driving, straight or through the covers, was perfection. The ball flashed from his bat literally scorching its track through the grass to the boundary. What must be a true story relates to an energetic young amateur darting about fruitlessly at extra cover trying to lay a hand on any one of his thundering drives. Hammond called out, 'Don't worry, sonny, I won't hit you.' He was just as deadly off his back foot. The ball was hit with the same certainty and force through the gaps.

Bowlers without the surest control were destroyed and right arm leg spinners were particularly vulnerable. Tommy Mitchell, Derbyshire and Test leg spinner, was once driven to such distraction that he left the field in despair. Wally Hammond perfected the sweep to leg. Front foot outstretched, bat parallel with the ground, and the best googlies to drop outside the off stump were casually swept to leg at the angle of Hammond's choosing.

Gloucestershire cricket with Wally Hammond in the full flow of his run making was not quite the soliloquy it had been when W.G. held the stage. It must have held good in both cases that often the others tended to be mere cyphers. When batting with him the main responsibility of the other batsman, besides admiring his superb craftsmanship, was to run when called, generally for two, but above all to learn to count to five and run on the sixth ball of the over to give him strike.

There was an aloof side to his character. Keeping the world at arm's length, like all great batsmen (the same doesn't seem to apply to bowlers) he could become bored with the mundane. Some personal animosity with an opposing bowler or a challenge, perhaps mischievously engineered by Bev Lyon who alone could motivate him; or a great occasion would bring to the fore his competitive instinct.

Wally Hammond made the first of his 167 centuries in 1923. It was his third at the end of the following season in that sensational game against Middlesex when Charlie Parker took a hat-trick in each innings, that gave the cricket world a foretaste of his exceptional talent. In the second Gloucestershire innings he made 174 not out in less than four hours on a turning wicket.

He reserved cricket's greatest ever all-round performance for the 1928 Cheltenham Festival. He had made his first overseas tour to the West Indies during the winter of 1925 to 26. He contracted a disease there which kept him out of the 1926 season and he spent most of the summer in hospital where one of his visitors was Gilbert Jessop. He celebrated his return to cricket in 1927 with 1,042 runs in May and so emulated W.G.'s feat of 1895, with the significant difference that all his (Hammond's) runs were for Gloucestershire. The first of the Cheltenham Festival games in 1928 was against Surrey. He made 139 and 143 in the two innings and took 10 catches in the game. Worcestershire followed. In 10.2 overs his cutters and off spinners brought him 9 wickets for 23 runs. Charlie Parker took the tenth wicket – caught Hammond. In the second Worcestershire innings his analysis was 6 for 105 in 33.3 overs. Charlie Parker was the only other bowler involved. His 33 overs brought him 4 wickets for 31 runs. Wally's batting was almost a failure in the only innings Gloucestershire needed to defeat them; he made 80 out of a Gloucestershire total of 370 for 6 wickets.

In two successive games he had made 363 runs, taken 16 wickets and made 11 catches. That season his tally was 2,825 runs, 84 wickets and 78 catches.

Greater than Grace?

Gloucestershire had now returned to the top echelons of the game. They were fifth in the County Championship of 1928 and fourth in 1929 although in many senses it had been a better year. They had lost their chance of winning the Championship in a one run defeat by Sussex at the Cheltenham Festival. They had won 16 games. They were second in 1930 and second again in 1931.

In the period 1923 to 1930 two others were to establish themselves as main stream cricketers. The first was Charles Christian Ralph Dacre, son of the Auckland harbourmaster from nearby Devonport, New Zealand, born 15 May 1899, who came over on that country's first tour as batsman and reserve wicket-keeper. He introduced himself dramatically to Gloucestershire, playing for New Zealand at the Cheltenham Festival in 1927 having already scored 101 and 107 in his first two games of the tour. He opened the innings and in thirty minutes had made 64, including five sixes, out of 82 for the first wicket. This was the very nature of his batting. Small of stature, immensely strong and nimble footed with a devil-may-care approach to both life and the game, he thought only in terms of attacking the bowling. Too often this led to his downfall. He had to serve the stipulated two-year qualification for the County. He made a century, 100 not out, against Oxford University in the first game when he officially joined the County in 1930.

In 1926 the Committee, in its increasingly discouraging search for new talent, set up a Cricketer Nursery at the Fry's Ground. Percy Mills, who was approaching the end of his long career, was the coach. When he moved on to Radley College, Charlie Dacre was temporarily in charge. The Bristol Rugby Club had kindly made its facilities available for the cricket nursery and the gym was used for the indoor nets, with the outdoor in the dead ball area at the club house end of the ground. Charlie Dacre's batting philosophy seemed to be directed entirely to hitting the ball out of the ground. He batted like Jessop must have batted; all exciting, explosive aggression.

Charles John Barnett, born in Cheltenham in July 1910, was the son of C. S. Barnett who had played for the County in 1904 and had occasionally captained the team before his retirement in 1926. From his earliest days Charles had shown himself a cricketer of the greatest potential and made his debut in 1927 when still a boy at Wycliffe College. He never did completely lose the inherent impetuosity that at first led too often to losing his wicket and slowed his maturity. He did not make 1,000 runs in a season until 1930 and his first century in 1933. Having become a professional in 1929 he might be classed as a batsman who bowled and he was at all times a brilliant out fielder. A serious minded cricketer with supreme confidence and a deep perception of the game, in 1930 his greatest cricket was yet to come.

Soon after daybreak on Tuesday, 26 August 1930, spectators began to gather outside the Fry's ground. The Australians were in town and Wally Hammond was 76 not out. Crowded trams trundled up the Gloucester Road and disgorged their passengers who poured off down Nevil Road to join the queues at the entrance. Long before the start of play the gates were closed on the eighteen thousand lucky people crammed inside. They were to live through the most dramatic day's play in the history of the Club.

The Australians had arrived in Bristol cock-a-hoop after thrashing England by an innings and 39 runs in the Oval Test. They had made 695 in their one innings and their brilliant young star, Don Bradman, still only twenty-one, had made 232.

Rain delayed the start on Saturday and play was not possible

GLOUCESTERSHIRE v AUSTRALIANS

At Messrs. J. S. Fry & Sons Ltd. Athletic Ground (by kind permission)—August 23-25-26, 1930

GLOUCESTERSHIRE

	First Innings		Second Innings	
1 Sinfield	c Walker, b Harwood	1	c a'Beckett, b Hornibrook	16
2 Dipper	c Richardson, b Harwood	1	c a'Beckett, b McCabe	26
3 Hammond	c a'Beckett, b Hornibrook	17	b Hornibrook	89
*4 B. H. Lyon	b Harwood	8	b McCabe	8
5 Dacre	c a'Beckett, b Grimmett	4	c McCabe, b Grimmett	17
†6 Smith	c Richardson, b Hornibrook	16	b Hornibrook	23
7 F. J. Seabrook	c and b Grimmett	19	lbw, b Hornibrook	2
8 Barnett	b Grimmett	2	c Walker, b Grimmett	6
9 Neale	c Walker, b Hornibrook	2	b Hornibrook	0
10 Parker	not out	0	not out	3
11 Goddard	c Kippax, b Hornibrook	3	run out	0
	Extras b- lb-2 nb- w-		b-6 lb-6 nb- w-	12
	Total	**72**	**Total**	**202**

FALL OF THE WICKETS
1-2 2-3 3-17 4-30 5-35 6-33 7-67 8-69 9-69 10-72
1-21 2-101 3-113 4-166 5-187 6-192 7-199 8-199 9-201 10-202

ANALYSIS OF THE BOWLING—First Innings

Bowler	Overs	Mdn	Runs	Wkts	Nbs	Wds
a'Beckett	8	4	9			
Harwood	11	5	13	3		
Grimmett	18	3	28	3		
Hornibrook	14.3	6	20	4		
McCabe						

Second Innings

	Overs	Mdn	Runs	Wkts	Nbs	Wds
	9	4	16			
	11	4	29			
	28.2	4	83	2		
	25	5	49	5		
	10	3	13	2		

AUSTRALIANS

	First Innings		Second Innings	
1 W. H. Ponsford	b Sinfield	51	run out	0
2 A. Jackson	b Goddard	5	lbw, b Goddard	25
3 D. G. Bradman	c Seabrook, b Parker	42	b Parker	14
4 A. Kippax	lbw, b Sinfield	5	lbw, b Parker	0
*5 V. Y. Richardson	lbw, b Goddard	12	st Smith, b Parker	34
6 E. a'Beckett	c Sinfield, b Goddard	0	c Lyon, b Parker	5
9 A. Harwood	b Goddard	0	lbw, b Parker	2
10 P. M. Hornibrook	b Goddard	9	lbw, b Parker	14
8 C. V. Grimmett	not out	7	c Seabrook, b Parker	12
†11 C. Walker	c Seabrook, b Parker	1	not out	0
	Extras b-5 lb-7 nb- w-	12	b-2 lb-7 nb- w-	9
	Total	**157**	**Total**	**117**

FALL OF THE WICKETS
1-42 2-78 3-88 4-96 5-129 6-131 7-131 8-131 9-140 10-157
1-59 2-63 3-67 4-73 5-73 6-81 7-86 8-98 9-115 10-117

ANALYSIS OF THE BOWLING—First Innings

Bowler	Overs	Mdn	Runs	Wkts	Nbs	Wds
Sinfield	14	5	18	2		
Barnett	4	3	3			
Goddard	26	7	52	5		
Parker	30.5	9	72	3		

Second Innings

	Overs	Mdn	Runs	Wkts	Nbs	Wds
	34.2	10	54	2		
	35	14	54	7		

Australia won the toss.   *Captain   †Wicket-keeper

Scorers—B. Bloodworth, A. Ferguson.   Umpires—Messrs. Buswell and Huddleston.

Scorecard – Gloucestershire v Australians 1930; the famous tie.

before 4 o'clock. Victor Richardson, the Australian captain, won the toss and put Gloucestershire in to bat. Two and a quarter hours later, at the end of the day's play, they were all back in the pavilion for 72 runs. The wicket had not dried completely by Monday morning. The great crowd seemed re-signed to spend the day watching the Australians amass another great total. Then suddenly their batting began to fall apart. It started when Reg Sinfield brilliantly caught Bradman off Charlie Parker for 42. Tom Goddard then bowled brilliantly, 5 for 52, and the Australians were all out for 157. The wicket became easier for Gloucestershire's second innings. By the end of play they had cleared their deficit and were 147 for 3. Wally Hammond was at his absolute best.

He continued for only a short while on the third morning. Gloucestershire made little headway after he was out for 89. Their innings closed at 202, just 117 ahead.

Bev Lyon opened the second Australian innings with Charlie Parker and Tom Goddard bowling. Jackson and McCabe opened for Australia and soon made 59. The game seemed set for conclusive formality. It is reported that some of their lower order batsmen took the opportunity to change and go down to Gloucester Road for a haircut! Suddenly the score slipped to 67 for 3 wickets. They were hurriedly recalled.

The final drama really began when Charlie Parker bowled the young Bradman. 81 for 6 wickets was soon 86 for 7. Then began an electric battle of attrition between the Gloucestershire bowlers and the Australian tail enders. Slowly the score rose to 108 for 8 before Jim Seabrook brilliantly caught Grimmett for 12. He had batted an hour for his runs. Ten runs and two wickets to go. Each run was fought for. The crowd cheered every successful ball. The ninth wicket fell at 115. Three runs to win. A wicket or a boundary would settle the game. Walker, the last of the Australians, reached the wicket. The batsmen conferred. Bev Lyon set out his fielders. A leg bye. Two to win. Amid the tension Tom Goddard bowled a faultless maiden. Hornibrook, the other batsman took a swing at Charlie Parker and edged the shot. They scampered a run. The scores were level.

Now came the real drama. Two balls of that over were still remaining. The buzz of excitement snapped to a frightening silence before he bowled each ball, only to burst out again as each moment of crisis passed. The tension persisted through

Tom Goddard's next over, a maiden. Now it was Charlie Parker's turn again.

It was indeed palpitation time. The silences and the explosive cheering greeting each ball increased. The Bristol ground was no place for trembling knees or weak stomachs. Imperturbable as ever he drew on all that experience gained from many a long day's exhausting bowling. A maiden. Fourteen balls had now been bowled with the scores level. Tom Goddard came up for his thirty-fifth over. The first ball rapped Hornibrook's pads. Goddard swung round at umpire Buswell, boomed off his foghorn appeal. Up went his finger with the assured finality that brooks no argument. Pandemonium broke out. The excitement that had been building throughout the day and during those fifteen final balls exploded. The crowd shouted its relief, swarmed on to the field, engulfed the Gloucestershire players, chaired Charlie Parker and Tom Goddard to the pavilion steps. They had bowled every ball of that never-to-be-forgotten final innings.

The crowd gathered in front of the pavilion and demanded speeches from the two captains, who replied suitably, and acclaimed the Gloucestershire players. A memorable day.

It is only right that Bev Lyon should have had the final word. Someone asked him for his impressions of the day. He replied, 'Any captain can win or lose a game against the Australians, but there are bloody few who can tie one.'

7

The Lyon Legacy
1931-1939

'During the past year the Council have made arrangements with the Directors of Messrs J. S. Fry and Sons, Ltd., to purchase the County Ground, and the Club will take possession at December 31st 1932.' So reports the Year Book for the 1931 season. This indicates that negotiations were far advanced over the winter 1931/32.

Fry's were paid £10,000 for the ground which is what it had cost them in 1915. The details had been agreed by 31 December 1932 with 4 April 1933 as the date of the Registration of the Gloucestershire C.C.C. Ground Company Ltd. A. J. Gardner, the Chairman of the Cricket Club, was its Chairman, Messrs R. E. Bush and P. F. C. Williams, co-directors and the Club Secretary, Gilbert Tunnicliffe, the Company Secretary.

Fry's had made the fullest use of the ground for their employees. In sporting terms this consisted of numerous football, rugby, hockey, cricket, athletics and cycling, as well as tennis, netball, bowls and quoits teams, and in the pavilion billiards, table tennis and skittles. Len Corbett, the great Bristol and England rugby centre three-quarter, who also played five times for Gloucestershire C.C.C. in 1921, was an employee and began his sporting career on the ground.

The Chairman and the two Directors each took out shares to the value of £500. The Cricket Club promoted a special Appeal Fund in 1932 that raised £4,266 18s. 9d. Debentures carrying an interest of 3½ per cent were issued to bring another £10,500. M.C.C. made a grant of £300 and Wally Hammond postponed his promised Benefit to 1934. The Ground Company charged the Cricket Club a rent of £500 per annum.

The composition of the Ground Company changed during the years preceding the 1939/45 War. As A. J. Gardner, P. F. C. Williams and R. F. Bush retired, Lt. Col. D. C. Robinson, R. E. Giles and F. O. Wills replaced them.

The annual losses increased as the years passed. £1,656 in 1931, £3,691 in 1933 and £3,327 in 1934. A second Special Appeal Fund for £13,000 'to free the County Ground from debt' was launched in 1935. This raised a further £10,370. Debentures were redeemed and the overdraft at the bank was reduced but the financial problems had been held at bay rather than removed. The Club was well on the way to solvency when the Second War came.

These years also saw a comprehensive shake-up of the administration. This resulted in, as much as from, the appointment of Major H. A. Henson as Secretary. His primary responsibility was membership. Gilbert Tunnicliffe became Assistant Secretary and ran all the games at the home venues. The Secretary's office, which since E.M.G.'s day (he had run the Club from his home in Thornbury) had been in the Albion Chambers of Small Street, now moved into the County Ground.

The establishment of a Management Committee directly responsible to the Council gave a sharper cutting edge to the control of its affairs. There was, for the first time, a two-tier constitution with the Council as overall watchdog which, in general terms, was to persist to the present day. The County was keeping pace with the business world and developing an executive-like operation.

In spite of the team's prodigious success on the cricket field there was never a comparable increase in membership. For almost its complete life span lack of members has been the main weakness of the Club. Successive Chairmen have literally demanded increased membership. The plea in 1936 'If every member would enrol one new member this year, 1937 would be outstanding in the annals of the Club,' was to be repeated verbatim almost half a century later.

One of the inherent responsibilities of any organisation is to keep a clear vision of the road ahead and not to become over-absorbed in the inevitable day-to-day problems that arise. This is particularly the case in the cricket field where great and loyal players come to the end of their careers. There is always a restless search for young professionals of the necessary potential and five years is still the recognised time factor in their development.

Charles Barnett had served his apprenticeship by 1932. Success came to him the hard way. He had made his debut in 1927 as a sixteen-year-old Wycliffe schoolboy amateur, turned professional in 1929 and the following year made his first 1,000 runs in a season. There had been little to suggest that soon he

Charles Barnett.

would be thrilling cricket crowds round the world with his exciting batting. His father and his uncles, who had both played for the County, had taught him from the very beginning that the basic element of batting was to play straight. They had played with him for the Tewkesbury Club. His straight driving in the arc between wide mid-on and extra cover was perfection. To him a half-volley was a half-volley was a half-volley. It was there to be hit through or over the fielders and that meant from the very first ball of the innings. Once in full flow he hit good length balls 'on the up' with the same assurance.

At first he batted in the middle of the order. As Alf Dipper's prowess declined during 1930 and 1931 he moved up to take his place beside Reg Sinfield. Dipper retired in 1932 and the opening partnership of Sinfield and Barnett went into business. Charles Barnett was Bev Lyon's idea of an opening batsman. He set the momentum of the whole innings. There were occasions when he moved up Charles Dacre to join him. The results could be explosive. In 1933 Worcestershire caught the full blast. 196 runs before lunch on the first day. Charles Dacre went on to make 119 and Charles Barnett 107. Wally Hammond next in made 122. In the second innings of this game at Worcester the scores were Dacre 123 not out, Hammond 111 not out, Barnett 18. The following year at Dudley, Charles Barnett redressed the balance with 170, but Charles Dacre repeated the onslaught, Dacre 104, Wally Hammond 265 not out. The team total was the fourth highest in the Club's history – 625 for six wickets.

Back in 1933 Barnett had signalled his maturity with his first century. The dam burst with his 146 against Kent at the County ground. There were to be four more centuries and an aggregate of 2,280 runs before the season's end. He was no ordinary opening batsman watching the balls go by. He probably hit more sixes than any other opening batsman.

Before Barnett came on to the scene a century before lunch was a rarity; now it was always a possibility with him at the wicket. The statistic made no difference to him. On more than one occasion at a certain point he could have achieved it with a little more caution. In 1934 he scored a hundred before lunch against Glamorgan at the County Ground, and against Somerset at Bath. By then he was an international cricketer. He first played for England at the Oval against the West Indies in 1933 and made 52 batting at number 8. The best remembered of his pre-lunch exploits will be against Australia in the Trent Bridge Test of 1938. Against a formidable attack he reached 98 in the penultimate over before lunch. He completed his 100 off the first ball of the next over. He went on to make 126 in a mammoth England total of 658 for 8. This was Reg Sinfield's only Test, and only the fourth occasion when three Gloucestershire players were in the same England side although Wally Hammond, Charles Barnett and Tom Goddard played in the Second Test and were included in the party for the Third Test at Old Trafford when, to the delight of the cartoonists, not a ball was bowled in five days!

He was now supremely confident in his own ability. His batting carried the stamp of his personality. His team mates called him 'Guvnor'. Match winning innings by batsmen nearly always refer to innings later in the game; Charles Barnett won games from his very first visit to the wicket. The Australians became so concerned with his destruction of some of their front-line bowlers that they paid him the compliment of delaying the choice of their team until they had seen if his name appeared in the English line-up. He was considered too impetuous and adventurous for some English selectors but never for England's cricketing public. His adventurous batting was so exciting to watch that his failures were as much a surprise as a disappointment. He was a very good outfielder and no ordinary seam bowler, that rare cricket combination of opening batsmen/ opening bowler.

He was one of *Wisden*'s five cricketers of 1936. He toured Australia and New Zealand in 1936/37 where the hard Australian wickets suited his style of batting. He played in each of the five Tests. Against Queensland at Brisbane he made 259, his highest ever score.

In 1932, after four wonderful years on the cricket field the County were beset with problems. Besides the sad yet inevitable decline of some of its long serving and loyal cricketers, the captaincy and the wicket-keeper positions were the cause of much concern.

Bev Lyon, the directing force of those successful years, could spend less time away from his increasingly demanding business commitments. Jim Seabrook was the only other amateur with the necessary experience to take his place and he was only available towards the end of the season during the Haileybury School vacations. The appointment of a vice-captain had been left open to allow one of the senior professionals to take over. This had happened as far back as 1930 when an all-professional Gloucestershire team took the field for the first time. Charlie Parker was captain.

In 1932, when that boy who in the early 1920s had been shown the Jessop 'damage' high up on the terraced house outside the Gloucester Spa Ground first came into the County side, he found Bev Lyon and Wally Hammond away and Charlie Parker the captain for the game. He was astonished to find that his Gloucestershire cricket heroes addressed him as Mister Parker. However, that did not restrain the captain delivering to him and Basil Allen, the other young amateur who had also run himself out, a never-to-be-forgotten lecture on the art of running between the wickets. The professionals, behind his back, nodded in amused but sympathetic agreement. The pay off

130

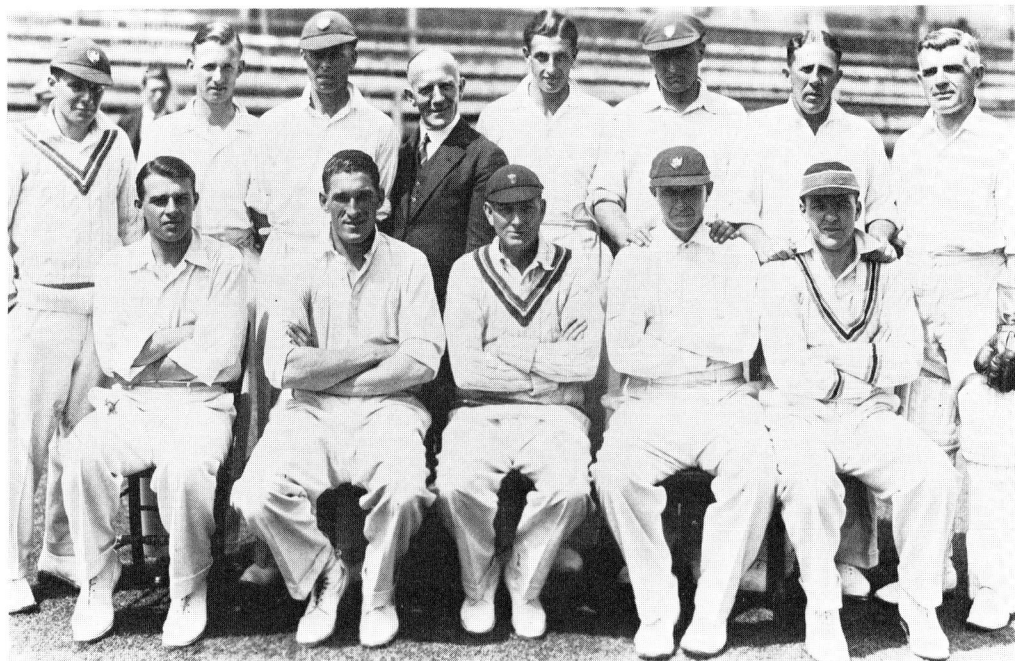

Gloucestershire C.C.C. 1932. Back row left to right: *E. Stephens, R. Ford, W. Neal* (scorer), *J. Rogers, C. Barnett, C. Dacre, B. Bloodworth.* Front row: *G. Parker, T. Goddard, C. Parker, A. Dipper, B. Allen. Gloucestershire*

came later in the game when Charlie himself was almost run out after it had rained. There had arisen some inevitable confusion with Tom Goddard over a call. Charlie was in mid wicket when Tom sent him back. He slipped and fell, charged back to the end from which he had come and horizontally regained the crease in a flurry of mud, sawdust and grass cuttings. A few balls later he was out. Having shrewdly assessed the strength of the approaching storm the professionals suddenly found they were needed elsewhere. The dressing room door burst open. Basil and I stood in awed silence as our muddied captain flung his bat like a strong armed discus thrower at the far corner. It clattered on to the lockers. The superlative flow of expletives drowned the stifled shrieks of distant laughter.

There was another of Glevum's sons who played during those years, Eric James 'Dick' Stephens, born 23 March 1909. Left-handed batsman and a brilliant fielder he played 216 games for the County from 1927 to 1937 and must have appeared as many times as twelfth man. During those summers it was a feature of Gloucester life to see him and Tom Goddard, 5′ 2″ beside 6′ 2″, taking three paces to Tom's one, hurrying to catch the train to Bristol.

The County was also experiencing a wicket-keeper problem. Harry Smith, for so long anchor in this critical position, did not play at all in 1932. Three wicket-keepers kept during the course of that season. At first it was Bernie Bloodworth, who had first been engaged as a batsman and who, when not playing, was scorer and general factotum to the team; then Bert Thomas Lewis Watkins, the Gloucester Club professional and groundsman, Charles Gordon Raikes of Oxford U.C.C. who stepped in after the Varsity match and also J. F. Maclean.

In 1933 no doubt the Committee saw the opportunity to solve both problems at a stroke. Paul Ian Van der Gutch was appointed Deputy Captain to take over the team when Bev Lyon was away. He had, in fact, played against India at Clifton College the previous season. This game, the last the County were to play on the ground, saw Wally Hammond take a quite remarkable catch on the deep square leg boundary. Amar Singh hooked Reg Sinfield flat and square. Wally Hammond did not move a step. He nonchalantly caught the ball with his right hand head-high to his left.

Paul Van der Gutch was a gangling 6′ 2″. He had been to Radley College where Percy Mills was cricket coach, played in the cricket XI for four years, captained it for the last two and represented the Rest *v* the Lord's Schools as opening bat and wicket-keeper. He was now a trainee engineer with Lister's of Dursley. Born in Nottinghamshire he needed to serve the necessary two year qualification period before making his debut against India at Clifton College in 1932 when he nervously dropped his bat on the way to the wicket. Mr (later Sir) Percy Lister allowed him to be away for the season. It says much for his courage and modesty, as well as his friendly reception by the professionals, that the season was not entirely unsuccessful. The County finished tenth in the Championship Table but this could be no more than a temporary state of affairs. He did not obtain leave from Lister's for 1934 and was posted to Calcutta. At the outbreak of War he joined the Indian Army Engineers, was captured in the Western Desert, returned to Calcutta in 1945 and to this country in 1949.

Dallas Alexander Chancellor Page, son of H. V. Page of the W.G. era, was appointed in his place for 1934. His father was a master at Cheltenham College where he had been at school. He went to Sandhurst, destined for a military career in the

Gloucestershire C.C.C. 1937. Back row left to right: C. Barnett, M. Cranfield, W. Neale, R. Sinfield, C. Dacre, V. Hopkins. Front row: G. Parker, B. Allen, D. Page, J. Goddard, W. Hammond, C. Parker.

Gloucestershire Regiment. He first played for the County in 1933. A good outfielder and a stylish rather than a sound batsman, he now captained the team when Bev Lyon was away. The latter left his mark on the season with five centuries but this was his last season as captain. His influence had been so great that the direction and impetus continued under the captaincy of Dallas Page in 1935.

Gloucestershire games against touring overseas teams began way back in 1878 when, at Clifton College, the Australians handed out their compliments to W.G. for his kidnapping of their Midwinter, inflicting the County's first ever defeat on a home ground.

South Africa's first tour of this country was in 1894 when the party included Cyril Sewell, a future Gloucestershire captain. The County later beat the South Africans by six wickets in 1929. When the two teams arrived for the Cheltenham Festival game in 1935 there was nothing to suggest that the County was to record one of the most sensational wins in the Club's history. The South Africans were carrying all before them and had beaten England at Lord's by 157 runs in the second Test, while Gloucestershire were in the throes of a disastrous season, having lost the seven previous games.

Dallas Page won the toss, always a vital factor at Cheltenham. Reg Sinfield slowly accumulated a fine century, 102, supported in the middle order by the dependable Billy Neale's 61. A most significant event had occurred higher up the order. Zenophon C. Balaskas, small with a short flicking darting action, had bowled Wally Hammond for 38 with a googlie. The great man left the field indignant and angrily vowing revenge. Gloucestershire made 279. South Africa replied with 289. The second Gloucestershire innings was all Wally Hammond. He made 123 out of 289. The wicket now belonged to the spinners, but he destroyed Balaskas just as surely as Peter May and Colin Cowdrey were to destroy Sonny Ramadhin at Edgbaston in 1957. Balaskas, who had taken 9 wickets for 103 in that Lord's Test, never bowled effectively again – nor for that matter did Ramadhin.

Gloucestershire made 298 in their second innings to give them a lead of 289. It rained before the completion of the second day's play and South Africa did not commence their second innings until the following morning when the rain had helped the wicket to recover. They moved forward confidently. It was not until mid afternoon with the score at 150 for 3 that Reg Sinfield came on to bowl. In less than an hour the lower South African batting collapsed and his 15.3 overs brought him 5 wickets for 31 runs with a final analysis of 8 wickets for 72 runs. With his first innings century this was his best ever performance for the County in a great victory.

The South Africans went on to Essex to lose only their second game of the tour, and Gloucestershire to much better things. The wicket-keeper problem remained. Victor Hopkins of Dumbleton had been brought straight into the side from Club cricket but it was not the happiest of occupations for an in-experienced wicket-keeper to face. He did so stoically. In the face of great adversity, and by a sheer persistence he held the unenviable post until the arrival of the next great Gloucestershire wicket-keeper. Harry Smith recovered sufficiently from his heart ailment to keep wicket for most of the 1935 season. He carried on to the very last game of the season against Warwickshire at Gloucester. He had played 393 games for his County, made 13,300 runs, stumped and caught 706 batsmen, but statistics alone can never indicate fully this fine cricketer's place in the annals of Gloucestershire cricket.

Now the fourth of the great Gloucestershire wicket-keepers stepped on to the Road. Arthur Edward Wilson played his first game for the County against India at Cheltenham in 1936 although this was not his first experience of Gloucestershire cricket. Andy was born in Paddington a cricket ball's throw from Lord's. Not surprisingly his first cricket inspiration came from that ground and Patsy Hendren was his schoolboy hero. He joined the M.C.C. ground staff in 1932, the same day as two other young cricketers, Denis Compton and George Emmett who were destined to become great names in the cricket world. All threee of them played for the Young Professionals against the Young Amateurs. Originally Andy had been engaged as a slow left arm spinner, but Mr W. H. Findlay, the Secretary of the M.C.C., spotted his potential as a wicket-keeper when 'just for fun' he kept wicket in the nets. As fate would have it, he made his first-class cricket debut for Middlesex at the County Ground in 1933. Fred Price the Middlesex wicket-keeper could not play and Wilson was called to Bristol hurriedly to take his place. Middlesex easily beat Gloucestershire by 8 wickets, but significantly Wilson had made three stumpings in the second Gloucestershire innings.

He played a few more games for Middlesex, but sensing that they had a well-established wicket-keeper and that Gloucestershire seemed to have a problem in that area, he wrote to the County inquiring if they might have a place for him. They did. He was engaged in 1936. He played for Stinchcombe Stragglers, for Gloucester C.C. and other clubs around the County during his two-year period of qualification.

Wilson became Gloucestershire's regular wicket-keeper in 1938. They had been waiting for him for six years. The problem had been solved at last. Here was a wicket-keeper with the mental and physical courage to master the daunting task of

Gloucestershire C.C.C. 1937. Back row left to right: *W. Neale, E. Stephens, B. Watkins.* Middle row: *R. Sinfield, C. Barnett, M. Cranfield, J. Crapp, R. Haynes, B. Bloodworth (scorer).* Front row: *W. Hammond, B. Lyon, B. Allen, G. Parker, T. Goddard.*

keeping wicket to top class spinners, particularly Tom Goddard's lifting off breaks from round the wicket. A left hand batsman, he slowly worked his way to the top of the batting order and made the first of his centuries in 1938.

Alf Dipper of many centuries and the shuffling feet had left the Road in 1932 to become a first-class umpire. He had played in 478 games for the County, made almost 28,000 runs and taken 161 wickets, most of them in his earlier days. He died in London on his birthday – 9 November 1945. Now in 1935 two more of those great corner stones of Gloucestershire cricket, whose careers had begun before the First World War, departed. First it was Harry Smith and then Charlie Parker.

Charlie Parker, who had first played for the County as far back as 1903 against W.G.'s London C.C.C. at Crystal Palace, was then in his fifty-second year. He had taken more than a hundred wickets in every season since 1920 – more than two hundred on five occasions. His last game was against Middlesex at Cheltenham, the game following the sensational victory over the South Africans. He bowled 54 overs in the game, but his three wickets had cost him 166 runs. It was probably of more concern to him that Middlesex had won by 4 wickets. He left to join the first-class umpires list with Alf Dipper, his Tewkesbury colleague from those days so long ago at the beginning of the century.

Charlie continued his association with the County and became the cricket coach for a few years after the Second War. A new generation of cricketers had been born. No doubt he found delight in expounding to them the mysteries of spin bowling but, above all, the art of batsmanship. At the beginning of each season he bought two new bats threatening to make 1,000 runs but his deeds in the middle bore no resemblance to his brilliant late night exposition of the arts of batsmanship. He was a severe batting coach who judged every batsman against Wally Hammond standards. Perhaps he will be remembered for his sad countenance and caustic words, but at heart he was a gentle person and a devoted father. Following his wife's death he brought up his son and daughter almost single handed, even to the extent of washing and repairing their clothes. He moved on to coach at Cranleigh School, Surrey. A friend associated with him in those years so aptly described him, 'Cricket was in Charlie's very soul'. It certainly was. He coached and talked cricket to the very end. He died at Cranleigh on 11 July 1959 aged 76.

He had played 602 games for Gloucestershire and taken 3,170 wickets in 25,307 overs. He had played in more games, batted more times, bowled more overs, taken more wickets and talked more cricket than any other cricketer in the long history of the Club.

There was another departure in 1936. After a boisterous career Charles Dacre returned to his native New Zealand. Reluctantly he had played through the season, scored 1,092, but suddenly he was gone. Originally he was an electric cover point but he threw out his arm which restricted his value in the field. A most versatile cricketer, he had kept wicket in New Zealand and was drafted into that hazardous position during the County's recurring wicket-keeper deficiency.

There was an occasion during the second innings of the 1934 Cheltenham Festival game against Sussex when Maurice Tate and Jim Langridge held up the County with a long ninth wicket stand of 120 runs, defying Bev Lyon's constant switching of the bowling. Finally he persuaded Wally Hammond to try a second spell. Normally he bowled at a gentle pace off a lollypop run but probably egged on by his captain, he let one ball fly. It reared off the pitch and hit Charlie Dacre standing up on the shoulder. He didn't flinch. The bowler and wicket-keeper never did have anything in common but now the battle flags were flying. Wally Hammond added a few yards to his run and put his whole formidable frame behind the next ball. It flew past Dacre's head for 4 byes. Wicket-keeper and bowler retreated in opposite directions. Hammond was bowling off about a good dozen yards, Dacre was that distance behind the stumps, more goal-keeper than wicket-keeper. At the end of the innings Hammond had taken two wickets for 41 runs. Spectators had been privileged to see him bowl his fastest and to catch a glimpse for a few dramatic overs the forgotten third dimension of his cricket artistry. There were 41 byes in that second Sussex innings.

Over the years little news came back from New Zealand concerning Charlie Dacre who had returned there in 1936. Life was not easy for him. For a time he worked as a groundsman at Christchurch but he was repeatedly ill and died at Devonport on 2 November 1975. In all he made sixteen centuries for the County, his highest score being 223 against Worcestershire at Worcester in 1930. He was a brilliant cover point until he threw his arm out.

Wally Hammond continued on his imperious way. He was leaving W.G. behind. He had made his first century in 1923 and now in 1935 he had made his hundredth. As in the case of W.G. in 1895, it was against Somerset at the County Ground. It had taken W.G. twenty-nine years. Hammond celebrated his in twelve and he had missed completely the 1926 season. W.G.'s was celebrated with universal acclaim, toasted with champagne on the field, subscriptions, presentations, a dinner, celebratory plates and eulogy by the page. Hammond's passed almost unnoticed.

The 1936 season was one of the most eventful in the Club's history. It has already been seen that the great administrative shake-up of 1935/36 had effected remarkable improvements off the field. On it the season had got off to a slow start, mainly because Wally Hammond was recovering from an operation and missed the earlier games. It was also another of those wet

English summers. The excitement was left to the second half of the season. Once again the Cheltenham Festival proved to be the turning point. Six of the last seven games were won and by the season's end the team had recovered to fourth in the Championship.

In the cricket context the season will be remembered best for the very last game of the season against Nottinghamshire at Gloucester on 29, 30 August and 1 September. Triumph and tragedy attended the game.

Tom Goddard had chosen this game, on his home ground in his home town, for his benefit. A benefit is the reward for long and distinguished service to the Club. In those days its financial success depended solely on the gate receipts for the game. The crowds poured in on the Saturday. The wicket prepared by Arthur Paish was not going to last. Charlie Parker had retired the previous season. The spin bowling was now shared between Tom Goddard, Reg Sinfield and Lionel Montague Cranfield, the son of that other Lionel Cranfield who had played occasionally for the County between 1903 and 1922; all of them were off spinners. They bowled out the opposition before tea. Gloucestershire soon lost two wickets. With some anxiety Tom Goddard watched Wally Hammond preparing to go out to bat on a turning wicket. If he was out before the close of play very few spectators would be present on Monday. As he moved away he turned to Tom Goddard and said, 'Don't worry Tom, I will bat all day Monday'.

On Monday, before a record crowd of seven thousand, he and the ever dependable Billy Neale resumed the innings. They were still there at lunchtime. Before the day's end Wally Hammond had scored 317 runs in six and a half hours of superlative batting. This was the ultimate Hammond. The challenge and the pride were the driving force.

Tuesday saw another great crowd gathered to acclaim Gloucestershire's tenth Championship win of the season. This duly came by an innings and 70 runs. Dallas Page, the captain, took the final catch to close the game. A memorable game saw Tom Goddard the beneficiary by £2,090. That August Wally Hammond had beaten another of W.G.'s records. He had scored 1,281 runs against the Old Man's 1,279.

Then came the tragedy. The players departed after their season's work. Dallas Page was killed tragically in a car crash returning to his home at Cirencester. His sports car collided with a motor cycle a few hundred yards beyond the Five Mile House and crashed into the low Cotswold stone wall. He climbed from the wreckage, was taken to the Cirencester Memorial Hospital where he died just after 2 am on Wednesday, 2 September. He had handled the side with increasing confidence during his two years of captaincy.

Once again Gloucestershire was faced with the captaincy problem. Bev Lyon was playing occasionally but he was beyond recall. In the period 1931 to 1936 he had made five of the nine amateur centuries scored. Basil Oliver Allen, Clifton and Cambridge U.C.C., the only amateur with the potential and the time was the only contender. He was appointed for the 1937 season.

England were soon to be faced with the same problem. There was no amateur worthy of the post for the 1938 series against the Australians. The matter was settled at a stroke. Wally Hammond became an amateur. He had joined the regional board of a tyre company after the 1937 season and could now play as an amateur. He was appointed captain for the 1938 series, but not without some criticism. Once again he had caught up with W.G., the only other Gloucestershire cricketer to captain England.

This proved to be just the challenge to stimulate and concentrate his supreme talents. With little experience he was to confound his critics. His batting did not suffer; he made 240 in the second Test at Lord's. The series will be remembered best for Len Hutton's 364 in the final Test at the Oval. Batting first, England made 903 for 7 wickets and won by a phenomenal innings and 579 runs, to draw the series, leaving Australia to retain the Ashes.

Gloucestershire retained their fourth position in the 1937 Championship. With four of their best players away at Test Trials and in the Tests it was not surprising to find they had dropped to tenth in 1938. It was not without its compensations. A number of younger players were waiting to step into their places, gladly accepting the opportunity to gain invaluable experience.

John Frederick Crapp, born in St Columb Minor, Cornwall, on 14 October 1912, whose parents moved to Bristol in 1921, was taken straight into the County side from Stapleton C.C. in 1936. He demonstrated the great strength of Bristol Club cricket by making 1,052 runs in his first season. A left handed middle order batsman, phlegmatic to a degree, with a wistful sense of humour, of great patience and sure technique, a fine slip fielder, his place was assured for many years to come. Although Cornish born and because of his long residence in Bristol there was no need for him to serve the two years' qualification period. There was, however, for George Malcolm Emmett, born in Agra, India on 2 December 1912 where his father was serving in the Indian Army. The family were Devonians. George Emmett joined the M.C.C. Ground Staff the same day as Andy Wilson. Together they came to Gloucestershire in 1936. They made their County debut on the same day, and appropriately received their caps from Wally Hammond, the captain, on 13 May in the Long Bar at Lord's following Gloucestershire's defeat by Middlesex. At first George Emmett was considered a logical replacement for Charlie Parker's left arm spinners, but he soon established his position as a fine attacking batsman. Small of stature, agile, he was a beautiful striker of the ball. From the very beginning it was manifest that his reflexes and his timing were in accord. He played his shots with effortless ease to all parts of the field. He and Andy Wilson both made more than 1,000 runs in their first full season, 1938. Gloucestershire were indeed gathering their forces together for an assault on the prime position in the national scene.

Jack Crapp.

Bev Lyon had been denied the ace in his pack and had never been able to operate with a fast bowling combination. That was arriving. The first to come was Colin John Scott, like Jack Crapp from Bristol Club cricket, but this time it was from W.G.'s old village, Downend. A 6′ 1″ blond, he was an athletic fastish right arm bowler. He bowled the perfect out swinger but, being double jointed, he could vary these with an occasional inswing. A bowler of immense potential, a superb thrower from the outfield and no mean batsman, he had all the hallmarks of a Test cricketer. He took 121 wickets in 1939, his first full season.

The other half of the partnership came to the Club, like Andy Wilson and George Emmett, by way of M.C.C. Ground Staff. George Ernest Edward Lambert was born in Paddington, London, on 11 May 1919. He also needed to qualify for two years. A tall, muscular, inswinging fast medium bowler who may not have been blessed with the natural ability of Colin Scott, he proved to be the perfect foil in the opening bowling partnership.

George Emmett.

They made a lively pair on and off the field with a Flanagan and Allen Bristol/Cockney repartee that bubbled to the surface in any situation.

The 1939 season started with a recognisable declaration. Bev Lyon captained the side in the first game of the season against his old University at Oxford. Oxford made 286 in their first innings. Gloucestershire began their innings, but it rained the whole of Monday and play could not take place before lunch on the Tuesday. Over lunch Bev Lyon persuaded Dixon, the Oxford captain, to bring the proceedings to life. He would declare the Gloucestershire innings where it stood at 213 for 8, 73 runs behind. Then both sides would bat for two hours. The cricket world had not then appreciated that the answer in such a situation was to bat for a certain number of overs; perhaps Lyon had already grasped the point. Oxford made 132 runs for 8 wickets in their two hours, but he so arranged his bowling that slow bowlers, Goddard and Sinfield, bowled 21.4 of the 31 overs. They had contained the batsmen and taken 7 of the 8 wickets.

Gloucestershire then needed 206 to win in their two hours. Bev Lyon batted at his extravagant best. He hit a six and nine fours in his 83 not out and concluded the day seven minutes before the close with the winning hit. All in the day's work to him. The University had bowled 29 overs.

Bev Lyon played only one other match that season and Wally Hammond replaced Basil Allen as captain. His captaincy of the County side was modelled on Lyon's as far as the cricket was concerned, but he lacked his flair and his happy command of affairs. Technically his captaincy was of the highest order. The result was an outstandingly successful season and his side was acknowledged widely as the most attractive in the country. At one time it looked as if they might win the Championship but they were unable to sustain the winning momentum to the season's end. They finished third, the County's highest Championship position since 1931, with 15 wins to their credit.

The Winds of Change
1939-1952

8

Gloucestershire were travelling happily along their Road, confident of the way ahead, when on 1 September 1939 the barrage balloons rose into the foreboding Bristol skies. It was to be six long years before two Far Eastern apocalyptic blasts ended hostilities and their cricketers shook the dust off their cricket gear and continued their journey.

The Gloucestershire cricket position was so different from the beginning of the First War in 1914. Then it was doubtful if the County would survive for another year and the players were advised to find employment elsewhere. Now, at a sparsely attended A.G.M. on 5 April 1940 'a message was sent to the Gloucestershire players recording the thanks of the Meeting for their splendid services in 1939, and wishing them a speedy and safe return'. The Club also hoped to make a token payment to their professionals.

An emergency committee, chaired by F. O. Wills, was set up to look after the Club's affairs and they met a number of times throughout 1939 to 1945. The War Department took over the ground and the buildings. The army, the navy and finally the American services were the successive occupants. There are many who remember baseball being played on the ground and the two unexploded bombs which were dropped during the night of 11 April 1941. The explosives were removed but the empty cases remained near the pavilion for a number of years.

Much more cricket was played during the Second War than in the First. Many Gloucestershire cricketers joined the sports staffs of the services – F/O W. R. Hammond, F/O C. J. Barnett, P/O T. W. Goddard and P/O A. E. Wilson in the R.A.F. and Sgt G. E. Lambert in the army. G. E. Emmett and several of the others joined the army and were posted overseas. Tom Goddard was largely responsible for games in Gloucestershire, at Cheltenham in September 1940, Newnham on Severn in May 1941, Gloucester in June 1942, fives games at Gloucester during June 1943 and Clifton College in 1944, all containing many well-known West Country cricketers.

By 1944, and with a great number of Commonwealth cricketers in this country, almost a full season of representative
games was played at Lord's. The bombs of the European conflict were still flying. On a personal level Wally Hammond, who
had spent much of the War in Egypt and South Africa, and
Learie Constantine forgot their private cricket battles to become
friends and captain some of the sides. The War in Europe ended
on 5 May 1945 and that summer saw a five match Victory Test
series between England and Australia. The War in total was
concluded on 2 September 1945, six years and one day after it
had begun.

On 19 April 1945 the Gloucestershire Emergency Committee
handed back to the Management Committee the responsibility
of running the Club. F. O. Wills, who had so ably managed the
Club's affairs, continued as Chairman and was so much the
driving force during the coming post-war years. The War
Department relinquished its hold on the ground and later paid
£6,473 11s. 11d. for compensation and dilapidations. The meeting reported, 'We are very thankful that so far we have been
spared the loss of any of our players,' and that 'the development
and reinstatement of Gloucestershire C.C.C. is in hand'. They
had also applied for the release of Lt Col H. A. Henson from his
position of Assistant Secretary of M.C.C. at Lord's.

Four more Management Committee Meetings were held during 1945 and another in March 1946. Gloucestershire were well
prepared to continue journeying along their Road. The world
may have changed but cricket had not. In many ways the 1946
cricket season was just another pre-war season. Wally Hammond led almost the same set of Gloucestershire cricketers on
to the field. They batted and bowled the same way to the same
field placings as their past experience directed them. There
were five elder statesmen, Wally Hammond, Tom Goddard,
Billy Neale, Charles Barnett and Basil Allen, with some younger
but much wiser pre-war colleagues, Jack Crapp, George Emmett, Andy Wilson, Colin Scott and George Lambert. They
had all missed six years of cricket. What might they and Gloucestershire have not achieved during those lost years! Reg Sinfield was the only missing face. He had moved on to be cricket
coach at Clifton College. There were no young apprentices.

However, there was Cecil Cook of Tetbury, born 8 August
1921. He was in his twenty-fifth year, had served in the R.A.F.

and whilst playing cricket in Rhodesia had come to the attention of A. P. 'Sandy' Singleton, previously of Oxford U.C.C. and Worcestershire. He advised him to apply to Gloucestershire for employment at the end of the War. Sam Cook reported for a trial, was accepted by Wally Hammond (self appointed coach), played in the season's first post-war game at Oxford and took a wicket with the first ball he bowled in first-class cricket – J. O. Newton-Thompson caught Lambert, bowled Cook, 3 – and by the season's end he had bowled more than 1,000 overs and taken 133 wickets. The Gloucestershire spin tradition continued. Luckily Gloucestershire had found a perfect foil for Tom Goddard and a successor to Charlie Parker. He never possessed the subtlety of the latter, but he too spun the ball viciously under the greatest control, laboured long hours for the cause and was mightily effective. He bothered little about the deeper aerodynamics of flight that had so preoccupied Charlie Parker but in the end it mattered little. Both of them were to play only one game for their country and both became Gloucestershire cricket legends.

The members who had kept faith with the Club and the vast crowds that gathered around the County to welcome the return of their heroes were amply rewarded. An exciting season's cricket with 12 wins saw the County finish fifth in the Championship. The Club made a profit of £3,466 2s. 6d. and crowds and membership set new records. So it was to be for a few more years.

Wally Hammond enjoyed a tremendous Gloucestershire season in 1946. He scored seven centuries with an aggregate of 1,519 and an average of 104.6, again leading the national averages as he had done since 1929. Five others scored more than 1,000 runs and Tom Goddard settled for 177 wickets. Wally Hammond missed many County games, having experienced fibrositis in his back, but his major cricket commitments were at a higher level. He captained the England side against India and was appointed captain for the 1946/47 tour of Australia. As he left the field in a drawn match against India at Cheltenham Festival on 13 August there was nothing to suggest that he had played his last real innings for Gloucestershire.

It could only be expected that England would select a party mostly of older, with a few younger and untested players. It was a most unhappy tour. Australian cricket had moved on a generation and left far behind England's more leisurely and less technical approach. England were thrashed unmercifully. Wally Hammond was criticised heavily for his uncommunicative approach to his own players, to Don Bradman and to the Australian public. He had lost the respect of his colleagues and the cricket world. He wrote to the Club over the Christmas period saying that he did not wish to captain the County again. He wanted no more captaincy. However, he did indicate that he would be prepared to play under another captain.

He moved with his family to South Africa but returned to Bristol in 1951 to lend his presence to a County membership drive. He played in the Bank Holiday fixture against Somerset at the County Ground. It was to prove a sad cricket occasion. He was acclaimed as he came out to bat, but he had not played any serious cricket for five years. Almost every semblance of that finely tuned batting mechanism had disappeared, so had that once superb physical movement. This was a travesty of the old Wally Hammond. He was now forty-eight, only a year older than W.G. had been in his Indian summer year of 1895 when he made a thousand runs in May and scored his hundredth hundred.

Basil Allen was appointed captain for 1947. As in 1938, the last time he had captained the side, he was the only amateur available with sufficient experience. E. D. R. Eagar was offered the post of Assistant Secretary, no doubt with the future prospect of captaincy. Born in Cheltenham, Desmond Eagar first played at the College Ground in 1935 direct from school. The son of Lt Col E. F. Eagar, who had been a most active Cheltenham member of the Gloucestershire C.C.C. Council, Desmond had captained the College and O.U.C.C. Unfortunately for Gloucestershire he moved on to Hampshire where some of his declarations would have satisfied Bev Lyon.

Success on the field in 1947 began at once. For much of the season Gloucestershire and Middlesex engaged in a neck and neck race for the Championship. The matter was resolved in a closely fought game at Cheltenham which the County lost by 68 runs. This is the game locally remembered for Cliff Monk's remarkable catch. His favourite remark, 'I do fear the worst,' when matters were going drastically wrong on a cricket field would never have passed through his mind as he clambered in amongst the overspilling spectators on the lower boundary to

B. O. Allen.

take the ball above his head. A great competitor with a sparkling, piquant humour and a man of many talents – artist, composer, monumental mason, church organist and choirmaster.

As these post-war years unfolded the main problem was a shortage of wickets rather than runs. Tom Goddard and Sam Cook spun away day after day with continuing success, but that promising pair of strike bowlers was not producing the expected returns. George Lambert, the stronger of the two, firmly established his position. Colin Scott never recaptured the pre-war rhythm and control that promised so much. In 1950 and 1951 he switched to off-spinners, no doubt hoping to emulate Tom Goddard's conversion twenty years previously but there was to be no fortuitous meeting on the road to Damascus for Colin Scott. He reverted to his original style in 1952 and celebrated with 101 wickets, the first time since 1939 he had taken more then 100 wickets in a season.

George Lambert.

'Bowlers of all categories are our greatest need,' so commented a Management Committee minute in 1947. Forecasting can be dangerous. In that season the side won eighteen games, the greatest number in its history. The oldest question in cricket – who wins games, batsmen or bowlers?

Between the wars the Bristol wicket had earned a reputation of being a batsman's paradise. When dry it was no place for pace bowlers, nor for that matter, for anyone but top class spinners. Then the high clay content produced a billiard table surface that provided the material for many a marathon innings. The matter came to a head in 1946 when it was proposed that the next year's Test trial game be played on the ground. This was killed off point blank by a knowledgeable Yorkshire captain at a Lord's meeting with the forthright remark that 'the Bristol wicket was not worth playing on'. There were touches of irony in what followed. The County approached a Yorkshire organisation, the Bingley Ground Keeping Research Unit, for advice. They prescribed a sprinkling of sand to balance the clay content of the top soil. This must have been applied too heavily. Tom Goddard (222) and Sam Cook (138) were at times unplayable at the County Ground in 1947. That was the season the latter thanked Yorkshire for their advice by turning in his best ever bowling performance, 9 for 42, in the first innings of Charles Barnett's Benefit game. On the strength of his early season performances he made what was to be his only Test

147

appearance, against South Africa in the first Test at Trent
Bridge.

Visiting sides to the County Ground rarely made over 200
runs, although the home batsmen dealt more satisfactorily with
the problems. A crowd of over twelve thousand packed the
ground on the August Bank Holiday Monday of the Somerset
game. The County had made 244 runs on the Saturday, to
which Somerset replied with 98, Goddard 7 for 61 in 10.4 overs.
Left with 342 to get after the Gloucestershire declaration of 195
for 9 on Monday, Somerset were removed for 25. Tom Goddard's analysis of 5 wickets for 4 runs in 3 overs (he had, in fact,
taken those 5 wickets in seven balls which included his fifth and
final career hat trick) illustrated the nature of the wicket which
in a season had gone from one extreme to another. Jack Meyer,
the Somerset captain, acidly summed up the situation. 'It was
like batting on the Weston-super-Mare beach.'

By 1948 the tide must have turned and washed the sand away.
The Australians, without Bradman, made the highest ever
score, 747 for 7, against the County. Arthur Morris scored 290
composed of a century before lunch, the second before tea, and
well on schedule before the close to complete the third. Tom
Goddard's analysis that day was not particularly flattering, 32
overs, 186 runs and no wickets.

During 1947 a young ex-Royal Marine Commando officer,
himself destined one day to captain the Club, overtook perhaps
the greatest of the County's captains finishing his journey along
the Gloucestershire Road. Bev Lyon played only a few games
after the War. At the end of that year a Management Committee
minute correctly assessed his contribution, 'He played in the
early matches and imbued all those around him with a spirit of
enthusiasm and cheerfulness.' He continued as captain of the
Second Eleven. His last visit to a Gloucestershire game was to
the Gillette Cup game against Sussex at Hove in 1969. He
watched the proceedings with gentle amusement. He would
have relished the challenge of these limited overs games. His
former spinners would have bowled, but he shuddered at the
thought of some of their fielding in this modern context. One of
his last remarks to the new Secretary/Manager (who almost
forty years previously had started his first-class career under his
direction) as they walked in his spacious garden looking into a
neighbouring fold in the Sussex Downs exemplified the man,

'There are not many people living in this country who can look out of their garden and say "I own all I can see".' He died on 22 June the following year having willed his body to medical science. Such was Beverley Hamilton Lyon.

Most of the new post-war generation of Gloucestershire cricketers were born, or educated, in the county. Sam Cook was the first to arrive, but John Kenneth Richard Graveney, born 16 December 1924 in Hexham, Northumberland, was really the first of the younger generation. When his father, a good all-round sportsman in his own right, died in 1933, the family of three boys and two girls moved to Bristol in 1938. The boys attended Bristol Grammar School. He and his younger brother, Thomas William Graveney, born at Riding Mill, Northumberland, on 16 June 1927, both represented their school in a number of sports. They both became officers in the forces from school, Ken to be a Royal Marine Commando Officer who landed in Normandy at dawn on 'D' Day, and Tom in the Gloucestershire Regiment from 1945 to 1947. In those immediate post-war years the younger generation of cricketers served little cricket apprenticeship. They were thrown into the deep end. The Graveneys swam. Strangely the eventual course of their careers was reversed. Ken, who had distinguished himself as a left handed batsman in school and club cricket, is now best remembered as a lively paced seam bowler whilst conversely Tom, who at first promised to be a bowler, became one of cricket's greatest batsmen.

Ken Graveney's debut was against Worcestershire at Gloucester in 1947, and as expected did not bowl but made 37 runs. It was not until 1949 that he became a regular member of the team. His 6 wickets for 65 runs against Surrey at the Oval first attracted interest, but it was against Derbyshire at Chesterfield that he added his name to cricket's history books.

Before that game three Gloucestershire bowlers, all spinners, had once taken all ten wickets in an innings; George Dennett, 10 for 40 versus Essex at Bristol in 1906, Charlie Parker, 10 for 77 versus Somerset at Bristol in 1921 and Tom Goddard 10 for 113 versus Worcestershire at Cheltenham in 1937. Now a fourth was to be added.

At the end of the Gloucestershire second innings on the second day, Derbyshire faced a deficit of 352 runs. There is a pecking order for bowlers in cricket and the ritual here was for

149

the slow bowlers to be brought on at once to pick up the crumbs on a worn wicket. Tom Goddard, as shop steward of the Gloucestershire Spinners Union, no doubt had firmly stated his members' case in the dressing room between innings. The Union executive decided to rub the ball in the dirt so that they could commence their work as soon as possible, hopefully to be back in Gloucestershire that night. On the way out to the wicket Jack Crapp persuaded the captain, Basil Allen, to keep the shine on the ball to allow George Lambert and Ken Graveney two overs each and then to take them off. George Lambert did not get a wicket so he was removed after his second over to make way for Tom Goddard but Ken Graveney upset the scheme of things by taking a wicket with the penultimate ball of his second over. The captain decided he could have one more over and if he did not take a wicket in it he would join Lambert in the deep. He took a wicket in his third over and again in the fourth and the fifth. Failing to capture another in the sixth he was replaced by Sam Cook. This proved no more successful and Graveney finished the day with a few more overs. Derbyshire's score at the close of play was 69 for 4 and Ken Graveney's analysis 4 wickets for 5 runs.

The following morning the same arrangement was to apply for both seam bowlers; one over and, if no wickets, then off. George Lambert failed the test. Ken Graveney started his third spell and in his first over of the day Dusty Rhodes fired a shot at a ball outside his off stump into the safe hands of brother Tom at extra cover for his fifth wicket. His sixth and seventh wickets followed in consecutive overs. He failed to get a wicket in his fifth over and was about to take his sweater under the agreement, but skipper Basil Allen said 'Having got seven wickets you had better continue'. The eight and ninth wickets fell to him in his next five overs.

A stubborn stand developed between Bill Copson and Les Jackson. Eventually the skipper announced he was to be allowed three more overs to get his tenth wicket, if in that time he had not he would be taken off. It came in his eighteenth and when Copson lofted a shot into the extra covers to be caught by George Emmett. His final analysis was 18.4 overs, 66 runs and 10 wickets. Such is the contrariness of cricket. In the dressing room after the game Tom Goddard congratulated him on his ten wickets, 'Well bowled young 'un, but they didn't bat very well did they?' From Tom that was indeed a compliment.

In less than a full season he had made 505 runs and taken 59 wickets. A career of high all-round potential never materialised. Recurring disc trouble in his back forced him to retire in 1952. He returned to the Road as captain in 1963/64, but that is for later.

In 1947 Ken Graveney introduced his younger brother, Tom, to the County. Tom was on leave from the forces at the time and destined for an eventual career in accountancy. He played for a County XI in a charity game and made such an impression that he was offered, on the spot, a contract for the 1948 season when he would be demobilised from the Army. Like his elder brother he had been playing cricket, and golf, for as long as he could remember. Tom Graveney's first County game was against the University at Oxford at the beginning of the 1948 season. Topping 6 feet and slim of build it was immediately apparent from the smoothness of his movement and the classic elegance of his batting that here was an exceptional talent. The critics were soon using glowing terms to describe his cultured batting. His first full season brought him 973 runs. Now they were writing that Gloucestershire had found a successor to Wally Hammond. He played the first of his 79 Test Matches in 1951.

Another great Gloucestershire batsman made his debut in 1948. Clement Arthur Milton was born in Bristol on 10 March 1928, and educated at Cotham Grammar School. From the very beginning his sporting activities lasted all year long. He played for his school at cricket, rugby and football from a very early age, and in the summer for the Stapleton C.C. Such was his great natural ball game ability that before he left school for National Service in the Army he had attracted the attention of Gloucestershire C.C.C. and Arsenal F.C. He could have become successful as a seam bowler but he concentrated on his batting. This may not have attracted the attention Tom Graveney's was soon to do, but he was to display a complete range of shots that dealt severely with any but the most controlled bowling. A fluid coordination of a sharply tuned analytical mind, precision and action squeezed defensive shots into the 'come on' areas nearer to the wicket. His footwork was light as a ballet dancer's. He started as a middle order batsman but gradually and most effectively he advanced up the order. He opened the innings first with George Emmett and later Martin Young, until eventually he was opening the innings for England. He made 100 in his first Test. He played football on the right wing for Arsenal and for England against Austria in 1951/52. He became the last of the England cricket/football internationals.

If there are to be those who join the Road there are to be others who will leave it. Billy Neale and Charles Barnett, two members of the 1920s generation, ended their Gloucestershire cricketing days. Billy Neale played on until 1948 to return to his beloved Breadstones Farm near Berkeley. He had played 452 matches for his County, scored 14,752 runs, taken 100 wickets and made 228 catches. There is much more to cricket than statistics. For many years he had batted at the critical No. 6 position where, when things had gone wrong before his arrival, he had taken over and cemented together many a crumbling innings. As Andy Wilson has so aptly written, 'He may have been a cricket professional but he was one of Nature's gentlemen'. He died in the Gloucester Royal Infirmary on 26 October 1955.

Charles Barnett's departure was less felicitous. To the very end with his no nonsense batting he continued to thrill crowds everywhere. He took a well deserved benefit in 1947, departed abruptly in 1948 to join the Rochdale Lancashire League Club before returning to his business interest. He continued to take a close interest in the Club's affairs and ride with the Beaufort and Berkeley Hunts. His style of batting was far removed from the contemporary style of batting that was evolving.

During 1948 the Club indulged for a moment in nostalgia. On 14 July, the nearest cricket date to his birth on 18 July 1848, they celebrated W.G.'s centenary with a match against Derbyshire at the County Ground. His Grace the Duke of Beaufort, the Club's President, attended by the Lord Mayor, and the Sheriff of Bristol, unveiled a plaque to the Old Man at the Nevil Road entrance to the Ground. Little would have changed from those days in 1887 when he was so involved with the planning and layout of the area. A suggestion that it should be renamed the Grace Ground was not approved.

The Bristol wicket may often have been referred to as 'lifeless', but as the 1940s gave way to the 1950s ominously the word was being applied to cricket as a whole. What was taking place was not so much a revolution as evolution. The Australians had led the way, but a combination of other factors had to be applied; weather, lack of cricketers of real ability, wickets, character and leadership. Afterwards the end of a process is always self evident, it is the means that are so confused. The whole philosophy of the game was changing.

Cricket legislation between the wars had appreciated accurately that much of the attraction of the game derived from games won. Many batsmen now refused to play any ball not directly aimed at the stumps. Bowlers cut down their margins of error. Wrist spinners were soon to disappear. Life was also more difficult for off spinners and left arm leg spinners. The pundits began to talk of lower trajectories, flight was a lost word, captains and bowlers studied defensive field placings, gullies retreated towards third man and coaches demanded that slow bowlers bowl faster. A mediocrity settled over the game. Medium paced seam bowlers (known disparagingly as 'Military Mediums' to the pre-war cricket world) became the new heroes. Stopping bowlers taking wickets and batsmen making runs became the object of the exercise. In rugby and football it was to be the scoring of tries and goals. Cricket was more difficult and less fun to play. The crowds stayed away. There were more interesting ways of spending leisure hours. Some cricket had become no more exciting than watching runner beans grow.

By necessity Gloucestershire complied with the universal pattern, but happily there were shafts of sunlight across this increasingly dismal scene. Charles Barnett never did subscribe to the new style; George Emmett's way of batting belonged to an earlier era; so did Jack Crapp's when the occasion demanded. Tom Graveney had that great ability which laughed off any suggestion of playing defensively unless the wicket or the bowler was imposing impossible odds. The Gloucestershire traditions of batting lived through those years.

So did Basil Allen. Tom Goddard had captained the side when Basil broke a thumb fielding in the suicide position to the off spinner. He gave up the captaincy in that year (1950) and played occasionally in 1951 before he too was gone. He had served the County loyally in those difficult years when Wally Hammond changed his status and replaced him as captain but he returned when the great man departed and held Gloucestershire cricket on course. He became the President of

Sam Cook.

the Club in 1979 and 1980. He and Barbara, his wife, were Joint Masters of the Mendip Hunt for seventeen years. He died in his sleep at his home near Chewton Mendip on 1 May 1981.

Gloucestershire cricket maintained another characteristic – it never lost its sense of humour. The running between the wickets of Tom Goddard and Sam Cook is a piece of Gloucestershire cricket folklore. As the years pass the gap between fact and fiction widens but each often ran out the other by the length of the pitch. Like many a bowler Tom thought he could bat. The same thought never entered Sam's head. His great shot was referred to parochially as 'the Tetbury chop' and less generously by his colleagues in the dressing room as 'killing the rat'. The bat was brought down at an angle on to the ball as it passed by. When he came out to join his partner an air of expectancy and urgency settled on the proceedings. His arrival at the wicket to take guard brought into play a ritual exchange of repartee with the umpire. 'What do you want, Sam?' Sometimes it was 'Gin and tonic', at others 'Half a pint'. He was always given middle and leg.

There was an occasion when the County was playing at Lord's. They were well behind the Middlesex score on the first innings when Sam Cook came out to join Tom Goddard who already had a few runs on the board and a misplaced confidence that outran the logic of the moment. If he could only get to the Nursery End he would then be taking on the better bowler and the last two Gloucestershire batsmen would close the gap. A conversation something like this occurred as Sam passed him to the other end:

'We can get these, Sam.'

'What! You must be joking!'

'I want to get down to your end. When you hit it I'll run.'

'O.K.' Sam snorted.

The first ball arrived. Sam aimed the Tetbury chop at it, snicked it somewhere into the slips, put his head down and charged for the Pavilion end where he bumped into Tom who had seen the slip stop the ball and lobbed it to Leslie Compton, the wicket-keeper, who removed the bails. A flash of conversation followed:

'What the hell are you doing here, Sam?'

'You told me if I hit the bloody ball, I was to run and here I am. What do we do now?'

'Keep running, this is H.Q.'

Tom Goddard of the great off spinning fingers saw out the euphoric post-war years. His powers seemed to be everlasting but the real break came in 1951. He was severely ill with pneumonia and pleurisy during July and announced his retirement. This was the first season in which he took less than 100 wickets since his conversion to an off spinner in 1928. However, it was not to be the end. Monty Cranfield, so long his understudy, had already retired while the new spinners had not yet established their authority. It was also a season of injury and illness and he was recalled for odd games during 1952. He was fifty-three when he returned to his furniture business. He died in his Gloucester home on 22 May 1966. In 1980 his home town honoured him by naming a new road Goddard Way.

Douglas Martin Young was born in Coalville, Leicestershire on 15 April 1924, educated at Wellingborough School, Northants. from 1936 to 1941, played his first senior games for Worcestershire and then moved to Gloucestershire C.C.C. in 1948. Did he understand that the last step from his school cricket pavilion before he stepped on to the field was a piece of Gloucestershire cricket history? Murray Witham, the

Martin Young.

cricket master at the school and a life-long devotee of W.G., read just before the war that the Grace home, the Chesnuts, was to be demolished. He was outraged and took the very first opportunity to go to Downend, found there was considerable local interest and that steps were being made to save the house for a museum. This proved to be of no avail. He drove back to Wellingborough with the doorstep on the back seat of his car and a square of turf from the orchard where W.G. had learnt his cricket watched over by his knowledgeable mother, Martha. The step was inscribed, 'This stone was once the threshold to the home of Dr W. G. Grace at Downend, Bristol, "Not of an age but for all time". Laid July 10th 1940 by Henry Grierson Founder of the Forty Club.' Martin Young was playing for the school XI the day the stone was unveiled. The piece of turf was set in the school quadrangle but did not survive. In the process of some extensions to the school buildings the workmen removed it not knowing its history.

As so happens the move to Gloucestershire proved beneficial. He played his first game for the County at the beginning of the following season. In 1950 he made 135, the first of his forty centuries, against Worcestershire at Worcester, then two more centuries to finish the season with 1,558 runs in what was his first full season's cricket. He soon became one of the County's leading run makers. An undramatic, stylish, stubborn batsman of the highest technical skill and an outfielder of some repute.

Sir Derrick Thomas Louis Bailey, Bart., D.F.C., the eldest son of wealthy South African Sir Abe Bailey, was another batsman to be recruited from outside the County in that period. Born in London, educated at Winchester, Derrick Bailey entered the gold mining industry in South Africa before the outbreak of War. He joined the South African Air Force, was seconded to the R.A.F. and served in the Mediterranean area. After the War he studied at the Royal Agricultural College, Cirencester. Tom Goddard was playing for a County XI against the R.A.C. and persuaded him to play for the County Second XI. He captained the County in 1951 and 1952 and it was during this time that he was confronted with the decision to replace Tom Goddard by John Mortimore. He made himself into a batsman and displayed great courage against hostile bowling. In his first season of captaincy he made two centuries in his season's 1,003 runs.

His players of those years remember his strong competitive urge. They recall an incident during the Yorkshire game at Bradford in 1951 when batting with Colin Scott he heaved a long hop into the deep square leg sky exactly bisecting Harry Halliday and Frank Lawson. Each regardless of the other set off on a collison course and crashed headlong. Both fell as pole-axed. The batsmen had run two. Colin Scott stopped running but Sir Derrick shouted for him to continue. They galloped on until life was restored to the corpses and the umpires stopped them. Some say they had run fifteen, others sixteen, but stories like this improve with the telling. The umpires discussed the matter and awarded him two runs. He was indignant.

John Brian Mortimore, five years Arthur Milton's junior, was also Bristol born on 14 May 1933 and was educated at Cotham Grammar School. His first game was in the 1950 Cheltenham Festival against the West Indies when he was seventeen and a few months. The mysteries of Ramadhin's bowling were too much for Gloucestershire who were bowled out for 69, with young Mortimore 4 not out. He was not asked

John Mortimore batting and right. *bowling.*

to bowl until the two W's, Walcott and Weekes, had played the other bowlers into submission. In no time at all he bowled Clyde Walcott for 126 and had taken the first of his 1,696 wickets for Gloucestershire. In a few more overs of his off spinners he had taken two further wickets. Gloucestershire batting again for 96 all out, Mortimore 5 not out. He remained unperturbed at his spectacular introduction into a cricket world that was not slow to appreciate his studious approach to the game. The County had found another young off spinner who was going to carry on their great tradition of spin bowlers. He served his National Service in the Signals Regiment of the Army, where his cricket apprenticeship carried on that excellent nursery for young future first-class cricketers.

There was yet another off spinner to come but in no way had he the same introvert character of John Mortimore. Bryan Douglas Wells of Gloucester, born 27 July 1930, came to the County by way of Tom Goddard's old Club, Wagon Works C.C. He played before his National Service and made his presence felt with 6 for 47 runs in his very first game against Sussex at Bristol in 1951. Bryan 'Bomber' Wells (nicknamed Bomber after boxing's Bombardier Billy Wells) was no person to deal in half measures. His comments in the process and the consequent confusion of making a few runs are legendary – comments which have been recounted so many times that they improve with the telling. Another character had arrived, destined in his time to become a Gloucestershire cricket legend. When he bowled, however, that was something else; but

B. D. ('Bomber') Wells.

whether batting or bowling his running commentaries on his own fallibility, the state of the wicket, the game or the world situation will ever be remembered. If he was batting, running between the wickets could be devastating to all concerned; he would run without calling, call without running or else change his mind in mid-wicket. Legend has it that on one occasion he managed to get two injured batsmen (one of them himself) and their runners at one end while all four were being run out at the other. On another he drove Peter Rochford to the point of desperation so that on recovering the end from which he had started, he turned around hands on hips and shouted back at him, 'For God's sake Bomber, CALL!' 'Tails', beamed back the irrepressible Bomber.

There is one more cricketer to introduce before this period is closed. Ronald Bernard Nicholls's name first appears in the same Management Committee minutes of 6 June 1951 which include the information that Wally Hammond had offered to play against Somerset later in the season. Ron Nicholls, closely associated with Cheltenham, was born at Sharpness on 4 December 1933. He first played in 1951 and was as modest and uncomplaining as Billy Neale of earlier days. They had much else in common; both matured to become thoroughly workman-like batsmen, both made an honoured contribution, and both bowled a few overs of 'spinners' in their time, but Ron Nicholls never did take 6 wickets for 9 runs.

The effects of the changing face of English cricket were not immediately apparent. The following Gloucestershire chart is self-explanatory. The total profit from these years was over £22,000, but these profit-making years were not to continue.

Year	Captain	Played	Won	Drawn	Position	Profit
1946	W. R. Hammond	26	12	8	5th	£3,466
1947	W. R. Hammond	26	17	5	2nd	£3,973
1948	B. O. Allen	26	9	10	8th	£4,624
1949	B. O. Allen	26	10	9	7th	£1,768
1950	B. O. Allen	28	6	18	7th	£1,471
1951	Sir D. L. T. Bailey	28	5	14	12th	£1,861
1952	Sir D. L. T. Bailey	28	7	11	9th	£202
1953	J. F. Crapp	28	9	12	5th	£4,760

HAMMOND. Walter Reginald. 1920-1951
Captain 1939 & 1946. 405 matches

BATTING AND FIELDING

b. Dover 19 June 1903 d. 1965	Innings	Not Out	Runs	Highest Innings	Average	50's	Centuries	Stumpings	Catches
DERBYSHIRE	37	3	2158	237	63.47	11	6	–	40
ESSEX	44	6	1888	244	49.68	4	6	–	48
GLAMORGAN	42	7	2774	302*	79.25	6	10	–	28
HAMPSHIRE	44	2	1576	192	37.52	11	3	–	31
KENT	48	3	2352	290	52.26	14	6	–	35
LANCASHIRE	47	4	2823	271	65.65	6	10	–	33
LEICESTER	27	2	1460	252	58.40	4	5	–	24
MIDDLESEX	49	5	2398	178	54.50	9	8	–	47
NORTHANTS	13	3	796	193	79.60	3	3	–	15
NOTTS	28	3	1935	317	77.40	1	10	–	38
SOMERSET	43	9	2483	214	73.02	11	10	–	41
SURREY	37	3	2066	205*	60.76	3	11	–	35
SUSSEX	42	2	1627	168*	40.67	10	4	–	24
WARWICKS	32	4	1545	238*	55.17	8	3	–	22
WORCESTER	44	5	1946	265*	49.89	7	6	–	45
YORKSHIRE	42	5	1517	162*	41.00	4	5	–	24
CAMBRIDGE	3	1	228	113*	114.00	–	2	–	1
OXFORD	16	2	915	211*	65.35	6	2	–	9
AUSTRALIANS	6	0	169	89	28.16	2	–	–	1
INDIANS	6	2	194	81	48.50	1	–	–	2
N. ZEALAND	3	0	183	108	61.00	–	1	–	–
PAKISTAN									
S. AFRICA	4	1	232	123	77.33	1	1	–	2
W. INDIES	7	2	399	264	79.80	–	1	–	6
TOTAL	664	74	33664	317	57.05	122	113	–	551

HAMMOND. Walter Reginald. 1920–1951

BOWLING

85 Tests for England 33 Australia 24 South Africa 13 West Indies 9 New Zealand 6 India	Overs	Maidens	Runs	Wickets	Average	Best Bowling	5 Wickets in Innings	10 Wickets in Match
DERBYSHIRE	290.2	72	675	17	39.70	5–57	I	–
ESSEX	432.3	97	1180	38	31.05	4–22	–	–
GLAMORGAN	440.3	108	1149	47	24.44	8–25	I	I
HAMPSHIRE	478.2	118	1271	60	21.18	6–59	3	–
KENT	356.3	67	1049	29	36.17	4–93	–	–
LANCASHIRE	377	101	897	25	35.88	4–58	–	–
LEICESTER	269	70	658	25	26.32	5–64	I	–
MIDDLESEX	484.2	102	1363	45	30.28	5–60	I	–
NORTHANTS	171.2	46	415	15	27.66	3–61	–	–
NOTTS	148.1	37	378	11	34.36	4–19	–	–
SOMERSET	294	80	666	25	26.64	6–26	I	–
SURREY	291.2	65	787	29	27.13	6–26	2	–
SUSSEX	394	98	1031	39	26.43	6–62	3	I
WARWICKS	221.1	45	669	9	74.33	2–47	–	–
WORCESTER	330	83	807	38	21.23	9–23	2	I
YORKSHIRE	290.1	76	813	23	35.34	4–44	–	–
CAMBRIDGE	17.3	5	55	4	13.75	2–29	–	–
OXFORD	122	30	364	11	33.09	3–39	–	–
AUSTRALIANS	19	3	100	–	–	–	–	–
INDIANS	70.1	19	169	4	42.25	2–25	–	–
N. ZEALAND	5	2	4	–	–	–	–	–
PAKISTAN								
S. AFRICA	61	7	186	7	26.57	3–47	–	–
W. INDIES	34	2	115	3	38.33	3–93	–	–
TOTAL	5597.2	1333	14801	504	29.36	9–23	15	3

9 The End of the Amateurs
1953-1962

*Gloucestershire
C.C.C. 1953.* Back
row left to right:
*C. A. Milton, F. P.
McHugh, D. Allen,
T. W. Graveney, J.
Griffiths, J.
Mortimore, D. M.
Young, A. E. Crew.*
Front row: *G. E.
Lambert, A. E.
Wilson, J. F. Crapp
(capt.), G. M.
Emmett, C. Cook.*

So the Second War cricket boom passed. The next decade was
to reap the bitter harvest which the passive style of play had
sown. The world had changed. All but the most dedicated
refused to watch three day long battles of attrition between
batsmen and bowlers idling to a draw. Cricket was rapidly
losing its attractive charm and excitement and much of it had
become a bit of a bore. It was biting the hand that had fed it for
so long. The committees blamed the cricketers, the cricketers
blamed the committees and the pitches; the quidnuncs in the
pavilion bars blamed all three, the weather, the price of beer
and anyone willing to take up an argument.

Gloucestershire cricket did not subscribe wholly to the

accepted pattern. All through the 1950s there are to be found some wonderful examples of the traditional, forthright style of batsmanship that would have delighted their illustrious ancestors.

But there can be no disputing the facts. Membership, the only sound financial base for the Club, fell alarmingly in spite of almost annual appeals and membership drives. The small working profit of £202 for 1952 served as the first warning of the financial strains ahead, but a profit of £4,760 for 1953 clouded the real issues. Other counties were experiencing the same disturbing picture. Warwickshire were the first to take a thoroughly business-like yet untraditional cricket appreciation of the situation. They set up a football pools organisation that in a few years led to the extensive development of their Edgbaston ground, now the envy of other county colleagues.

A committee minute for early 1953 reflects a completely different assessment of the problem. 'That in view of the financial position of the club and bearing in mind the representation of all parts of the County through our committees it is not considered necessary to form a Supporters' Club, or desirable to promote financial assistance by means of a football competition.' This statement brought unanimous support. The matter was discussed again in December 1953 but 'the committee saw no reason to change its opinion'.

The storm broke the following season when a record loss of £4,233 16s. 9d. was reported. A summary of the period 1954 to 1962 illustrates clearly that the performance of the team in the Championship Table bore no relation to the overall financial position of the Club:

Year	Captain	Played	Won	Drawn	Position in Championship	Loss on Year
1954	Jack Crapp	28	5	12	13th	£4,234
1955	George Emmett	28	9	6	12th	£ 416
1956	George Emmett	28	14	7	3rd	£1,769
1957	George Emmett	28	8	7	12th	£5,394
1958	George Emmett	28	5	14	14th	£4,829
1959	Tom Graveney	28	12	4*	2nd	£3,927
1960	Tom Graveney	28	9	15	8th	£3,645
1961	C. T. M. Pugh	28	11	7	5th	£3,362
1962	C. T. M. Pugh	28	11	6	4th	£8,654

* 1959 Also a Tie *v* Essex

Action/reaction was immediate. The Committee considered that the disappointing results were not only attributable to the bad weather, but also to Bristol apathy and the dull play of both sides. In more direct terms it was proposed at the Council Meeting of 18 March 1955 'That the Council of Gloucestershire C.C.C. approve in principle of the formation of a Supporters' Association to further the best interests of the Club throughout the County.' The motion was carried by seventeen votes to one. This was a complete reversal of the previous year's decision. A Supporters' Club went into business immediately with a Football Pool lottery.

Losses on the year's working continued throughout the decade. Revenue from the boom years, now in the form of various investments, was whittled away slowly in the battle for survival. No matter where the Committee turned they found urgent problems awaiting their attention. The Ground Committee manfully kept pace with members' demands for improved facilities in and out of the pavilion area, with a modernisation programme around the ground; the Cricket Committee answered the battle for brighter cricket by digging up a third of the placid Bristol square and relaying it with different top soil in an unsuccessful effort to produce faster wickets; the Finance Committee juggled with their figures and kept a watchful interest in the Supporters' Club operation. In direct terms the Supporters' Club saved the Cricket Club by providing the necessary funds to carry out the work. The greater credit in those difficult years must go to the respective Chairmen, Frank Wills (1946 to 1956), Sir William Grant (1957 to 1960) and Sir Percy Lister (1961 to 1962) for their wise direction of the Cricket Council and the General Committee.

There were administrative changes too. Hugh Henson retired as Secretary, an exhausting appointment he had held with much authority before, during and after the War. He was followed firstly by C. H. G. Thomas in 1956 and then by R. J. G. McCrudden in 1962.

Digging up the Bristol square was not the only problem confronting the Cricket Committee. This issue of captaincy in County Cricket had varying implications. The supply of amateurs with suitable qualifications was drying up rapidly. Some counties had already taken on 'amateurs' who also carried out Assistant Secretary work on a yearly basis. Gloucestershire

toyed with this idea. One obvious candidate was Desmond
Eagar who had played for the County from 1935 to 1939 and
who, unfortunately, was allowed to move to Hampshire to be
responsible largely for the great revival which led to their winning the Championship in 1961. Others were Donald Carr,
O.U.C.C., who was approached in 1952 but took up the post in
his native Derbyshire and afterwards became Secretary of the
T.C.C.B., and Raman Subba Row of Surrey and C.U.C.C. who
went to Northamptonshire. William Knightly-Smith, London
born, of Highgate School and C.U.C.C. did eventually fill the
post of Assistant Secretary in 1955 to take this avenue to the
captaincy, but much had happened before them.

Sir Derrick Bailey captained the team in 1951 and 1952 but
business pressures forced him to withdraw in 1953. The
appointment of a professional captain had been foreseen and
widely discussed. A Minute of the Council Meeting, 19 November 1952, reads, 'That the Management Committee be em-
powered to nominate a captain if their choice is an amateur, but

*Jack Crapp hits out in
a match against
Somerset.*

to report back to the Council if their recommendation is to nominate a professional'. Carried unanimously.

Jack Crapp was appointed for 1953.

There need have been no misgivings when Jack Crapp took over in 1953. His long experience and the respect he had earned both on and off the field were qualities that needed to be experienced to the full. 1954 turned out to be the worst season's cricket since 1935, with the lowest gates since that year, and membership plummeting. There was just not one amateur appearance in the team. Unfortunately the eczema on his hands from which he had suffered for so long forced him to give up the captaincy after the 1954 season and he eventually retired from the game in 1956. He became a Test Match umpire where his quiet bearing and slow, understanding smile cooled many a tricky situation. He died in Bristol on 16 February 1981. He had played in 422 matches and 708 innings for the County with 22,195 runs and 366 catches to his credit.

Captaincy of a first-class county team is immensely demanding. There is a delicate balance to be kept between the Committees off the field and the players on it, calling for chilling degrees of diplomacy in both respects. It was widely acknowledged that 'there was nothing wrong with the game of cricket that the captains could not put right'. The game was under the closest scrutiny. It was indeed lucky that at the moment when the game was being subjected to the closest scrutiny in its long history, Gloucestershire could call upon two such stalwart figures as Jack Crapp and George Emmett, both of whom were professional captains schooled in their earlier days under amateur captains.

George Emmett, with his slow, knowing smile, readily accepted his daunting responsibilities with a firmness that befitted his family background and his war career in the Gunners. He is remembered as a disciplinarian by those who played under him, every one of whom respected his authority to the full. He was a shrewdly calculating captain who led by example. His twinges of arthritis may have restricted his mobility in the field, but his shots, particularly off his legs, were never to lose that distinctive whip-like quality.

With characters like B. D. Wells in his team, there was never any suggestion that his days of captaincy were going to be without their humorous interludes. There was an occasion with the Bomber bowling when a run out situation developed. The ball was thrown to his end with both batsmen in mid-wicket. There was an easy run out at his end. He ignored it. In an ecstasy of self-confidence he took deliberate aim at the far end, threw and hit two stumps out of the ground before the other batsman had reached that crease. George Emmett, who had watched the proceedings with mounting alarm and disbelief, in a shout that would have boiled a kettle, demanded 'What's going on, Bomber?' To which Bomber countered with a finality that brooks no reply, 'Well, this bloke can't bat, it's the other ... we wanted out.'

It is to George Emmett's everlasting credit that the batting of many of his colleagues kept alive the positive style of batting that will always be associated with Gloucestershire, illuminating the comment Nevil Cardus has made that 'when Gloucestershire became an all professional XI the batsmen continued to play like amateurs'. His captaincy terminated in 1958 and he played his last game towards the end of the following season. For a time it looked as if he would continue to live and work in Cheltenham but he became Secretary to the Imperial Athletic Club. He died in Bristol on 18 December 1976. George Emmett played in 454 matches and 770 innings with 22,806 runs, 57 wickets and 262 catches, but cricket is always much more than statistics.

Before you have captains you must have cricketers. The flow of Gloucestershire born cricketers throughout the decade continued with only a few exceptions. It was most fitting that another of these should come from Cotham Grammar School which had already produced two Test cricketers and was now to produce a third. David Arthur Allen, born in Bristol on 29 October 1935, played his first game for the County against the Combined Services in 1953. A month later, in his fourth Championship game, cricket was introduced to that deceptively casual bowling action which in just a few seasons was to be seen around the world. In a tremendously exciting finish against Surrey, the reigning champions, at the County Ground, he took 6 wickets for 13 runs to win the game with two balls to go. His last 3 wickets had cost him 5 runs! His Cotham school friends chaired him in triumph from the field. National Service then claimed him. He returned in 1959 to take 84 wickets and score 743 runs in his first full season of cricket. He was picked to play in the

David Allen.

David Smith.

last Test against India, but unhappily a badly bruised finger, acquired in a weekend benefit match, forced him to withdraw.

Anthony Stephen Brown, born in Bristol on 24 June 1936, also played his first game in 1953, against Yorkshire at Sheffield, aged 17 years and one month. So began a career that was to have a great significance for Gloucestershire cricket for many years to come. The easy flowing action of his medium paced seam bowling later caught the attention but during his National Service, playing for the Combined Services XI, his batting so progressed that he became an invaluable middle of the order all-rounder.

With David Robert Smith, also of Bristol and born 5 October 1934, who had played football for Bristol City before he played for the County, he formed a formidable partnership of strike bowlers. David Smith's first full season in 1957 brought him 106 wickets. Both he and Tony Brown had the same lithe, whippy actions which gave them the fullest control over their pace, swing and movement off the pitch.

Injury forced Tony Brown to miss the best swing bowlers' bonanza of those years. Gloucestershire had beaten India by 192 runs at Cheltenham in 1959 and in 1960 they inflicted an even heavier defeat on South Africa. Denis A'Court, his understudy, had replaced him four games earlier for the game at the County Ground. The overcast sky, humid conditions and a green wicket were all tailor-made for a seam bowler's dream and a batsman's nightmare. So it proved. South Africa batted first for 116 runs; Gloucestershire followed with 81, but not before Arthur Milton had retired from the match with a broken thumb. The following morning Denis A'Court and David Smith so bemused the South Africans that half the side was out for 18 and all for 49. They had bowled unchanged, Denis A'Court for a career best of 6 for 25 and David Smith 4 for 20. The County fared little better in their second innings; Ron Nicholls saved the day with 35 not out of a winning total of 87 for 7 to give them victory by three wickets.

Andy Wilson, whose first visit to the County Ground had been in 1935 for Middlesex took his benefit against them there in 1953. During the intervening years he had proved himself a most competent wicket keeper and an invaluable batsman. As if to prove the point he celebrated the season with a world record of ten catches against Hampshire at Portsmouth, over a thousand runs for the sixth time, 56 catches and 19 stumpings.

Gloucestershire C.C.C. 1956. Standing: C. A. Milton, P. Rochford, B. D. Wells, J. V. C. Griffiths, J. B. Mortimore, G. J. Lake, R. B. Nicholls, D. M. Young. Seated: C. Cook, G. E. E. Lambert, G. M. Emmett, Lt Col H. A. Henson, J. F. Crapp, T. W. Graveney.

Barrie Meyer keeping wicket for Gloucestershire.

By the end of his career in 1955 he had played 318 games for the County, scored 10,532 runs and seven centuries in 486 innings. With 416 catches and 168 stumping this well qualified him to join that elite band of Gloucestershire wicket keepers, J. A. Bush, Jack Board and Harry Smith.

Peter Rochford from Halifax was his immediate replacement and Bobby Etheridge, a wicket keeper from Gloucester and another footballer/cricketer, became the reserve. Peter Rochford left the Club in 1957 when he shared the responsibility with Barrie John Meyer. Born on 21 August 1932 he was also a footballer. He became the regular wicket keeper in 1958 and so the fifth had joined that elite band.

George Emmett's last game was in 1959. By then Gloucestershire cricket was in the hands of the next generation. The Cricket Committee made provision for the best of the many young cricketers playing in the County. At the height of the boom the County was running in the 2nd XI Championship, the Minor Counties and the Gloucestershire Etceteras, captained by Arthur Derrick who for a time was also the Treasurer. All the County born members of the Championship XI had graduated through these years. As the financial strictures closed in, these activities were closed. The Etceteras stopped in 1956 and the Minor Counties in 1959 when the Second XI played a lengthened programme which was later restricted.

When cricketers of those teams meet it resembles a gathering of old boys recalling the happier days of their school life. They come from all around the County; John Griffiths, left arm spinner, and David Brown, Cheltenham; Derek Hawkins, Thornbury; David Carpenter, Tetbury; David Bevan, Gloucester; Graham Wiltshire, Chipping Sodbury who took a hat-trick against Yorkshire at Leeds in 1958 and distinguished himself by appearing on the field as a substitute for one ball and taking a catch and who followed George Emmett in 1962 as the Club's coach; Jim Andrew of Shirehampton, later cricket coach at Clifton College; Denis A'Court who bowled so spectacularly against South Africa in 1960 and took a hat-trick against Derbyshire at Gloucester in 1961. All of them did their two years' National Service before joining the staff. Then came a triumvirate of Cambridge Blues; Richard Bernard, whose great-grandfather, Dr David Edward Bernard, had married W.G.'s elder sister, Alice Rose, in 1867, and who himself took up a medical career; also from Clifton, Tony Windows who so easily could have become another Tony Brown middle order all-rounder but was already committed to a legal career. He introduced to the Club a fellow Cambridge Cricket Blue from Johannesburg, Raymond Christopher White. Overseas University students can play for any County whilst still in residence and he will always be remembered for the hurricane 102 not out he made against Nottinghamshire at Cheltenham in 1962. He returned to South Africa in 1964.

Fast bowlers were always in short supply in Gloucestershire. Sources outside the County supplied tall, ranging Frank McHugh of Leeds who unfortunately was forced to retire in 1956 when bowling so promisingly, and Martin Ashenden who came to the County from Northamptonshire.

Tom Graveney succeeded George Emmett as captain in 1959.

Tom Graveney
receiving the cheers of
the crowd after his
innings of 55 in the
Fourth Test at
Headingley versus the
Australians in 1953.

Arthur Milton batting at the Wagon Works Ground, Gloucester.

By then he had established himself as a regular member of that superb England batting line up, May, Cowdrey, Graveney, Dexter, that did so much to reestablish English batting. The pleasure and benefit that a County enjoys by having a Test cricketer in its ranks is somewhat counterbalanced by his absence. By now Arthur Milton, David Smith and David Allen had also played Test Cricket. George Emmett was recalled and shared the captaincy with Arthur Milton when Tom Graveney was away. To have three captains operating during a season can be disturbing, but such was the supply of mature cricketers that 1959 proved to be one of the most exciting in the Club's history.

English cricket everywhere reaped the benefit of that glorious summer. Gloucestershire, with a series of decisive wins in mid-season, looked set to topple Surrey from their position at the head of the Championship which they had held for the last seven years. The County played out the second tie in its history. This was against Essex at Leyton on 5, 6 and 7 August. In their first innings Essex made 364 for 6, Doug Insole 177 not out and 176 for 8, Insole 90. Gloucestershire replied with 329 leaving them 212 to win in 170 minutes. With a tremendous 91 out of 127 in 85 minutes Tony Brown was eighth out, leaving the two remaining batsmen 3 runs to get in the last six minutes of the game. Trevor Bailey bowled a wide, Barrie Meyer played a single leaving Sam Cook to display his bewildering array of shots with the scores level. The first ball he received disappeared from his bat into the leg field where it was caught brilliantly.

1959 was a batsman's year and as if to prove the contrariness of the game, two bowling battles in one week towards the end of August settled Gloucestershire's Championship challenge. The first was against Yorkshire at Bristol. Gloucestershire won the toss and with wide experience of the wicket, which had received so much expert advice over the last ten years, batted all the first day to accumulate 294 for 8 wickets. Tom Graveney declared the following morning and Tony Brown, with the best perform-ance of his career, 7 wickets for 11, and David Smith 3 for 16, bowled out Yorkshire for 35 runs before lunch. They followed on and struggled to 141 for 7 before bad light stopped play. The second innings closed at 182 and Gloucestershire had won by an innings and 77 runs. In this battle of the seamers, Messrs Brown and Smith had taken 17 of the Yorkshire wickets.

It says volumes for the power of the Gloucestershire bowling at that time that the following and decisive game that followed against Surrey at Gloucester belonged to the spinners. The wicket was of a doubtful quality and two classic combinations of off spin and left arm leg spin dominated the game. Winning the toss probably decided the issue. David Allen and Sam Cook restricted the Surrey first innings to 130. Laker and Lock then shot their way through the Gloucestershire second innings, at one time 26 for 7 wickets, for 71 runs. They had taken 19 of the 20 Gloucestershire wickets and Surrey had won by 89 runs. Yorkshire headed the Championship at the end of the season with Gloucestershire second and Surrey third after seven suc-cessive years at the top of the Championship Table.

1959 can be classed among the best in the County's history on the cricket field. John Mortimore had registered Gloucester-shire's first cricketer's double since Reg Sinfield's in 1937 and had played in two Tests. His studious approach to the game had brought him to the peak of his career. He accepted the problems of sequence bowling, that exacting art of bowling consecutive balls with the sole object of taking a wicket. Tony Brown and David Smith each took 110 wickets, Martin Young scored 2,090 runs and three other batsmen, Tom Graveney, 1,186, Arthur Milton, 1,061 and Ron Nicholls, 1,030 all claimed a share of the

John Mortimore.

runs. For the first time the Second XI won their Championship. All that and then a loss of £3,926 15s. 5d.

With the progression of John Mortimore and David Allen towards Test Match status and both of them promising to be batsmen of some stature, Bomber Wells could be classed as surplus to requirements. He may have batted like an engine shunting trucks but his bowling was something different. He was a top class off spinner with a bewildering run up which could vary from 0 to 7 yards as the whim took him. The County wanted to keep him but he chose to move to Nottinghamshire. The following season, 1960, he took 120 wickets for them. He had taken 544 wickets before he left Gloucestershire. His career ended for them in 1965 when he left cricket in true Wellsian fashion. During the season he lost a regular place in the Nottinghamshire XI but was recalled for a few games. When his total of wickets reached 999 he declared that he would not play again. The encouragement of his colleagues proved fruitless.

175

'No, plenty of bowlers have taken 1,000 wickets but no-one 999.' However, the cricket statisticians had the last laugh. They later credited him with 998 first-class wickets. A figure he disputes to this day.

There have always been strong North versus South feelings in the County. Gloucestershire folk want to see their County team playing in their area. When the Bristol Ground was bought back from Fry's in 1933 there was some talk that it should be sold immediately and the headquarters moved to Gloucester or Cheltenham. A stronger 'attack' from the North of the County might have proved successful, but by the late 1950s so much money had been spent on improving the facilities at the County Ground that this was no longer practical. There was also a shortage of alternatives in the North, but Council members from Stroud and Lydney pressed strongly for games.

One of the few likely venues was the Erinoid Ground at Stroud. Mr John Harvey, Managing Director of Erinoid Ltd, a cricket lover, was also a Council Member of the County Club. Rex Griffiths and members of the Stroud region had fought long for the games. The first to be played there was against Nottinghamshire on 9 June 1956. It was scheduled for three days but it was won by Gloucestershire by nine wickets in two days in spite of the remarkable bowling feat of Ken Smailes who, in the first Gloucestershire innings, almost unnoticed turned in a career best analysis of 41.3 overs, 20 maidens, 66 runs and all 10 wickets.

This game and the one against Essex the following season, which the County lost by an innings and 21 runs, amply demonstrated that bowlers were coming into the ascendancy. Both games had been well supported. A second game was added in 1958 against Oxford and Cambridge and in 1963 two Championship games. The difficult decision not to play there in 1964 was made for the County by Erinoid who extended their operations on to the playing area. It is doubtful if the County would have continued to play there. The ground and adjacent area were small by first-class standards, gates had by then fallen and were no longer covering expenses but it was the wicket which had caused so much concern. Ken Smailes had set the pattern in the very first game and by the early 1960s it was being referred to as Death Valley or a turnip pitch. The delicate balance between bat and ball that makes for a good game of cricket had

been too heavily weighted in favour of the bowlers.

Fourteen games were played at Stroud between 1956 and 1963. The wicket sorted out the Test batsmen from the rest; only Mike Smith, 182 not out in 1959, Arthur Milton 131 in 1963 and Peter Richardson 126 in 1959 and Ron Nicholls 107 in 1961 scored centuries in the 51 innings played.

Bowling figures abound. Frank McHugh's 6 for 41, followed Ken Smailes' 10 for 66 in the first game. David Smith's 6 for 36 against Essex in 1961 and 7 for 20 against Sussex in 1962 and Tony Brown's 7 for 24 in that game. However, it was the spinners who gave Stroud its reputation. Sam Cook's 5 for 13 against Warwickshire in 1959, but particularly the off spinners, John Mortimore's 5 for 32 against C.U.C.C. in 1959 and 3 for 8 against Surrey in 1960, then David Allen's 9 wickets against Middlesex in 1961 and finally his 11 wickets against Glamorgan in 1963 sealed the fate of cricket in Stroud.

Captaincy problems built up as the 1960 season approached its disappointing end. With rumours of disquiet in the dressing room and disturbing criticisms being voiced in the Cricket Council, the two sides took up their entrenched positions. The matter came to a head over the winter of 1960/61. After a number of protracted, and later abortive meetings, Tom

Tom Graveney who played in 506 innings for Gloucestershire between 1948 and 1960.

177

Graveney decided to leave the Club. Some of the bitterness was reminiscent of W.G.'s departure in 1899. The Old Man was by then nearing the end of his long career. Tom was only in the middle of his but the atmosphere was soured for many years to come. Sir George Dowty, later to be President of Worcestershire, persuaded him to join that County. He had played 506 innings for Gloucestershire between 1948 and 1960 bringing him 19,705 runs and 50 centuries.

Tom Graveney was a superb batting technician. Some of his forward or square shots through the covers had all the ease, grace and authority of Wally Hammond. He did not play in 1961.

Worcestershire won the County Championship in 1964 and 1965. He captained them in 1968 and was awarded an O.B.E. for services to the game. He retired in 1972 with 47,793 runs and 122 centuries and 79 Tests to his credit.

Whoever followed him as Captain of the Gloucestershire team, whether amateur or professional, would inherit an uneasy situation. The problems landed squarely in the lap of an Old Etonian, Charles Thomas Michael Pugh, who was born in London on 12 March 1937 and was appointed to succeed him. In every respect it was a difficult decision for the Committee to make. They hoped that the appointment of an amateur captain would solve their problems, but they were fighting against the current trend. By 1961 amateurs were almost an extinct species.

Tom Pugh, one of the country's leading racquets players, who had made a great number of runs in London club cricket, had been recommended by Percy Fender, the former Surrey and Test amateur, in 1958. He played his first game for the County in 1959. In his first full season in 1960 he scored 1,011 runs and with his captain Tom Graveney, took part in the existing second wicket partnership record of 256. He was an unlucky cricketer. In almost his first game as captain in 1961 he ducked into a full toss from David Larter, the Northants fast bowler. His jaw was broken in two places and he suffered the further indignity of being given out lbw.

At the time the side was in third position; by his return six weeks later it had dropped to sixth and completed the season fifth in the Championship Table.

Martin Young and Ron Nicholls had a great batting season under his captaincy in 1962. In the very first game against the

Ron Nicholls.

178

University at Oxford they set the County's first wicket partnership of 395 (Martin Young 198 and Ron Nicholls 217), so directly or indirectly Tom Pugh had been associated with Gloucestershire's only two post Second War partnership records. The side rose to fourth place in the table. He had captained them in twenty-eight games of which eleven had been won, a very high percentage. But still the Committee was not satisfied. He was not appointed for 1963 and returned to his business career in London.

Gloucestershire C.C.C. 1962. Back row left to right: *D. A. Allen, A. S. Brown, A. R. Windows, R. B. Nicholls, R. C. White, D. R. Smith, B. J. Meyer.* Front row: *F. Dudridge (scorer), D. M. Young, C. Cook, C. T. M. Pugh (capt.), C. A. Milton, J. B. Mortimore, H. White (masseur).*

Instant Cricket
1963-1968

During the first years of the sixties cricket continued along its path of self-destruction. Largely of its own volition it no longer excited a generation that had grown up with a much wider choice of entertainment options at its disposal. It is easy to elaborate in retrospect, but it is generally accepted that too much of the first-class cricket being played was about as entertaining as watching ice-cream melt. Adapt or die is Nature's Law. Cricket survived but it needed a revolution to save it. A crisis of confidence was at hand.

Several possible answers were explored. At the very centre of the problem was the fact that the three-day games in mid-week were sparsely attended. At first the controversy settled around the delicate issue of playing on a Sunday. Rothmans had already correctly assessed the potential of Sunday play with their International Cavalier games. After prolonged discussion and much heart searching a thoroughly British compromise of a limited overs knock-out competition of 60 overs a side was arranged for 1963. Thoroughly conservative to the last, it was called 'The First-Class Counties Knock-out Competition' and sponsored almost anonymously by Gillette. In 1964 it was openly referred to as the Gillette Cup. To complete the story of the introduction of the limited overs competition, the Sunday John Player League of 40 overs began in 1969, but in deference to the Lord's Day Observance Society, at first no direct charges were permitted. This matter was by-passed in various ways, but Gloucestershire allowed admission to the ground by enforcing the cumbersome purchase of a programme. Then in 1972 came the Benson and Hedges Cup, 55 overs, part regional league and part knock out.

Limited overs cricket changed the chemistry of the game, or as Wilfred Wooller, that Welsh rugby/cricket sage summed it all up, 'the orchestra is now expected to play Beethoven during the week and Boogie Woogie at weekends'.

Meanwhile Gloucestershire's exchequer continued to shrink. The investments gathered during cricket's euphoric post-war phase had been realised to keep in check the creeping dilapi-dations at the County Ground and to improve the amenities. The overall annual loss was now running at £10,000. The overdraft by the end of 1966 had reached £27,840 with atten-dant bank limits. Crisis point had been reached. Three acres of the ground at Ashley Down End were sold to the Bristol Edu-cation Authority for £30,000 on 21 February 1967. The result-ing immediate profit of £3,000 soon evaporated and by the end of the financial year the deficit stood at £11,380. The s.o.s. signals were brought out again.

Mr J. E. C. Clarke, appointed Chairman at the Council Meet-ing on 27 April 1962 to succeed Sir Percy Lister, inherited this Canute-like situation. He had come to the position through his Vice-Chairmanship of the Club and Chairmanship of the Sup-porters' Club and thus was acquainted closely with the debili-tating financial problems. The Club's Constitution, which he had for long considered 'democratic but cumbersome', largely through his efforts was recast and then approved at the Annual Meeting of 27 November 1962. This gave the Regional Com-mittees of the County a stronger representation in the Club's affairs and a consequent widening of their efforts within their Regions. A positive catalogue of fund raising activities resulted; the Bristol Region under the enthusiastic direction of Mr O. F. L. Brown ran the Badminton Ball, Donkey Derbys were organised at the County Ground and Race Nights during the winter; the Cheltenham Corporation, inspired by Councillor Aimbury Dodwell, initiated a series of highly successful func-tions to coincide with the Cheltenham Festival; Gloucester ran its fashion shows while Thornbury, in the most capable hands of Gordon Tovey, created a highly rewarding Ducie Cup six-a-side competition for cricket clubs.

The Club attended to its economies even to the dangerous expedient of reducing its cricket staff and its fixture list for the lower levels. Two pitches were rented to Bristol City A.F.C. until the sale in 1963, tennis courts, the Kildare Bowling Club, the bowling green, two hockey pitches to the Bristol Hockey Club during the winter months, two cricket wickets for Horfield C.C. and Messrs Jones C.C. during the summer, but all failed to halt the slide. Gloucestershire efforts paled into insignifi-cance compared with what Warwickshire had achieved at Edg-baston. They had started their immensely successful football pools operation at about the same time as Gloucestershire, but with courageous professional acumen. The result was the best developed cricket ground in the world. Gloucestershire's own Supporters' Club contribution of £70,000 between 1960 and 1970 may appear puny by comparison but it too had been expended largely on improved amenities at Ashley Down.

Amid all its financial worries the County received a much welcomed legacy of £6,000 from the estate of Mr Thomas Smith of Vancouver. Born in Bristol in 1870, he played club cricket, watched W.G. and Jessop play at the County Ground, emigrated to Canada in 1903 and continued to play in Winnipeg and Vancouver until he retired. He had never forgotten his early cricket days in Bristol and when he died in 1962 he left half his residual estate in trust to Vancouver C.C. and half to his old County.

In the whole wide range of the fund raising activities there was one of the greatest future significance. Sponsorship and advertising were at first only grudgingly accepted as a fact of life. A series of pictures taken at the County Ground in 1906 during that memorable win by one run over Yorkshire shows three big advertisements displayed. Fifty years later a Minute of the Management Committee Meeting for 24 June 1965 agrees to 'discreet advertising' at County matches and banners were allowed to be displayed at 'say £5 a match'. Thus unfolded another piece of history. The Ladies' Stand was partitioned into five boxes and hosting by organisations at lunches became an accepted feature of the day's play.

The almighty buck – or the lack of it – was saving the game.

If there is to be a dividing line in the internal affairs of the Club in the decade between 1960 and 1970, it could be 1968 with the immediate registration of an overseas cricketer, but if it refers to cricket as a whole it must be 1963 which saw the passing of the amateur.

It was not the moment for sentimental reflection but, for better or for worse, there were wider implications. Bev Lyon, Percy Fender, Brian Sellars and many other great County Captains had definite ideas about who ran the affairs on the field. Their professional counterparts soon found that the dressing-room provided a forum of discontent that needed delicate handling. Gloucestershire had appointed Tom Pugh after three professional captains. Now in 1963 when amateur cricketers joined the dinosaurs as specimens of an extinct race, paradoxically they appointed an ex-professional who was to play as an amateur.

Ken Graveney could claim to be the last of the amateurs. After a back injury had forced his premature retirement in 1951 he had continued to play golf and club cricket in Bristol, retained his close association with the Club, captained the Second XI in 1962, and now a year later, with surprising yet commanding logic, he was appointed captain of the Club. His career in industrial catering had progressed favourably. His employers gave him permission to take up the appointment on the understanding that he played as an amateur. This arrangement no doubt satisfied the Club's mood for economy. More pointedly he was given the authority to select his team but all was not well on the field. The side finished eighth and then seventeenth, winning twelve of the fifty-six games in his two years of captaincy, but it was agreed that 'his great contribution had been in leadership rather than in statistics'.

1964 saw the retirement of Martin Young to South Africa where he had coached from almost the beginning of his career in 1949. He had made an admirable contribution of 23,400 runs, including 40 centuries. Sam Cook also concluded his career before joining the Umpire's List. He had taken almost as many wickets (1,768) as he had made runs (1,937) in the 498 matches he had played for the County.

Wally Hammond died in Durban on 2 July 1965 following a heart attack, due in part to the serious injuries he had received in a motor accident a few years previously. His last visit to this country was to support the County's fund raising activities in March 1951. Frank Twiselton, a member of the Management Committee, made the arrangements for the tour sponsored by Chairman, Sir Percy Lister. Wally spoke at a number of dinners throughout the County, including the Annual Dinner held at the now demolished Bell Hotel, Gloucester.

When his business ventures in South Africa collapsed under the unhappiest of circumstances he took up an appointment as cricket coach to Natal University in Durban. The last letter he wrote is dated 28 June 1965 and was to Frank Twiselton. By a remarkable coincidence it arrived at the moment his death was announced on the morning radio of 2 July. Wally wrote that 'he was very well and the nippers are growing up fast, the three of them presenting me some difficulty in keeping up with them' adding that 'there was little chance of another visit to England'.

Following his death his wife Sybil, their son and two daughters were left in straitened circumstances. A Charitable Trust Fund helped the family over their immediate difficulties and in May 1967 became the Wally Hammond Memorial Fund to assist Commonwealth cricketers and their dependants in need of help. Previously in March 1966 the ground of the University of Natal Cricket Club at Durban was named the Hammondfield. Ray White who had made that thrilling century for Gloucestershire at the Cheltenham Festival of 1962 played in the Commemoration Game.

Wally Hammond's ashes were brought back to England and were scattered on the County Ground.

If the two seasons had not been rewarding collectively they had certainly been so for John Mortimore. He completed his

Gloucestershire C.C.C. 1965. Back row left to right: *S. E. J. Russell, D. W. J. Brown, M. Bissex, F. Dudridge (scorer), A. S. Brown, B. J. Meyer, A. R. Windows.* Front row: *R. B. Nicholls, C. A. Milton, J. B. Mortimore, D. A. Allen, D. R. Smith.*

second cricketer double, 1,425 runs and 102 wickets in 1963 and his third the following year, 1,118 runs and 104 wickets. C. Townsend, Jessop and Sinfield had completed the double twice and only the immortal W.G. more times. Such is the standing of John Mortimore in Gloucestershire's cricket history.

David Smith and Tony Brown shouldered the onerous burden as strike bowlers. Oh for a fast bowler to assist them. Little did they realise he had already visited the country touring with the South African Schoolboys.

Ken Graveney returned to his business duties after the 1964 season. John Mortimore, who had been his vice-captain, succeeded him in 1965. His quiet, methodical approach to the game was not enough to rejuvenate a side that had become stale. There had been so little for them to enthuse over in the last four years. Matters had improved in 1965, the side had risen to tenth in the Championship winning seven games, but a report at the end of that season underlined the problem 'after mid-season many of the batsmen walked to the wicket as if to face a firing squad'. With waning confidence comes a fatalistic acceptance of defeat. After Martin Young's departure Arthur Milton and Ron Nicholls were the only consistent batsmen. David Smith and Tony Brown continued to share the seam attack with occasional assistance from Tony Windows, with David Allen and John Mortimore wheeling away, sorely missing Sam Cook's alternative support. Almost inevitably the slide followed. They were fifteenth in 1966 and seventeenth (bottom) again in 1967.

There are two sources of supply of cricketers; you produce your own as Yorkshire has always done, or you import them from some other source. There are various alternatives. Mike Bissex, Somerset born, first played in 1961. Ambidextrous, bowling left arm spinners and throwing with his right, he was only now in 1965 beginning to establish himself as a middle order batsman. Then there was Syd Russell from Middlesex who had already scored two centuries against the County. He first played in 1965, scored 1,256 runs in the season but never did produce the regular quota of runs so necessary.

David Shepherd.

Gloucestershire had always cherished their West Country connections and with a coach named Graham Wiltshire scouting through the Minor Counties how could it have been otherwise? David Robert Shepherd of Bideford, St Luke's and Devon scored 108 in his Gloucestershire debut in 1965. Rotund in figure, a robust batsman, of genial disposition, Devonian to the core, Sir Francis Drake would have relished his company. So would he the other Devonian from his own Tavistock town, Jack Davey. Opening left arm fast bowler of the old pre-century Fred Roberts type, fastish, workmanlike but prone to injury, he took over some of the load from David Smith and Tony Brown. It took both of them a few years to adapt their particular qualities to the first-class game. Jack Davey did take 60 wickets in his first season but was not able to play a full season until 1971. Meanwhile David Shepherd had to wait until 1968 to pass the season's tally of 1,000 runs. Both of them proved invaluable in the limited overs games and Gloucestershire's Devonian twins helped the team's morale through many a long day.

Jack Davey.

During the middle sixties it became increasingly likely that another source of supply of cricketers would become immediately available. Flamboyant Caribbean cricketers became the hunting ground for most of the counties. The immediate registration of one overseas cricketer became the rule from 29 November 1967. Gloucestershire had sounded out Clive Lloyd and Joel Garner, but the strongest moves were made in the direction of Gary Sobers, already the target for other counties. It was not to be. The County refused to be drawn into a Dutch auction and he signed a contract with Nottinghamshire. However, the County did engage Roy Wycliffe Phillips, a righthand batsman from Barbados, but he had to serve the stipulated two-year qualification period before playing his first game in 1968. When the quest for Gary Sobers failed, Gloucestershire concluded a chapter of events that had opened in 1965.

In Michael John Procter, born in Durban on 15 September 1946, Gloucestershire found the fast bowler they had been waiting for all through their history. At sixteen he was Vice-Captain of Hilton College and he first came to England with the South African Schoolboys team in 1963, which outgunned most of the country's public school sides they met. He made 148 not out against Radley College. Graham Wiltshire, by now the County's cricket coach, had seen this score while browsing

Mike Procter.

through the School's Cricket Section of *Wisden*, and also that of another boy named Barry Richards who was the leading run getter of the tour. A letter was sent to David Allen who was on the 1964/65 tour with the England team in South Africa asking him to contact the boys' parents. This he did in due course. On his return to Bristol letters were sent inviting the boys to Gloucestershire for the following summer. These were the days of stringent economies. They came at their own expense, spent the summer playing for clubs around the County and for the County's lower teams with the satisfying exception of a rain spoilt game at the County Ground against their own country. They were the top scorers, Richards 59 and Procter 69, in the only Gloucestershire innings of 279. They returned home de-lighted with their reception in Bristol.

In 1966 they returned to this country with the Wilfred Isaacs South African tour party which contained many future Test cricketers. Unfortunately the game against a David Allen XI at the County Ground was rained off. Bristol did not see the aggressive batting and bowling that brought Mike Procter three Test appearances for South Africa against Australia over their 1966/67 cricket season. He took seven wickets in his first Test at his native Durban. For the first time the wider cricket world had witnessed the long run and remarkably powerful bowling action that was to cause so much devastation in the years ahead.

In 1967 the qualifying period for overseas cricketers was still as it had been for Charles Dacre in 1927, an 'unbroken' two years, but in 1967 the whole matter was now at the very centre of cricket controversy. Gloucestershire had attacked the rule vigorously and persistently. They paid return air fares for both young players foreseeing the problem of a 'dead end winter in Bristol when they could be employed and playing cricket in South Africa'. Eventually the County won their case on both counts. The 'unbroken' year was now only to refer to the cricket season, and then in November 1967 the immediate registration of one overseas cricketer became permissible. If the rule had not been passed then it is probable that both Mike Procter and Barry Richards would have become Gloucestershire cricketers. When it was passed Gloucestershire set off in earnest pursuit of Gary Sobers, the greatest attraction in cricket, as centre-fill for the approaching Centenary Year, a boost for their flagging membership and to be captain. When that failed they were forced to decide between Mike Procter and Barry Richards. They chose Mike Procter. Barry Richards was attracted to Hampshire where he was immediately successful, becoming a *Wisden* Cricketer of the Year for 1968. Gloucestershire had now acquired their second inter-hemisphere cricket season com-muter but his journeys by 'plane took him only hours where Billy Midwinter's in 1878–82 had taken him weeks by boat.

And that's how Mike Procter came to Gloucestershire.

In 1968 Gloucestershire supporters admired at close quarters for the first time the new dimensions that had come to their cricket; the smoothly increasing momentum of the long run, bursting into that awesome whirling action delivery, as much off the wrong foot as in mid-air, and the remarkable control those immensely powerful shoulders and a husky near six foot frame which brought him 69 wickets in the first season and many more in the years to come. When they added to that 1,167 runs, including three centuries, from no-nonsense but aggressive match-winning batting, and his baseball type throwing they knew that they had seen another cricketer of the W.G., Jessop, Hammond class and their long sought for fast bowler.

The right knee ligaments did not hold up to the shattering impact of that delivery stride. He returned home to South Africa at the season's end with his leg in plaster.

Gloucestershire acquired another worthy cricketer in 1968. David Michael Green, born 10 November 1939 at Llanergan, Caernarvon, he spent his early life at Timperley, Cheshire. He became another schoolboy prodigy, playing for the Lancashire Second XI while still a pupil at Manchester Grammar School. He played rugby for Sale and Cheshire before going to Oxford University to read history. He won Cricket Blues in 1959, 1960 and 1961. In the vacations he played for Lancashire and having been taken on to the cricket staff in 1962, he won his cap. He first made over 2,000 runs in a season in 1965, won four 'Man of the Match' awards, only to become disenchanted with first-class cricket in 1966 when he directed his attentions to school-mastering. When he was not retained by Lancashire at the end of 1967 he moved to Bristol to enter industrial catering. Joining Gloucestershire he thanked Lancashire with 2,137 runs, 4 centuries and with 233 in an opening stand with Arthur Milton. David Green had the Charles Barnett approach to batting off the bowlers from the very first over. He was a teasing seam change bowler with a pithy off field repartee that shrewdly commented on the game, rugby or the world at large.

John Mortimore gave up the captaincy after 1967. It had been hoped that Gary Sobers would follow him but with his non-arrival it passed to Arthur Milton, the senior member of the side. The results remained disappointing; two games only were won; the County could recover only one place from the bottom of the Championship Table. Cricket's own Law of Diminishing Returns was applying itself to Gloucestershire.

1968 was much more than just another cricket season for Gloucestershire. There were also changes in the Club's

In the winter Mike Procter returned regularly to his native South Africa to play for Natal. He is seen here having won the Western Province single wicket championship in the Currie Cup 1968. With him on the right is runner-up Barry Richards.

administration. The Chairman, Jack Clarke, who had been so deeply involved with the affairs of the Club for most of the post-war years, thought fit to stand down. Michael Jarrett, a life-long Lydney and Gloucestershire cricket enthusiast, was appointed in his place. It was through his energetic efforts that Lydney took over from Stroud in 1963 as a venue for first-class cricket. During the next decade Gloucestershire tried successfully to satisfy the demands of the North of the County by playing limited-over games at Moreton-in-the-Marsh, Tewkesbury and even Swindon.

Richard McCrudden, the Club's Secretary, died towards the end of 1967. The responsibility of running the Club temporarily passed to Mr H. R. S. Bishop, until a new Secretary took up his appointment on 15 July 1968. Long ago he had been shown the supposed Jessop rocket mark high up on the Beaufort Terrace outside the Spa Ground at Gloucester, first played for the County in 1932, and in 1937 had taken part in a record Gloucestershire debacle at Dover when Kent scored 219 runs for 2 wickets in 71 minutes. Now he found he had returned to cricket at a most interesting stage of its development and that a new era had already begun for Gloucestershire.

Almost immediately I had earned myself another title. I found that one of my duties was to make announcements over the public address system at the County Ground. Nervously approaching the microphone for my first announcement, I switched on the apparatus and launched myself into an already carefully prepared statement. I had not yet appreciated that the set took a little time to warm up.

'They can't hear you!' shouted someone from the adjacent press box.

'Will somebody show me how this bloody machine works', plaintively came over the air.

'They heard that', came back from next door.

I looked out to find the spectators fully enjoying my comment. From that moment I gently puffed into the microphone to catch the echo before I started my announcement. Alan Gibson, cricket historian and writer of the nimble word, christened me Puff the Magic Dragon!

The Road to Nowhere Again   11
1969-1973

John Mortimore had taken over the captaincy in 1965, his benefit year. Now in 1969 Tony Brown took it over in his. Captaincy tests the man probably more than the cricketer. He had a shrewd idea of the responsibilities which he was inheriting

Geoffrey ('Noddy') Pullar.

Gloucestershire C.C.C. 1969. Back row left to right: D. M. Green, M. J. Procter, G. Pullar, J. Davey, B. J. Meyer, D. R. Shepherd. Front row: D. R. Smith, J. B. Mortimore, D. A. Allen, C. A. Milton, R. B. Nicholls.

and was younger than most of the seven other captains he had played under since 1953. For many years he had shared the new ball with David Smith. Batting in the middle order he had always threatened more runs than appeared in the score book. He relished the opportunity the captaincy presented and brought to it the much needed drive and confidence that had been missing for too many years.

Geoffrey ('Noddy' to those in the game) Pullar, born at Swinton in Lancashire on 1 August 1935 followed David Green to Gloucestershire in 1969. His first-class career began in 1954 and by 1959 he had established himself as a Test opening left hand batsman of phlegmatic temperament against any type of bowling, with an immaculate defence and punishing batting style that brought him 40 centuries and 28 Test appearances.

Ron Nicholls and David Green had established themselves as a successful partnership. Pullar batted at No. 3 or 4 and he played 41 innings for Gloucestershire with one century and 1,038 runs. The injury that was to plague his later career and impede his mobility in the field forced him to retire from the game in 1970.

It was in 1969 that the potential of the side exploded into successful action. After a slow start the method and the pattern were established until, by the end of July, the County was 51 points ahead of the nearest challenge. Glamorgan proved to be the bogey team. Previously they had won decisively at Cardiff, but the climax of the season's work was decided in the return game at Cheltenham. The Gloucestershire innings opened shakily and the game was lost before lunch on the first day. A psychological paralysis had gripped the leading batsmen but the sum of their collective experience should have carried them through. For too long they had been looking over their shoulders at Glamorgan on the charge behind them. Glamorgan's win by an innings and 50 runs carried them to the second Championship in their history. Gloucestershire, with ten wins, had to be satisfied as runners up.

1970 was Centenary Year no matter what some cricket historians may have decided. The target in financial terms was £100,000; £1,000 for every year of the Club's history or £1 from 100,000 of the County's 2,000,000 inhabitants; in cricket terms the Championship. In both respects the results were bitterly disappointing; £16,150 from the Centenary Appeal and by a rule bottom of the Championship. There were more excuses to be found on the cricket field. The proposed tour of the South Africans was cancelled and replaced by the World Test Series. Mike Procter's comings and goings to join the World XI completely disrupted any chance of establishing a confident momentum, but he would have been lost to the County if his country's tour had gone ahead.

'The lesson of 1970 is that Gloucestershire C.C.C. must be pulled away from the road to nowhere' so summarises the foreword to the 1971 Year Book. It continues: 'There is always a strength to be gathered from disaster. The controversy over the constitution, the management of the Club, the poor performances on the cricket field, put all of us under pressure. That is right. The time for antidotes is past, now for the stimulants.

Commemorative Cover June 2

GLOUCESTERSHIRE C.C.C.
1870 CENTENARY 1970

GLO'SHIRE C.C.C.
CENTENARY

JUNE 2 BRISTOL 1970

W. G. Grace

GLOUCESTERSHIRE COUNTY CRICKET CLUB
NEVIL ROAD,
BRISTOL. BS7 9EJ

Special commemorative cover issued to celebrate the centenary in 1970.

The time has come for new and younger faces to appear on the scene, a new direction given to our affairs. Some will have despaired, others will have maximised our shortcomings; all who love Gloucestershire cricket must keep faith and continue to give us their support.'

As ever finance was at the centre of the problem and, at its very core, the crippling burden of the County Ground. Even before the sale of the football area at the Ashley Down Road end in 1967 suggestions that the whole area should be turned into a sports complex or sold to the Bristol Corporation had been discussed more than once at Committee. The matter had been shelved only to reappear as the seasonal losses continued. By the end of 1971 the overdraft had risen to £30,000 and the bank was again sounding the alarms. Every avenue of escape from the closing tentacles had been explored from 1968 onwards. Discussions advanced to feasibility studies. A sports/ leisure centre, blocks of flats along the Kennington Avenue side of the ground, sale to one of at least three interested developers or directly to the Bristol Education Authority were pursued optimistically to flounder on the Planning Authority's refusal to allow the area to be used for other than recreational uses. The County's lack of funds denied them any extravagant adventure.

Gloucestershire's Road lay ahead. There were many ghosts from the past pressing the present occupants for some action. As ever in a crisis the Club took another look at its Constitution. The foreword of the 1971 Year Book again: 'The basic problem of the management of a County Cricket Club is that it is at once and the same time a democracy and a business. These can be poles apart, the one demands the widest possible representation and the other a small nucleus of executive decision and action.'

The Supporters' Club which continued to make vital contributions to the Club's welfare significantly appointed a full-time Secretary to widen its activities in the ever changing pattern of the 'games of chance' business, letting and staffing what facilities the buildings could offer.

Tony Brown became the Assistant Secretary directing his attention to public relations, setting up a target golf range for use during the winter months and to the widening of advertising in all its aspects. The Secretary was now referred to as the Secretary/Manager with overlapping responsibility for the cricket, the administration and the rapidly developing field of sponsorship at the County level. The Club's expanding business led to the appointment of Group Captain Brian L. Davis as Administrator in September 1973. The results were in no way dramatic but they did reflect an awareness of the potential of the business field, to be seen in a slowing down of the increase in the overdraft.

The winds of change which had blown through cricket brought the Cricket Council, as the governing body of cricket, under three headings – The Test and County Cricket Board, M.C.C. and The National Cricket Association which became responsible for all other cricket. There was no overall body for clubs, umpires, junior cricket and groundsmen in Gloucestershire in 1968. It became the duty of the County's administration to form one. This was not easy. The love/hate relationship between the North and South of the County, that was apparent before the birth of Gloucestershire C.C.C., had in no way lessened over the years. The Bristol and District Cricket Association, founded in 1892, had been the authority for most of the clubs in the Bristol area. There was no such body for the

North of the County. Matters evolved slowly and painstakingly until in 1971 a Gloucestershire Cricket Association was formed.

The County's involvement in these affairs brought its rewards. Besides a deeper and wider appreciation of the problem caused to clubs by the severe lessening of schoolboy cricket, it also illustrated clearly the necessity for the County's deepening involvement in youth cricket.

In the unlikely event of Orwell writing that all cricket coaches are unique and that some are more unique than others, then he would have had Graham Wiltshire in mind. He had joined the cricket staff in 1952, played occasionally from 1953–60 and was appointed coach in 1961 when another career opened up. His largely self-appointed responsibilities as far as the cricket was concerned were directed initially towards courses for youngsters around the County and then to Gloucestershire Young Cricketers. He was the Pied Piper leading them out onto the Road. Humorously articulate, boasting his Chipping Sodbury accent and dedicated to the cause, as the years progressed he developed a wonderfully perceptive appreciation of an individual cricketer's technical problems.

During the winter months he visited many schools throughout the County. The following is one of the numerous letters of appreciation he received:

Dear Mr Wiltshire,

Thank you very much for sparing your time to come and see us. We were very grateful for it.

We especially liked your sponge balls. I am going to ask my dad if he will make me a ball on a string. Some of us are going to play the games at lunch-time, in the playground, and some of the games we are going to play in P.E.

When we discussed afterwards, most of us liked the cricket game best, but we wish the girls could have had a go. We all think you are very good at cricket, and I expect everyone envies you because you are so clever with a bat and ball.

We would be very pleased to see you again.

Yours sincerely,

Class 1

A stream of Young Glosters passed through his hands. Julian Shackleton, who would have bowled like his famous father,

Derek, of Hampshire but was forced to retire through a back injury; Jim Foat, fleet of foot, and David Graveney, son of Ken and nephew of Tom, all three of Millfield; Andy Stovold of Alveston, Robert Lanchbury, Howard Cleaton, Philip Thorn, Malcolm Dunstan of Cornwall, all played for the senior team. There were to be many others.

There were two future international cricketers who spent a formative cricket period under his direction. Geoffrey Howarth came over from New Zealand in 1968 as a school boy cricketer to widen his experience. He returned to join Surrey in 1969 to play and later captained New Zealand. In 1970 Gloucestershire discovered a most promising young Barbados born West Indian boy named Roland Butcher, playing for the Stevenage Club in Hertfordshire. They secured a place for him on the Lord's Ground Staff, assisted him financially, only to find that at the end of his two years' apprenticeship he had signed a contract to play for Middlesex. He went on to become the first coloured player to play in a Test Match for England.

Andy Stovold.

There was one strong addition to the team in 1971. Roger David Vernon Knight, born at Streatham, London, on 6 September 1946 and educated at Dulwich College and Cambridge University, was registered specially for 1971. He had played cricket for the University from 1967–70 but could not gain a regular place in a strong Surrey XI. A tall, left hand, upper order batsman, a useful right arm third seam bowler and an excellent fielder, he was the complete cricketer. His contribution was immediate, 1,215 runs and 16 wickets, but the limited over games were to prove his speciality.

There was a much greater consistency in the batting which became apparent as the County reached the eighth position in the Championship. Gloucestershire entered into the Gillette Competition at the second round. A third time visit to Hove in four years proved lucky – by 123 runs. Surrey were then defeated by 15 runs in a tense quarter final at Bristol. Gloucestershire's total of 214 seemed quite inadequate with Surrey at 193 for 5, 24 runs behind with 14 overs still to go. Roger Knight returned for his second spell and finished off the Surrey innings with four wickets in ten balls. He had earned Gloucestershire a place in the semi-final and for himself the first of his many Gillette Man of the Match awards.

The semi-final against Lancashire was a cricket epic, played

out before an Old Trafford audience of twenty-five thousand. There was enough sustained action and drama to fill a Bible. Gloucestershire's 60 overs brought 229 runs for 7 wickets, thanks to Ron Nicholls (53) and Mike Procter (65). Tony Brown, Jack Davey and Mike Procter so contained the Lancashire innings that with the lights of Manchester long since switched on in the gathering gloom, the game still hung in the balance.

Tony Brown now had a critical decision on his hands. He wanted to bring Mike Procter and Jack Davey back for their final overs but he knew that if he did the umpires would take the players off the field and continue the game the next morning. This would have brought angry reaction from the expectant

Arriving in Zambia; the team plus guest players Don Shepherd and Roger Davis.

Lancashire spectators, already well over the boundaries into the field of play. He really had no alternative but to carry on with the slower bowlers. Then David Hughes in one devastating over, the fifty-sixth, took 24 runs off John Mortimore to settle the issue at 8.56 pm.

Lancashire went on to beat Kent in the Final at Lord's.

Gloucestershire made their first overseas tour in 1962 under Tom Pugh's captaincy. In 1971 a party of fourteen, which included Don Shepherd and Roger Davis of Glamorgan set off from Heathrow on 5 October. Early in May the Zambia Cricket Union had invited the County to make a tour at the end of the season. It was not until late August, when Surrey withdrew from their scheduled tour, that permission was granted by the East African Cricket Association. The tour was composed hurriedly. Zaheer, having flown overnight from Karachi, joined the party at Lusaka. An exciting and wonderfully rewarding tour followed. David Shepherd, to be known in future as 'The Rev.' when it was assumed locally that he was the other cricketer of

Gloucestershire C.C.C., plus guest players in Zambia. Back row left to right: J. C. Foat, J. P. Sullivan, J. H. Shackleton, J. Davey, D. Shepherd (Glamorgan), C. A. Milton, D. R. Shepherd. Seated: G. W. Parker (secretary/manager), A. S. Brown (capt.). Front row: G. G. M. Wiltshire (coach), R. B. Nicholls, Sadiq, R. Davis (Glamorgan).

that name, kept wicket in all of the three successful games against Zambia in Lusaka and Kitwe and the two drawn games against Copperbelt and Livingstone XIs.

The party was housed privately by expatriates in Lusaka, Kitwe and Livingstone, some of them from Bristol and the County. Unhappily Tony Brown developed a stomach disorder which landed him uncomfortably (more through convenience than misconception) in the maternity ward of the Livingstone Hospital. This brought a tiny fragment of Gloucestershire cricket history. Don Shepherd, with unanimous approval, captained the side for the remaining games, thereby becoming the first player from another County to captain the Gloucestershire team.

We must now retrace the course of events to record how Zaheer and Sadiq, who both toured Zambia, came to Gloucestershire.

There are three matriarchs of cricket. Two of them are Gloucestershire's while the third is Mrs Foster whose seven sons played for Worcestershire. Of Martha Grace's three, William Gilbert, Edward Mills and George Frederick played for England but of Ameerbee Mohammad's sons, Wazir, Hanif, Mushtaq and Sadiq played for Pakistan and the fifth, Raess, was once twelfth man. Mushtaq played for Northamptonshire in 1966 following the stipulated two-year qualification. Sadiq Mohammad was born at Junagadh, India, on 5 May 1945. The family moved into Pakistan at the time of the partition in 1947. He arrived in this country on 28 May 1967 and in July came to Bristol for a trial. At the time the County was in the process of qualifying Barry Richards and Mike Procter and were looking to contract Gary Sobers, under the new Immediate Registration of Overseas Cricketers rule. Sadiq could not find a county to register him. In 1970 he was playing as a professional for the Poloc Club in Glasgow, but Tony Brown played with him for D. H. Robbins XI against the R.A.F. at Eastbourne. He came to Bristol for another trial and played for the Second XI against Warwickshire at Leamington, but although the omens did not look good (he took more wickets than he made runs) he seemed to be every inch a cricketer. He was contracted and served his qualifying period. The rest is history; but there were two further twists to come. Further changes to the rules came in 1971. An overseas cricketer could now play for a county after five years' residence in this country, in Sadiq's case 28 May 1972. This allowed the County to play another at the completion of Sadiq's five years' residence; the County therefore pounced at the opportunity to contract Zaheer who would be eligible to play for Gloucestershire one year after the conclusion of the Pakistan tour, i.e. 16 July 1972, for by then each county would be allowed two overseas cricketers.

If Sadiq's apprenticeship had been prolonged as soon as he came to the County his progress was positively meteoric. He played for Pakistan in the three Tests of their 1971 tour in the opening position where it is always useful to employ a left handed batsman. Compact, watchful, with the technical ability, courage and application to see off any opening attack he patiently waited for the bounty of runs to be gathered in later. Twirling his bat around in his hands, waiting for the next ball, he cut drove and dabbed his way through many a century. He was an odds and ends leg spin bowler, with the occasional expensively bought wicket to his credit and a close catcher of the highest order.

Zaheer Abbas, born in Sialkat near Lahore, first came to Britain with the Pakistan tour of 1971. He made 110 in the opening game against Worcestershire, but it was his 274 in the first Test at Edgbaston (the highest score ever by Pakistan against England) that had the cricket statisticians sharpening their pencils. Some counties took a closer look at their bank balances.

He went to school and college in Karachi where he captained both at cricket before moving to the Pakistan International Airways organisation. He had already played for Pakistan in one Test against New Zealand in 1969, toured Ireland with the P.I.A. XI and was scheduled to come to England with the Pakistan Eaglets, a tour that was cancelled because of the South African problem.

A gentle, modest, assured, shrewdly perceptive and self-contained person for whom the words 'grace' and 'graceful' fall easily into place. Bespectacled, of upright stance and higher than average back lift, his lithe, slight build is equipped with a steel-sprung frame. When in full flow, Z bats as if in a mesmeric trance, detached from the world around him. For ordinary batsmen the bat goes searching for the ball. For him it seems to find its own way onto the exact spot on his bat as if under some

Sadiq Mohammad.

hypnotic influence. He plays a great variety of shots off his back foot to all angles of the field, but such are his sharp reflexes that a bowler can never be certain that anything over or under pitched is not sent like a rocket high into the distance. There is that precision of his shots snapped through the unattended areas that makes fielders seem quite unnecessary, which is the hallmark of only the greatest batsmen. Where Wally Hammond or W.G. physically destroyed bowlers Z clinically takes them apart.

Gloucestershire immediately set off in pursuit following his 274 at Edgbaston, caught up with him during the following rain affected game at Bradford and finalised the details at the next match at Oxford for his registration to take effect late in July 1972. He was a Wally Hammond class slip fielder but with a strong right arm from the boundary and was honoured as one of Wisden's five cricketers of 1971. He returned home to Pakistan following their tour to join the Gloucestershire Zambia Tour Party.

So in 1972 Gloucestershire found that a South African and two Pakistanis had joined them on their Road. But others had left them. David Smith finally succumbed to his persistent knee

Gloucestershire C.C.C. 1972. Back row left to right: Zaheer, D. R. Shepherd, D. A. Allen, J. H. Shackleton, R. D. V. Knight, A. G. Avery (scorer), J. Davey, B. J. Meyer, G. G. M. Wiltshire (coach), M. Bissex. Front row: J. C. Foat, Sadiq, J. B. Mortimore, A. S. Brown (capt.), G. W. Parker (secretary/ manager), M. J. Procter, C. A. Milton, R. B. Nicholls, R. Swetman.

injuries in 1970. He had played in five Tests and 357 games for the County, bowled 11,360 overs for 1,159 wickets and made 280 catches; he had proved himself as one of the most effective strike bowlers in the Club's history. Then in 1972 David Allen played his last game. Since 1953 he played 349 games for Gloucestershire and 39 Tests for England. Those long fingers and that economical action brought him 882 wickets for the County. He took a wicket with every 10 overs he bowled compared with Tom Goddard's 8, John Mortimore's 9 and Charlie Parker's 7. Like Mortimore he had mastered the difficulties of bowling on shirt front wickets; on worn wickets he could be unplayable and he too developed into a thoroughly dependable middle order batsman with a temperament that thrived on adversity.

Great cricketers are lauded most when they have retired, wicket keepers doubly so. So often their worth is not recognised until someone else takes up the unenviable position at the focal point of the game. Barrie Meyer retired at the end of 1971 to turn to umpiring and later became a Test umpire. He took his place in the line of great Gloucestershire wicket keepers with J. A. Bush, Jack Board, Harry Smith and Andy Wilson. To satisfy the curious and to help them to decide which is the greatest of these, here are the relevant statistics:

	Games	Innings	Caught	Stumped	Runs	Centuries	Tests
J. A. Bush 1870–1890	137	208	190	82	1,195	—	—
Jack Board 1891–1914	430	755	699	317	13,092	8	6
Harry Smith 1912–1935	393	645	442	263	13,330	10	1
Andy Wilson 1936–1955	318	486	419	168	10,534	7	—
Barrie Meyer 1957–1971	406	569	707	119	5,368	—	—

It became necessary to find a replacement for him. At first the responsibility fell to Stuart Westley. Lancashire born, special registration thus becoming essential, he had kept wicket for Oxford U.C.C. in 1968 and 1969. But it was not to be. Roy Swetman had finished his career with Surrey and Notts and it was not difficult to persuade him to return to the game. He made his Gloucestershire debut in 1972. Diminutive, highly competitive, he fitted admirably into the scene. Experience gained with Surrey and twelve Tests proved invaluable. There was a Young Gloster in the wings ready to step on to

*Andy Stovold – a
batsman who has done
much for his county
over the years.*

the stage. Andrew Willis Stovold of Alveston played his first
game during the 1973 Cheltenham Festival when Roy Swetman
was absent through injury. With the advent of the limited over
games the selection of the wicket keeper became more heavily
weighted in favour of those who could bat. Andy Stovold had
proved himself to be as much a wicket keeper/batsman as a
batsman who could keep wicket. He took over the duties in the
Gillette Cup semi-final against Worcestershire at Worcester
and carried on into the successful final against Sussex at Lord's.

With the approaching demise of Gloucestershire cricket at
Stroud's Erinoid ground, Lydney, on the other side of the
Severn, came into the first-class cricket scene in 1963. Lydney's
cause had been represented strongly and persistently by
Michael Jarrett and his active West of Severn Regional Committee. Their reward came with the game against Surrey on 24, 26
and 27 August 1963. Unhappily that game and the following two
in 1964 and 1965 against Derbyshire and Yorkshire were also
disrupted severely by rain, as was the first experiment of playing
on a Sunday, against Cambridge U.C.C. in 1966. The first
result did not come until 1967 when Lancashire beat the County

by an innings and 60 runs. The Sunday experiment continued in drawn Championship games with Glamorgan in 1967 and 1968, but it was the two games against Sussex over the weekend of 29 June 1969 that really closed the short chapter of cricket at Lydney. Unfortunately these proved to be the most successful played there. Gloucestershire looked set for the Championship title at the time. The weather belonged to the Mediterranean not to the Forest of Dean. The gates were closed just after the start of the new John Player League on Sunday, with local traffic at a standstill and the County taking its first £1,000+ gate; a spectacular black cloud rose from a nearby fire in the closing stages of a wonderfully exciting game, won by the County in the last over. The great work of the Lydney C.C. and the regional committee had been rewarded, but they were too soon to be bitterly disappointed. The following day David Allen proved unplayable claiming 8 wickets for 34 runs in a Sussex second innings of 88. Gloucestershire had won by an innings and 39 runs. The pitch was already under suspicion, but now it was reported and classed as unfit for Championship cricket. This was the last of the Championship games to be played there. John Player League games continued until 1973.

As Tony Cordle of Glamorgan bowled the first ball to Sadiq in the Gillette Cup game at Sophia Gardens, Cardiff, at 11 am on Saturday, 30 June 1973, there was nothing to suggest that 5 games, 2,141 minutes, 3,151 balls, 90 wickets and 2,124 runs later, Gloucestershire would be celebrating their first major success since 1877.

After Zaheer (43) had parted company with Roger Knight at 166 (44 overs) the Gloucestershire batsmen came and went with uncomfortable regularity. He and David Graveney had given the County no more than a workmanlike 230 for 9 at the end of 60 overs. The opening overs by Tony Brown and Jack Davey showed the Glamorgan batsmen that runs would have to be fought for throughout the innings. The normally aggressive Majid took 25 minutes over three runs before falling to a brilliant leg side catch by David Graveney. Later Tony Lewis and Alan Jones battled on, but even at its most prolific the Glamorgan innings never matched the Gloucestershire run rate. The innings ended at 196 (57.1 overs). The first fence had been cleared thanks to some masterful batting, bowling, fielding and captaincy.

The second round game against Surrey at the County Ground was a nerve-tingling battle of attrition, despair and elation from first ball to last. John Edrich won the toss and sent Gloucestershire in to bat. By the eleventh over they had scored 24 for 5 wickets. Geoff Arnold, using his abundant skill and experience to the full, had driven the County's front line batsmen from one disaster to another. David Shepherd was already firmly holding out when Tony Brown arrived at the wicket following Mike Procter's stunning dismissal for a duck, to be greeted:

'We're in a bit of a mess, captain. What's the form?'

'You're to stay here for 60 overs, Shep', came the clipped nervous reply.

Never were a captain's orders more faithfully and courageously carried out. Unexpectedly John Edrich took Geoff Arnold off at 4 wickets for 17 in 8 overs before he had completed Gloucestershire's destruction. It was left to David Shepherd to see the innings through to a modest 169 for 7 in the 60 overs.

The wicket had dried out and the total was well within Surrey's batting potential. They approached the matter with safety in mind and never acquired a dominant momentum. Crisis point was reached with Roope and Younis in partnership establishing some authority when John Mortimore from the distant leg boundary threw out the latter. Sensible caution and a few strong arm blows kept Surrey in the chase. In the fifty-third over, with Surrey wanting 35 runs with 4 wickets in hand, Tony Brown brought back Mike Procter for his final fling. Jackman was run out with 22 yards to spare and then he removed two of the last batsmen with Surrey still 19 runs short of the Gloucestershire total.

History had repeated itself. The whole match resembled the 1971 quarter-final tie. Again Gloucestershire had not made enough runs and Surrey had arrived at the position of requiring 24 runs with 5 wickets and 14 overs to spare, but still lost by 15 runs.

In the quarter-final against Essex at Chelmsford, for the third time in three successive Gillette Cup games Gloucestershire were put in to bat. Brian 'Tonker' Taylor, the Essex captain, won the toss and with typical dry humour announced to Tony Brown, 'We will bat – after you!', acknowledging realistically that he would prefer to begin the day with Mike Procter and Jack Davey watching proceedings from the dressing-room than

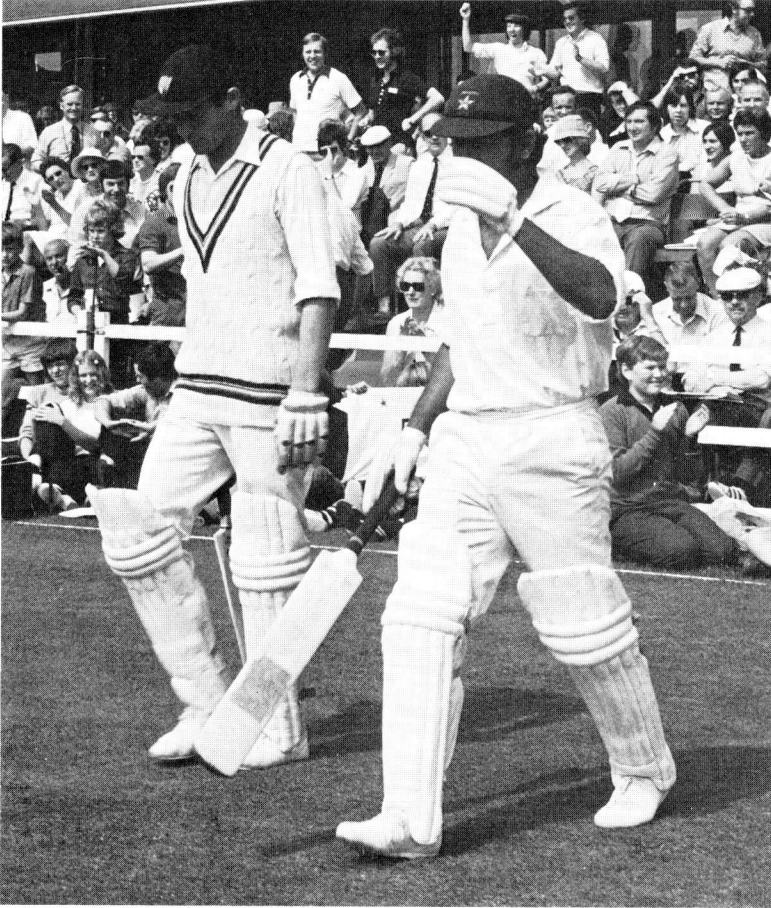

Ron Nicholls and Sadiq Mohammad opening the innings against Essex in the 1973 quarter-final of the Gillette Cup.

tormenting his batsmen on an early morning seaside pitch. He was justified to the extent that Ron Nicholls soon joined them, but Sadiq (56) and Knight (60) confidently applied bat to ball. Zaheer (45) and Procter (22) continued; no other Gloucestershire player reached double figures.

Essex in reply were coasting along at 104 for 2 wickets in 27 overs, but by the fortieth had slumped to 130 for 7. In the next fifteen Ray East and Stuart Turner had restored the Essex ascendancy to 205 for 7. Jack Davey and Tony Brown removed both of them in one final burst to bring to an end a hard fought day's cricket with Gloucestershire the winners by 30 runs. Mike Procter had not taken a wicket.

The Duke of Wellington's verdict after Waterloo that it had been 'a damned nice thing – the nearest run thing you ever saw

Some of the Gloucestershire supporters at Worcester, 1973.

in your life,' aptly fits the semi-final against Worcester at Worcester. Tony Brown won the toss for the first time in the competition and wisely decided to bat. The Gloucestershire alarms sounded at once. At 29 for 2 wickets (9 overs) Mike Procter arrived at the wicket to be dropped in the slips first ball. He survived another chance before he reached double figures. As the day progressed he began to bat at his majestic best, striking the ball to all corners of the field with the lazy, powerful elegance that had made him one of the most exciting batsmen in cricket. The others played their supporting roles and the momentum was maintained. When he left with 101 and the score at 226 for 7 (57 overs) the Young Gloster, Andy Stovold, who had taken over from the injured Roy Swetman, experienced for the first time the exhilarating atmosphere of a limited overs pressure cooker.

243 for 8 wickets was too few for comfort on a perfect Worcester batting wicket. The first wicket did not fall until 123 (40 overs). Tony Brown had used his varied attack cleverly to keep some control over the run rate. Slowly the score mounted until

he disposed of Imran Khan, 188 for 3 (52 overs). This exposed Glenn Turner, once again the mainstay of a Worcestershire innings. Mike Procter returned for his final three overs. He removed Turner (109) in the first over and another two in each of his last two overs. Rodney Cass and John Inchmore ran for everything. Some ragged Gloucestershire fielding heightened the tension. Twelve runs were still required from the last over, to be bowled by Jack Davey. With five runs and two balls to go Cass drove the ball hard at him. Jack Davey, never renowned for his fielding, stopped it, cleanly whipped round and ran out John Inchmore backing up. Now the game could only be won by a six. Everything depended on the last ball of the day. It was 7.39 pm. Tony Brown spread his fielders around the boundary. Jack Davey's main concern was not to bowl a no ball. He bowled well short of the crease, Ormrod hooked it behind the umpire. It landed well short of Ron Nicholls on the square leg boundary, who gathered it from beneath the feet of an advancing horde of ecstatic Gloucestershire supporters.

Gloucestershire had won their Waterloo but unlike the Iron Duke there was one more battle to be fought and won on Saturday, 1 September 1973.

Wishful thinking had now become reality. The special trains, the coaches and the cars collected up the faithful from all corners of the county and set off for the final at Lord's before the rest of the world had put the cat out. The players arrived in London late on the Friday, following three gruelling days at Old Trafford but in time to analyse meticulously the opposition and the likely course of events. The following morning Chairman Frank Twiselton pinned a W.G. linen square above Tony Brown's place in the dressing room. That made sense, for the Old Man had also been captain when Gloucestershire had last won something. The team arrived with a quiet confidence to the sharpened atmosphere of the final. They had already weathered every kind of storm they were likely to encounter here.

Tony Brown won the toss and had no hesitation in deciding to bat. The score had reached crisis point at 22 for 3 wickets in 10 overs when Mike Procter strode in, head up to take on the world. He saw off John Snow's opening spell then heaved a couple of sixes over the long on boundary. He and David Shepherd brought the urgent stability Gloucestershire required. When the latter left at 74 for 4 in 23 overs Andy Stovold met his ordeal with a mature confidence. Just before and after lunch Tony Greig brought back John Snow to land Mike Procter but he netted Andy Stovold instead. Tony Brown played himself in. Gradually he and Mike Procter thrust back the fielders to guard the boundaries, to pick up the twos and threes in the resulting vacuum. The flood gates were really opening when Procter swinging for another six that would have brought him a century, was caught at deep fine leg for 94, from the first ball of the fifty-second over and the score 180 for 6 wickets. It had been a superb 'Hammondesque' innings of precision, power and elegance.

The remainder of the Gloucestershire innings belonged to Tony Brown supported mainly by Jim Foat who, with some electrifying running to give him the strike, brought 49 more runs in the next 7 overs. Jim Foat returned to the Pavilion, with only seven of these runs to his credit, acclaimed by the knowledgeable Lord's crowd. With David Graveney now carrying on where he had left off, Tony Brown showed a healthy disrespect for Greig's bowling by hitting two towering sixes into the laps of Gloucestershire supporters over the long leg boundary before the innings closed at 248 for 8 wickets. He had scored 46 of the 68 runs from the last 8 overs. He had given more pleasure and excitement in that one innings of 77 not out than most cricketers give in a lifetime.

If the Gloucestershire innings was reminiscent of the Surrey game then the Sussex opening stands were all Worcestershire – slow but safe – 51 for 1 wicket (22 overs), 121 for 2 wickets (39 overs). John Mortimore came on early to bowl 12 immaculate overs before and after tea while Tony Brown interspersed Davey and Procter to keep the run rate in check. At 155 for 3 wickets (44 overs) the Sussex innings suddenly burst into flames. Tony Greig entered to face Procter. A short mid-wicket conference with Graves, the other batsman, indicated that he would much prefer to be at the other end. The covers were alerted. The second ball thumped Greig on the pads. He set off. Graves sent him back but Jim Foat had flashed in, picked up the ball and broken his wicket before he had recovered his crease. 156 for 4 wickets (45 overs).

Later left handed Michael Buss was taking advantage of some wayward bowling from Roger Knight when Tony Brown imposed a re-adjustment of his field posting David Graveney at

Opposite; Score sheets of Final.

Gloucestershire C.C.C. won toss — Final. — Gillette Cup (60 overs)

Gloucestershire C.C.C. CRICKET CLUB V Sussex C.C.C. — C. CLUB

INNINGS OF Gloucestershire C.C.C. PLAYED AT Lords ON 1st Sept 1973

BATSMEN	HOW OUT	BOWLER	TOTAL
1 Sadiq	l-b-w	Buss	9
2 Knight R.D.V.	bowled	Snow	2
3 Zaheer	bowled	Buss	9
4 Procter M.J.	ct Morley	Buss	94
5 Shepherd D.R.	ct Griffith	Marshall	11
6 Arnold R.W.	ct Griffith	Snow	10
7 Brown A.S.	not out		77
8 Foat J.C.	bowled	Snow	7
9 Graveney D.A.	Run out		6
10 Mortimore J.B.			
11 Davey J.			
			225

BYES 4 — LEG BYES 4 — EXTRAS 23 — TOTAL 248 FOR 9 WKTS

RUNS AT THE FALL OF EACH WICKET: 5 22 27 74 106 180 220 248
2 3 1 5 6 4 8 9

BOWLERS	OVERS	M'DNS	RUNS	WKTS
Snow J.A.	12	4	31	3
Greig A.W.	12	1	53	–
Buss M.A.	12	5	46	3
Marshall R.P.T.	12	3	29	1
Spencer J.	12	–	66	–
Extras			23	
Run outs				1
	60	13	248	9

UMPIRES 1 A.E. Fagg 2 T.W. Spencer SCORERS 1 R.G. Avery 2 W.S. Denman

---

Gloucestershire C.C.C. won by 40 runs — Match award A.S. Brown presented by R. Bedser

Gloucestershire C.C.C. CRICKET CLUB V Sussex C.C.C. — C. CLUB

INNINGS OF Sussex PLAYED AT Lords ON 1st Sept 1973

BATSMEN	HOW OUT	BOWLER	TOTAL
1 Greenidge G.A.	bowled	Knight	76
2 Morley J.D.	ct Zaheer	Brown	31
3 Prideaux R.M.	bowled	Davey	28
4 Graves P.J.	not out		36
5 Greig A.W.	Run out		0
6 Buss M.A.	ct Graveney	Knight	5
7 Griffith M.G.	bowled	Knight	3
8 Faber M.J.J.	Run out		9
9 Snow J.A.	bowled	Procter	4
10 Spencer J.	bowled	Knight	2
11 Marshall R.P.T.	bowled	Procter	0
			194

BYES 4 — LEG BYES 5 — WIDES — EXTRAS 14 — TOTAL 208 FOR 10 WKTS

RUNS AT THE FALL OF EACH WICKET: 52 121 155 156 173 180 195 204 207 208
2 3 1 5 6 7 8 9 10 11

BOWLERS	OVERS	M'DNS	RUNS	WKTS
Procter M.J.	10.5	1	27	2
Davey J.	10	1	37	1
Mortimore J.B.	12	3	32	–
Brown A.S.	12	1	53	1
Graveney D.A.	2	–	18	–
Knight R.D.V.	10	–	47	4
Extras			14	
Run outs				2
	56.5	6	208	10

UMPIRES 1 T.W. Spencer 2 A.E. Fagg SCORERS 1 R.G. Avery 2 W.S. Denman

Tony Brown receiving the Gillette Cup.

Tony Brown receiving the Gillette Cup.

boundary deep point. Buss hit the very next ball with mathematical accuracy into his hands; 173 for 5 (48 overs). The Sussex run rate was still in front of Gloucestershire's at the same stage, but they had no Tony Brown to take over. Suddenly the structure, so carefully built up by the earlier batsmen, disintegrated in a flurry of flying timber. The remaining wickets had fallen by eight minutes to seven in the gathering gloom. Sussex had made 208 runs and Gloucestershire had won by 40.

Tony Brown collected the Gillette Cup and his own 'Man of the Match' Award. W.G. looked down on the celebrations that followed. How mightily he would have enjoyed them.

Slowly the turbulent tide flowed out of the Lord's dressing room leaving its flotsam and jetsam behind until only Tony Brown and Mike Procter remained. They had not changed, and exhausted talked over an amazing day. You can be certain their own immense contribution that had made it so successful was never mentioned. It was 10 pm before Tony Brown took down W.G.'s square pinned above his locker and they left to continue the celebrations.

Two victory parades by the players and some officials passed round the County during the week. First it was around the

Bristol area which included a visit to the great Concorde hangar at Filton, and out into the county through Downend, Chipping Sodbury, then Wotton-under-Edge, Dursley, Cheltenham, Gloucester, Painswick and Stroud. Local dignitaries cordially welcomed and toasted the team. With commendable confidence and foresight the Gloucester City Corporation had set in motion their arrangements before the Final at Lord's.

There was another Gloucestershire cricket occasion to celebrate in 1973. The Gloucester Diocesan Clergy Cricket Club won the *Church Times* Cricket Cup!

As part of their victory celebrations the team visited the B.A.C. factory at Filton.

215

12

Gloucestershire Rises Phoenix-Like from the Ashes
1974-1980

In most respects Gloucestershire and Somerset are similar West Country counties of small towns, villages and rural communities. The Bristol conurbation is the exception with its orientation to Gloucestershire rather than to Somerset. The Local Government Act of 1972, which became operative on 1 April 1974, introduced the County of Avon into the local geography. This did not affect the historical County cricket boundary between the two first-class counties, which had always been the River Avon, but it did bring a latently alarming division between the North and South of Gloucestershire – the one was to be Gloucestershire and the other Avon.

During the early 1970s there was a much bigger problem than the adjustment of local administrative boundaries: survival. As it had been for much of the County's existence the problem was financial. The relief brought by the sale of the area at the Ashley Down Road end of the ground in 1967 lasted for only a few months. The losses on each year's working continued. The options were becoming fewer.

'As sure as God is in Gloucester' runs the ancient proverb. 1974 was the critical year. A way had once opened up across the Red Sea for the Israelites and it seemed that nothing short of a similar intervention was going to save Gloucestershire cricket. In 1914 the County had been on the road to nowhere, now in 1974 there was no Road at all, just a seemingly trackless empty horizon. Every one of the possible avenues of escape had been explored exhaustively. The Club was insolvent. A crucial point of decision was at hand. Crisis management meetings were held in September and October. Then one afternoon in the first week of December 1974, Charles W. Chown, Secretary of Phoenix Assurance Sports and Social Club, walked into the County Office. He had heard it reported that Gloucestershire had just experienced a disastrous cricket season, had made a loss of £26,158 on the year's working and were thinking of selling their ground. Phoenix Assurance were in the process of moving a major portion of their administration into Redcliffe, Bristol, and were looking for a Sports/Social Centre to accommodate their eventual staff of a thousand. Charles Chown had already visited two sites which had not materialised and now at the third attempt he had come to the County Ground. He found a welcoming reception party awaiting him on his return.

The first mention of any forward progress is to be found in the Minutes of the Annual General Meeting held on 15 March 1975. The Chairman, Frank Twiselton, reported that 'a possible solution to the financial problems was being negotiated with a commercial organisation who require sports facilities in the (Bristol) area and might be prepared to finance the setting up of a complete sports complex and leisure centre which the Club would be able to share and reap a percentage of the profit from their use.' A Special General Meeting was called for 19 September 1975 'to consider the proposed agreement with Phoenix Assurance'. Almost two hundred members attended this Meeting which was held at the County Ground and the details were approved by an overwhelming majority. Chairman, Frank Twiselton, Vice Chairman, Ken Graveney, Treasurer, Dickie Rossiter and guided throughout by the Club's President, R. F. P. Holloway, conducted the protracted negotiations with Phoenix. The Joint Venture Agreement was signed on 15 March 1976. This brought into being the Gloucester and Phoenix Assurance Amenity Company (Bristol) Ltd. Planning permission for the development of the ground had also been obtained. Phoenix paid £125,000 for the ground and the Amenity Company was granted a 99 year lease at a peppercorn rent. Gloucestershire surrendered their freehold, paid off £55,330's worth of debts immediately, entered into a 50/50 shareer partnership with Phoenix, retained complete use of the playing area for all their fixtures and with £10,000 of assistance moved their Social Club over to the refurbished Jessop Tavern to allow the Phoenix Social and Sports Club to occupy their old premises. The County Ground was renamed the Phoenix County Ground.

These were the conditions under which Gloucestershire cricket retained its heritage. The skies had cleared and the mirages of financial problems, magic solutions and wishful thinking had disappeared. There was the Gloucestershire Road again clearly visible and yet to be travelled.

From the very beginning the Phoenix/Gloucestershire C.C.C. relationship has been most cordial and eminently suc-

Top: *The Grace Suite.*
Bottom: *The Jessop Tavern.*

cessful. The Amenity Company is composed of three Phoenix and three cricket club members of Committee under the Chairmanship of John Norman, Administrative General Manager of the Phoenix Assurance Group, and directs the day to day working of the ground. Every square inch of the pavilion and the adjoining area has been developed to make way for six squash courts and ancillary facilities. The Ladies' Stand and the remains of the cycle track have been demolished and the space used for car parking; the cricket school was not forgotten and a new score board was erected. Many a wit watching the remark-

The Hammond Room.

able transformation remarked that 'Gloucestershire rose Phoenix-like from the ashes'. A superbly equipped Grace Suite became the centre piece of the pavilion and would have given the Old Man so much pleasure. He had been largely responsible for the original layout in 1888. So now Gloucestershire's three greatest cricketers were remembered at the ground – The Grace Suite, the Hammond Room and the Jessop Tavern. Who's next? Parker's Piece – C.W.L.P. of course!

It seems appropriate to summarise the financial details over the period 1973-79. They reflect the position leading up to the sale of the ground to Phoenix, and subsequent recovery, and also the daunting increase in the annual budget facing a County Cricket Club. The exciting advance in the Club's income derived from the great success of the wide-ranging Glosda (Gloucestershire Development Association) Promotions, since 1976 in the enthusiastic hands of Roger Northam, together with the expansion of the sponsorship and advertising programme.

Year	Income	Expenditure	Profit or Loss (+ or −)
1973	£83,083	£78,961	+£4,122
1974	£66,926	£93,084	−£26,158
1975	£96,420	£95,575	+£845
1976	£102,824	£123,078	−£20,254
1977	£173,895	£155,085	+£18,810
1978	£201,701	£190,667	+£11,034
1979	£230,586	£232,191	−£1,605

Unforgiving time saw some great names drop out of the Gloucestershire scene in 1974. Arthur Milton's career stuttered to finality. He was recalled to play a few games after his initial retirement in 1970 when, for the first time in twenty years, he scored less than 1,000 runs. His was a massive contribution. He had batted more times for the County than any other cricketer and only Wally Hammond and Alf Dipper had scored more centuries: 585 matches, 1,017 innings, 30,218 runs, 52 centuries, 718 catches and 79 wickets. John Mortimore's was just as remarkable. Only Charlie Parker had played in more games for Gloucestershire: 594 matches, 928 innings, 14,918 runs, 4 centuries and 1,696 wickets. He had achieved the cricketer's double in 1959, 1963 and 1964. With commendable strength of character and purpose John had taken correspondence courses in accountancy in the cricket season to supplement his work in the off season and was now approaching his Articles. He played out the 1975 season. The last of the great Gloucestershire off spinners had left the Road. Ron Nicholls too could claim some formidable batting statistics and with characteristic modesty he captained the Second Eleven and devoted his attention to local and youth cricket in Cheltenham.

In 1975 Roger Knight departed for Sussex. He had continued to teach Modern Languages at Eastbourne College during the winter months. Besides his eleven centuries and one hundred wickets for Gloucestershire, perhaps his greatest achievement had been in collecting three Gillette and two Benson and Hedges 'Man of the Match' Awards. He left Sussex in 1977 to return to Dulwich College, his old school, to captain Surrey and collect four more Gold Awards. Fellow ex-Surrey cricketer, Roy Swetman, handed on the wicket keeping gloves to Andy Stovold.

Gloucestershire finished third in the Championship Table in

1976. When Tony Brown led his winning team from the field at Worcester, little did he realise that he had played his last game for his County. In the chain reaction shuffle of responsibilities that was taking place he took over the duties of Secretary/Manager. I then took over the sponsorship and advertising, bequeathing to him the cricket administrator's lament:

'And when the Great Administrator comes to write against your name,
He'll not ask if you have won or lost, but how you took the blame.'

He had played in most of the games of 1976, but his bowling capacity had been restricted increasingly by a recurring shoulder injury. He had succeeded a flurry of captains and strengthened the team's confidence into a force that was to reach its full potential in 1977. He and David Smith had formed a

Zaheer Abbas.

highly competent strike-bowling partnership that was an eloquent illustration of a shrewd David Green comment, 'opening bowlers don't have to bowl at 2,000 m.p.h., 200 m.p.h. will do if they have the necessary control and technical skill.' Tony Brown's cricket statistics honour all three dimensions of his game. He is one of only four Gloucestershire cricketers who have made more than 10,000 (12,684) runs and taken more than 1,000 (1,223) wickets for the County, and in addition he held 485 catches.

By 1976 Z had established himself as one of the world's leading batsmen. That remarkable batting machine was now performing like a well programmed robot. In a sense his nine centuries and two double centuries took second place to his incredible performances against Kent at Canterbury and Surrey at the Oval. Only once before in the history of the game had a batsman made a double century and a century in the same match. Now in 1976 he made 230 not out and 104 not out at Canterbury and 216 not out and 156 not out at the Oval. Almost as if to prove a point it was to be 205 not out and 108 not out against Sussex at Cheltenham in 1977. One is wonderful, two is terrific, three is impossible! Not even a W.G. could manage one!

David Runyon would have labelled the 1977 season as 'more

Charts showing how Zaheer scored his remarkable double century and century in the match against Surrey.

Zaheer Abbas.

First Gloucestershire Batsman to score Double Century & Century in same match for the County.

Gloucestershire C.C.C. versus Surrey C.C.C

at the Oval on 12th, 14th & 15th June 1976. Gloucestershire C.C.C. won toss.

Gloucestershire 390-7 (100 overs) Zaheer 216* & 264-2 declared Zaheer 156*
Surrey.   185 all out & 325-8   Match Drawn.

Details of Record

1st Innings				2nd Innings			
1st 50 runs.	92 mins	73 balls	9×4	1st 50 runs	65 mins	52 Balls	6×4 & 1×5
2nd 50 runs.	57 mins	58 balls.	8×4	2nd 50 runs	68 mins	61 Balls	4×4
3rd 50 runs.	75 mins	56 balls.	6×4	3rd 50 runs	46 mins.		4×4 & 1×6
4th 50 runs.	51 mins	38 balls.	5×4 & 1×6	6 runs	7 mins.		
16 runs.	24 mins.	31 balls.	2×4				
216 runs	329 mins	295 balls	30×4 & 1×6	156 runs	186 mins		14×4. 1×5 & 1×6.

Charts and details compiled during match

by H.G. Avery

Gloucestershire C.C.C. Scorer.

222

Zaheer Abbas.   60 not out at Lunch.

Intikhab Alam

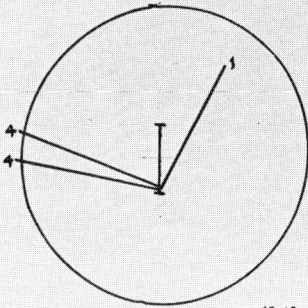

R.D. Jackman.

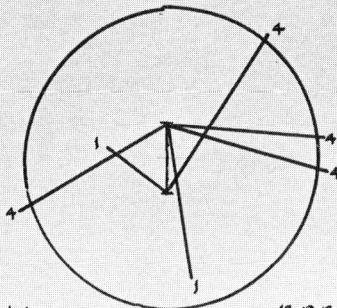

G.R.J. Roope.

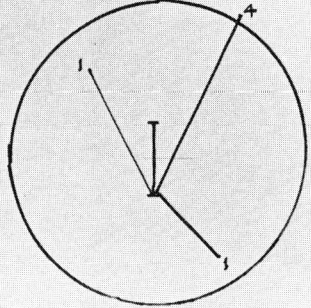

A.R. Butcher.

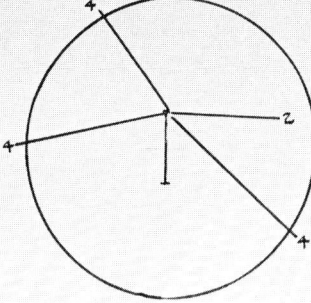

R.P. Baker.

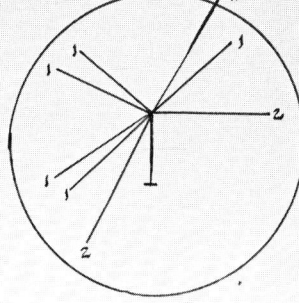

Intikhab Alam

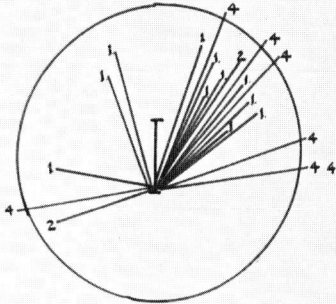

R.D. Jackman.

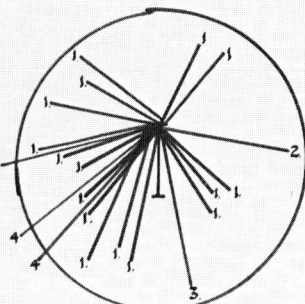

R.P. Baker.

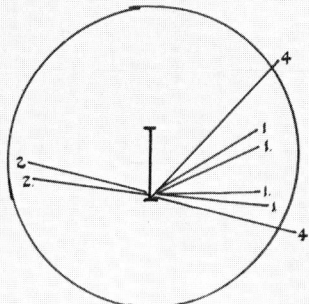

Zaheer Abbas.   148 not out at Tea

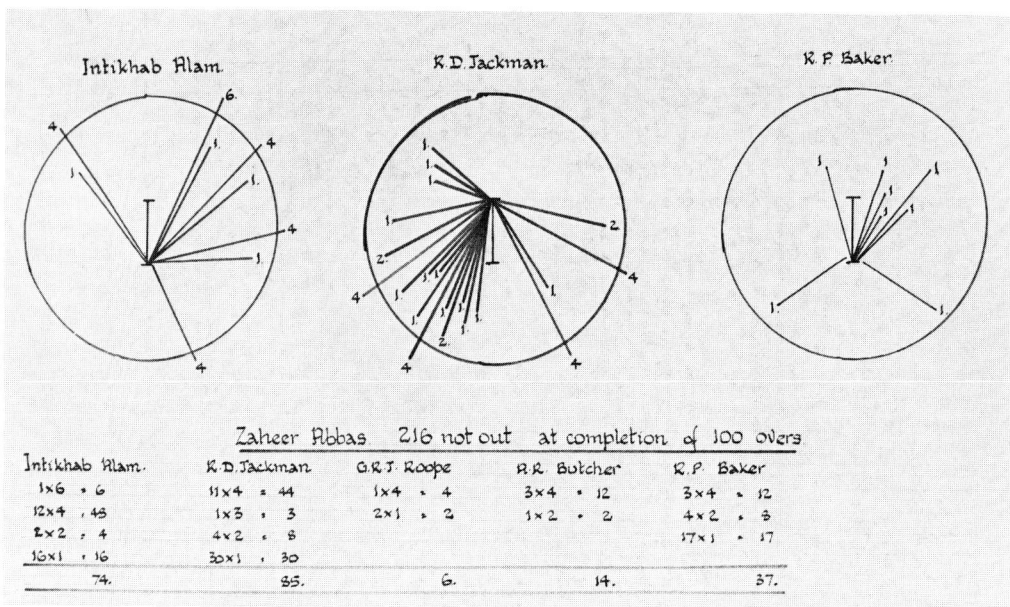

Intikhab Alam. R.D. Jackman. R.P. Baker.

Zaheer Abbas 216 not out at completion of 100 overs

Intikhab Alam.	R.D. Jackman.	G.R.J. Roope	R.R. Butcher	R.P. Baker
1x6 = 6	11x4 = 44	1x4 = 4	3x4 = 12	3x4 = 12
12x4 = 48	1x3 = 3	2x1 = 2	1x2 = 2	4x2 = 8
2x2 = 4	4x2 = 8			17x1 = 17
16x1 = 16	30x1 = 30			
74.	85.	6.	14.	37.

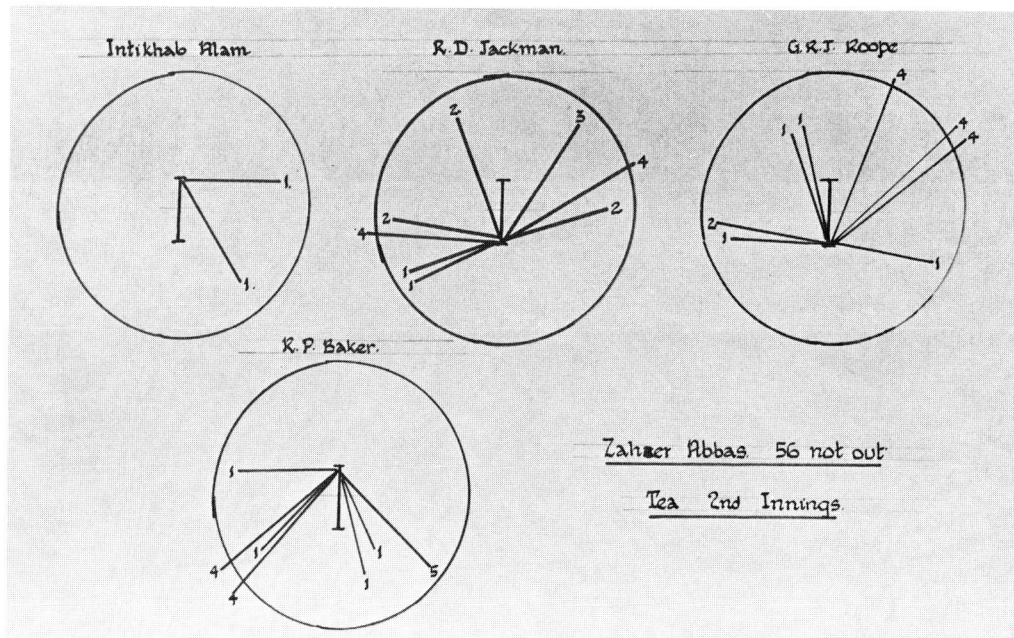

Intikhab Alam. R.D. Jackman. G.R.J. Roope.

R.P. Baker.

Zaheer Abbas 56 not out

Tea 2nd Innings.

than somewhat'. Mike Procter took over the captaincy, but the season will be best remembered for two outstanding details, the winning of the Benson and Hedges Cup and for the mounting excitement of the Championship challenge that was to be de-

Zaheer Abbas 156 not out at Close 2nd Day. 2nd Innings.

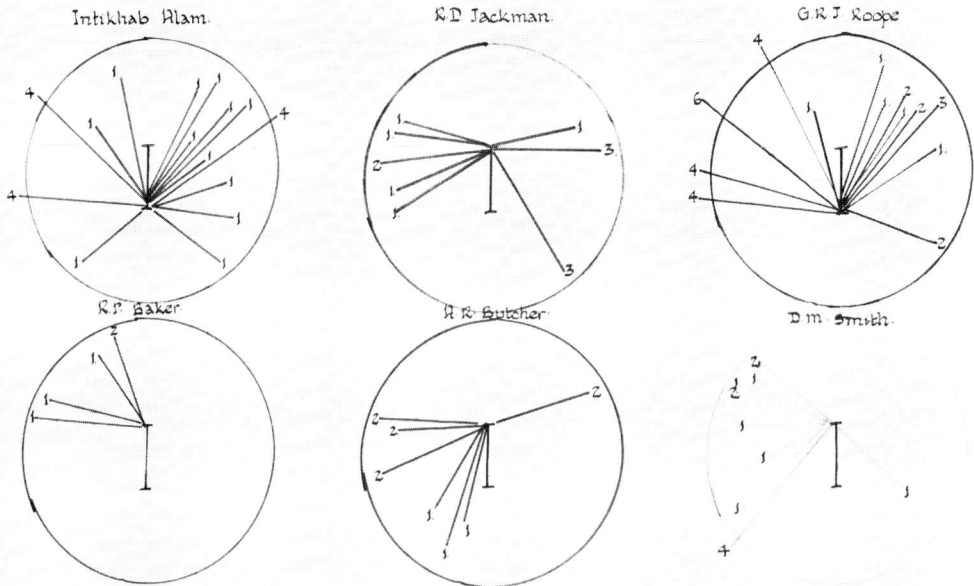

Intikhab Alam.

R.D. Jackman.

G.R.J. Roope

R.P. Baker

A.R. Butcher.

D.M. Smith.

stroyed in the very last game of the season against Hampshire at Bristol. All that and Kerry Packer, too!

In the Benson and Hedges Cup three of the four zonal games were won. Hampshire proved the winners at Bristol and the Lancashire game at Old Trafford, severely disrupted by rain, was decided in the County's favour on the technicality of a faster run rate. As leaders of the Group with Hampshire, Gloucestershire had qualified for the quarter finals. Middlesex were beaten by 18 runs after a tense day-long struggle at Bristol. David Shepherd played an innings (60 not out) of the same match winning quality as the one he played on the same ground against Surrey in the Gillette Cup game of 1973. With Middlesex at 163 for 7 wickets, facing a target of 194, Mike Procter returned to the action and blasted the tail back into the pavilion.

He was slipping into gear for his tremendous day on the 22 June against Hampshire in the semi-final at Southampton that was won by seven runs. Sadiq and Andy Stovold gave the County a century stand start, but the innings crumbled away to 180 in 54.2 overs. With a powerful batting line up Hampshire seemed set for an easy passage into the final; but matters at cricket are decided on the field, not on paper. Mike Procter

Gloucestershire C.C.C. 1977. Back row left to right: *A. J. Hignell, J. C. Foat, B. M. Brain, J. H. Shackleton, M. J. Vernon, J. H. Childs.* Front row: *D. A. Graveney, Sadiq, M. J. Procter (capt.), D. R. Shepherd, Zaheer, A. W. Stovold.*

exploded into action at once. He bowled Gordon Greenidge with the fifth ball of his third over. This was no more than the fuse. With the first ball of his fourth over he had trapped his Springbok friend, Barry Richards, lbw. Gloucestershire's cricket folk hero was now whirling in like a combine harvester in triple overdrive. Next ball Trevor Jesty suffered a similar fate and one ball later John Rice was bowled off his pads. That was the hat trick and the fourth wicket in five balls – a piece of Gloucestershire bowling history to compare with Charlie Parker's four wickets in five balls in his benefit game against Yorkshire on the Fry's ground in 1925. The next ball rapped Nigel Cowley on the pads. It looked as if he was prepared to walk back to the pavilion but he survived the confident appeal and went on to hold the remaining Hampshire innings of 173 runs together with a dogged 54, but the damage caused by those four balls was never repaired. Mike Procter bowled his 11 overs for 13 runs and 6 wickets and Gloucestershire had won by 7 runs.

On 16 July Gloucestershire folk set off once again for Lord's by car, coach and train. Kent had won the previous year's Benson and Hedges Final and had established almost a season ticket relationship with the Mecca of cricket that made Gloucestershire seem like a visiting team. Gloucestershire supporters, many from the more raucous surroundings of Kingsholm, were in no way to be overawed by the occasion. Banners declared 'Prayers at Canterbury won't stop Procter,' 'Canterbury we've got a HELL of a team,' and 'Jimmy Foat's like a butterfly, stings like a bee.'

Quietly confident the team had done their warm up net, sampled the atmosphere and returned to the pavilion before the Kent team appeared. Mike Procter won the toss. Andy Stovold and Sadiq gave the County a confident start by taking 19 runs off the first two overs. The former particularly dealt severely with some wayward Kent bowling. The first wicket fell at 79 and the second at 144 when Stovold was out for 71. Zaheer and Mike Procter maintained the momentum, relishing the opportunity to display their respective talents to the watching world. The innings progressed in abundance and finished at a formidable 237 for 6 wickets in 55 overs.

Kent were in difficulty from the start. Four for one, five for two and twenty-four for three. Only Bob Woolmer (64) and John Shepherd (55) could claim any degree of respectability. The concluding stages were marred by two premature invasions of the playing area. Firstly when Alan Knott skied a ball into the middle deep leg side for David Partridge to drop it and the concluding catch by Zaheer off Procter 64 runs short of the Gloucestershire total.

Andy Stovold won the 'Man of the Match' Award for his bustling opening innings which had given the whole Gloucestershire performance its match winning impetus. For the Benson and Hedges games alone 1977 had belonged undoubtedly to Mike Procter. Little wonder Gloucestershire was being labelled Proctershire.

Gloucestershire last won the County Championship in 1877 and with only a few hours of the last game to be played one hundred years later the odds were firmly in their favour to do so again. They had started the game leading the Table and needing only to beat Hampshire at Bristol, with their nearest challengers, Kent and Middlesex, needing also to win their games.

Mike Procter holds the Benson and Hedges Cup, chaired by D.R. Shepherd and Sadiq with D.A. Graveney supporting him.

Matters had progressed so favourably over the previous two days that Hampshire needed 271 runs from their second innings. The drama unfolded before a packed County Ground. The game moved surely in Gloucestershire's favour. The outcome rested in the hands of the bowlers – and the Bristol wicket where they had not won a game all season long. As the day progressed and news came in that both Kent and Middlesex were winning, the outcome of this game became critical. The opening Hampshire batsmen were back in the pavilion before lunch and the others were forced to fight for every run; only Gordon Greenidge of the recognised batsmen remained. He was dropped at mid-off. In that one mistake the season's work was destroyed. With nothing at stake as far as he and Hampshire were concerned he flung his bat to such purpose at everything the Gloucestershire attack had to offer that Hampshire galloped to a win by six wickets. The disappointed supporters gulped away their euphoria and gathered in front of the pavilion to greet their equally disappointed cricketers on the balcony. Once again the opportunity to head the Championship Table had been lost. Kent and Middlesex both won their games and shared the honours with Gloucestershire in third place, five points behind.

Devonians Jack Davey and David Shepherd left the Road in 1978 and 1979. Uncle Tom Cobley would have welcomed them both (Jack was no relation of Peter Davey!) aboard his strong backed grey mare on its way to Widdecombe Fair. They were just the sort of uncomplicated, humorous, loyal fellow Devonians he would have appreciated. They exemplified the finest qualities of the workaday world of English cricket.

Like all bowlers, Jack Davey would prefer to engage you in conversation about his batting. For many years his highest score was 17, but with the driest of humour he would inform you that in 1977 against Glamorgan this moved up to 53 – and not out! He laboured mightily in support of Mike Procter. For many years he had been referred to as J. J. Davey or Davy. One of his rewards was a small but highly selective fan club, the J.J.? Club, with a light blue tie and emblem J.J.? Certain match days are set aside for wearing the tie, another brain child of Alan Gibson's fertile wit. The forgetful pay a forfeit. One of the more sedate and less argumentative members admitted that he was not wearing the tie on the appointed day because he was at home gardening. His penalty, a rose to each of the members. The roses were on hand at a Cheltenham Festival day. Modern lapels only sport a dummy button hole. The search for pins by the vociferous few now sounds like an Odysseus task from Homer. Another member a respected Forest of Dean butcher, paid his penalty in lamb chops.

David Shepherd, the only Gloucestershire player to make a

Gloucestershire C.C.C. 1978. Back row left to right: A. G. Avery (scorer), B. M. Brain, J. H. Shackleton, N. H. Finan, A. J. Brassington, J. C. Foat, N. H. C. Cooper, I. C. Crawford, S. J. Windaybank, G. G. M. Wiltshire (coach). Front row: A. W. Stovold, J. Davey, M. J. Procter (capt.), D. R. Shepherd, D. A. Graveney, J. H. Childs.

century in his debut, followed in 1979. He made eleven more centuries, but his greatest innings was that 72 not out against Surrey in the Gillette Cup game at Bristol in 1973. He was accepted onto the umpire's list in 1980.

The worth of these two Devonians was far greater than their statistics would suggest, they had been at the heart of everything that had set Gloucestershire on its pedestal during these years.

Jim Foat also left in 1979. He had made five centuries, four of them in 1978 and 1979, but had not mastered the consistency required of a middle order batsman. He will be remembered for two flashes of Gloucestershire cricket history in the successful 1973 Gillette Cup Final; running like a hare for Tony Brown to receive that standing ovation from a discerning Lord's crowd for his own 7 runs and, above all, his lightning run out of Tony Greig at a crucial moment of the game.

There is a progression that applies to a young cricketer's development that can be paralleled with his schooldays. Many drop out at C.S.E. or O Level, some at A level, a few take a Scholarship and pass on to University before bumping into their ceiling. If they are more hard headed, more persistent and have exceptional academic ability, then a distinguished career should be open to them. So it is at cricket. Such are the grades to a Test career which any promising young cricketer has to pass through. He and a good coach (and the relevant committee behind them) together must appreciate and accept the high technical skills that the infinitely complex game of cricket demands. Patience is the key word. If County Cricket is the Scholarship stage, then five years is the time factor.

There is always a definite game when a cricketer's career terminates, but before his first he will have served his apprenticeship. The Young Glosters continued to thrive after the first arrivals in 1973. Alastair James Hignell, son of A. F. Hignell who had played one game for the County in 1947, first demanded notice as a brilliant scrum-half, cricketer, fives playing schoolboy at Denstone. The family house had always been at Almondsbury, but Tony Hignell was an R.A.F. doctor and his son was born on 4 September 1955 in Ely R.A.F. Hospital. He proceeded to Cambridge in 1974, immediately won Blues at Rugby and Cricket, became the first ever Cantab to captain his University at both sports and surprisingly was switched by the English Rugby selectors from scrum-half to full back to cover himself with distinction as a modern try scoring international full back before ankle injuries forced him to concentrate on his cricket. He passed through the Young Glosters, made his debut for the County in 1974, scored his first century (119 against the West Indies at Bristol) in 1976, gained his cap in 1977 and in 1981 had four centuries to his credit. He has a rumbustuous approach to batting with the eye and reflexes which befit a great ball game player, is a brilliant close fielder and in the open the fastest runner/thrower in the side.

Alastair Hignell.

By now Gloucestershire were spreading their net wider. Coach Graham Wiltshire was travelling the country and Young Glosters were coming in from far and wide. In 1974 the ever demanding need for a good wicket keeper brought Andrew James Brassington, born 9 August 1954 to the Club. In a few years he was being listed as a future England keeper, but now good keepers who can also bat are the necessity.

John Henry Childs, born in Plymouth on 15 August 1951, a slow left arm spin bowler of the George Dennett rather than the faster Charlie Parker variety, played his first game in 1975. By 1981 he had captured that unwearying precision that is the hallmark of great spin bowlers. Ball after ball dropped into the same few square inches and would have satisfied even the

greatest exponents of the art of controlled bowling, and he had moved into the mysteries of flight that had so intrigued Charlie Parker. A few years back the Gloucestershire spin attack had consisted of two off spinners, John Mortimore and David Allen, now it was two left arm spinners of equally dissimiliar yet complementary action and flight. David Graveney was coming in faster from a greater height, John Childs was teasing batsmen out in the style of George Dennett, but by then it looked as if these two fine bowlers were the final bastions of the spinners' art which was falling to the less demanding seam bowling.

Gloucestershire, always keeping a close watch on the market place, acquired the services of Brian Brain from Worcestershire in 1976. He was an opening bowler of the David Smith variety, tall, wiry in build and action, of great experience with plenty of notches on his six shooter but subject to injury. If both he and the equally suspect Mike Procter were working on all cylinders, then here was a strike bowling partnership that was as good as any the Club had seen in its long history. There was also the problem of third seamers to back them up.

Then in 1977 followed a batch of the most promising Young Glosters. Philip Bainbridge, of the same Sneyd, Staffordshire Club as Andy Brassington, had shown the promise that had attracted other counties. Gloucestershire set off in pursuit, as they had done for Zaheer a few years previously. He left school to go to Borough Road College of Education and made his debut in 1977. His is an outstanding example of the all-round patience necessary to develop the potential that is there for the world to see. There had been no doubt that W.G. and Wally Hammond at eighteen were future bright stars in the firmament, but it was not until 1981 that Phil Bainbridge played his first full season and moved up to the vital No. 3 position and, with Mike Procter and Brian Brain incapacitated, he took his place in the seam attack.

There were others; Brian Christopher Broad of Colston's School, tall, left hand opening bat, at times giving cricket enthusiasts a vision of the immortal Frank Woolley of upright stance and flashing bat. He first played in 1979, made a century before lunch against Oxford U.C.C. in 1980 and by 1981 had four centuries to his credit; David Partridge of Birdlip and Cheltenham, who for a time looked to be another Tony Brown seam bowler middle order batsman but who returned to his

Mike Procter holding the Lawrence Trophy which he won for scoring the fastest century of the season in a match against Northamptonshire 1979.

Civil Engineering in 1980; then Martin Stovold, brother of wicket keeper Andy Stovold, of Thornbury School and Loughborough College, to show a distinct but as yet unfulfilled promise.

Two other interesting cricketers briefly stepped on to the Road in 1977. Gloucestershire had established a liaison with Australian cricket clubs and exchanged players on a reciprocal basis. Alan Border of Australia, left hand bat, spent the season with the County and playing for Downend and the Second Eleven, played one first-class game against Oxford U.C.C., before returning home. Also Mike Garnham, Johannesburg born but at school in Barnstaple, a distinctly promising wicket keeper contracted by the County, who was persuaded to move to Leicestershire when he saw he was not likely to play for Gloucestershire.

An extrapolation of Gloucestershire's future prospects at the end of the 1970s must have pointed to bounding success on the cricket field and an amen to the litany of financial problems. It was not to be.

13

Nothing is Forever
1981-1982

There are few scenes in cricket to compare with the Cheltenham Festival on a sunny day. It embodies the very best traditions of the game. Business and Club marquees around the ground, rows of temporary stands, strong local and municipal involvement, receptions and functions, all against the back drop of that superb Victorian architecture and a cricket pitch that is no place for the negative or faint hearted. The first County game of three days was played in 1872 and in 1878 two games of six days were referred to as the Cheltenham Week. The Cheltenham Festival, three games in nine weekdays, appeared in 1906. The first Sunday John Player League game was played in 1969 to make ten consecutive days until in 1975 both Sundays were used and it became the present eleven days. From the very beginning the County had used the ground, thanks to the courtesy of the Council of Cheltenham College. Visitors to the Festival may be surprised to learn that originally the College and the County played on the same square, which was a little nearer to the College than the present one. The division came only after the last war. The County square is used exclusively by the County and the College square is much nearer to the buildings.

Ghosts, stories and echoes of the past haunt this famous ground. Phil Woof (grandson of W. A. 'Billy' Woof of Gloucester, first in the long line of illustrious Gloucestershire left arm spinners who was the College cricket coach from 1886 to 1926 and son of another Billy Woof), 'Woofie' to generations of Cheltonians, recalls a day in the late 1920s when the Festival finished early. It has been seen that Charlie Parker could have been a successful golf professional like his brother Arthur if he had not turned his talents towards cricket. Wally Hammond was also a low handicap golfer without Charlie's shorter game, but who could outdrive him. Eventually, after much goading during the Festival and no doubt egged on by Bev Lyon, Charlie accepted his challenge of a one drive only contest. Watched by team mates and a few spectators, they proceeded left from the dressing room to the top corner of the ground near the present

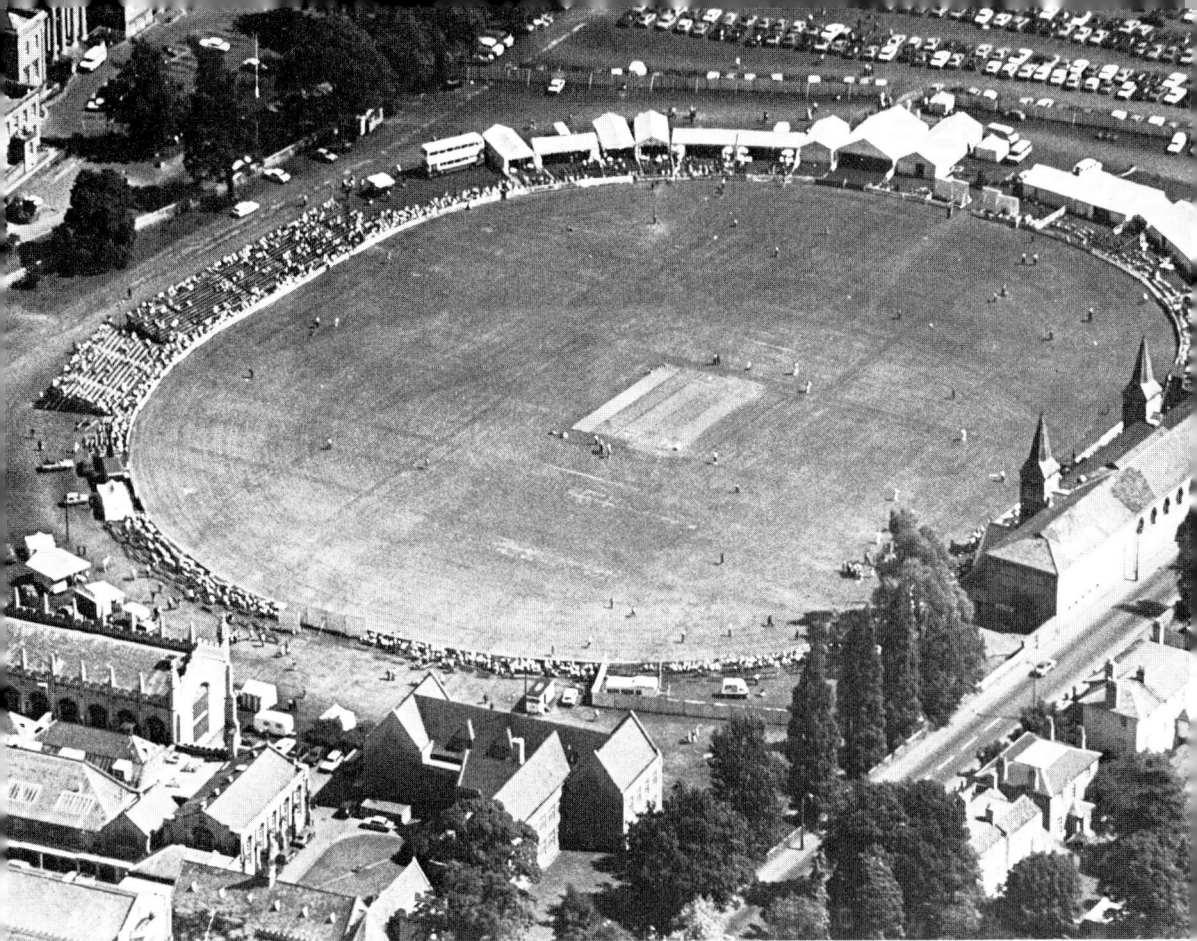

The College Ground, Cheltenham, 1980.

Centenary Block. The target diagonally across the field was the Christowe Gate, down in the bottom corner near the junction of Sandford Road and College Lawn Road, about 300 yards away. Charlie drove first and was a good 50 yards short. Wally followed; his ball pitched and ran on to finish only a few yards from the gate. He laughed his head off, claimed his bet, and as they walked back to the dressing room cadged a cigarette and a light from the crestfallen Charlie.

Nostalgia overflows at the Festival, old men tell tales of long ago. It never seemed to rain in those days. The present young, just as their fathers and grandfathers did before them, charge out on to the field of play at the intervals to look at the wicket, bat and bowl like their heroes or hopefully collect a few autographs. There goes Nico Craven, Gloucestershire's answer to Calvert, gathering snippets for another of his Diaries on the County's sporting occasions. Here come some Exiles on their annual pilgrimage.

235

The Cheltenham Festival is a great social occasion for Gloucestershire cricket folk who are attracted from near and far. Somerset Wyverns are a highly successful exiles' organisation supporting their County Cricket Club. As the 1971 cricket season progressed and as Gloucestershire widened the scope of their activities it seemed fitting that they should follow Somerset's example. There are references to an earlier Gloucestershire London Society, but on 9 July 1971, at a small meeting of members in London, the Gloucestershire Exiles were formally constituted with Vincent Coronel as Chairman, his wife Laura as Fund Raiser/Treasurer and Ken Daniels as Secretary. The aim of the organisation is to promote the affairs of Gloucestershire C.C.C. among Gloucestershire people living outside the County, to arrange 'Meet the Players' social events when the team is playing against Surrey or Middlesex, to recruit new members and support the Club's wide ranging activities.

Subsequently the Exiles became an established part of the Club's constitution with two members elected to the Council. The original target of 200 members was reached during 1979 and included members from around the world. All keep in touch with the Club's affairs in quarterly News Letters, and congregate at the Exiles' Reception Marquee at Bristol or Cheltenham. In 1980 the Exiles contributed towards the salary of a Young Gloster and in 1981 gave £500 for the Club's use.

In 1981 Gloucestershire passed the 111th milestone along its Road. 111th! There is an English cricket superstition that 111, Nelson, is an unlucky number. The Gloucestershire counter is that all of those directly involved must keep their feet off the ground. 1981 may have been a memorable year for English cricket, but for Gloucestershire it was no more than hardly adequate. The superstitious may just as well have kept their feet on the ground.

Once again the tide had turned during the Cheltenham Festival but by then the County had ceased to be interested in the outcome of any of the four competitions. At the season's end they were fourteenth in the Schweppes and sixteenth in the John Player League, all they had to show for their labours.

Mike Procter's time on centre stage of Gloucestershire cricket seemed to be running out. After a few painful games his knee finally gave out necessitating another major operation. He returned home to South Africa during the course of the season.

The years were also catching up with Brian Brain. He too, did not complete the season. Gloucestershire were now back with the problem they had encountered for much of their life – a deficiency of strike bowlers. Alan Wilkins, left arm seam bowler, who had arrived from Glamorgan the previous season, shouldered one half of the responsibility with 52 wickets (including a career best 8 for 57 against Lancashire at Old Trafford). But it was two other arrivals who roused the most 'historic' interest. The constant search for opening bowlers led to Michael Whitney, aged 23, of Sydney, Australia. A left arm bowler he was playing for Fleetwood in the Lancashire League. Arrangements were agreed, allowing him to play for both Clubs.

The T.C.C.B. rule in force meant that one of the County's three cricketers from overseas had to stand down. At the end of the 1980 season Mike Procter had been classed as a home based cricketer and in any case was absent through injury. The result was that Sadiq could not play if Whitney did. He made his Gloucestershire debut against Sri Lanka at Bristol and his first registered game against Derbyshire at Gloucester. After the Test Match at Old Trafford the Australians found that two of

Gloucestershire C.C.C. 1981. Back row left to right: A. S. Brown, P. Bainbridge, J. H. Childs, B. C. Broad, D. Surridge, S. J. Windaybank, A. W. Stovold, A. G. Avery (scorer). Front row: M. W. Stovold, Zaheer Abbas, D. A. Graveney, A. J. Hignell, Sadiq Mohammad, A. H. Wilkins.

Mike Whitney.

their seam bowlers, Rodney Hogg and Jeff Lawson, had broken down. Mike Whitney was playing against Hampshire at Cheltenham. Gloucestershire had won the toss and were batting when a telephone call from Fred Bennett, the Australian Manager, asked him to report to Headingley to play in the Fifth Test beginning the next day. Hurriedly the necessary formalities were satisfied and he left. He played for Australia in that Test and the Sixth at The Oval, returning to play in two more games for Gloucestershire.

Then there appeared a wicket keeper who discovered belat-

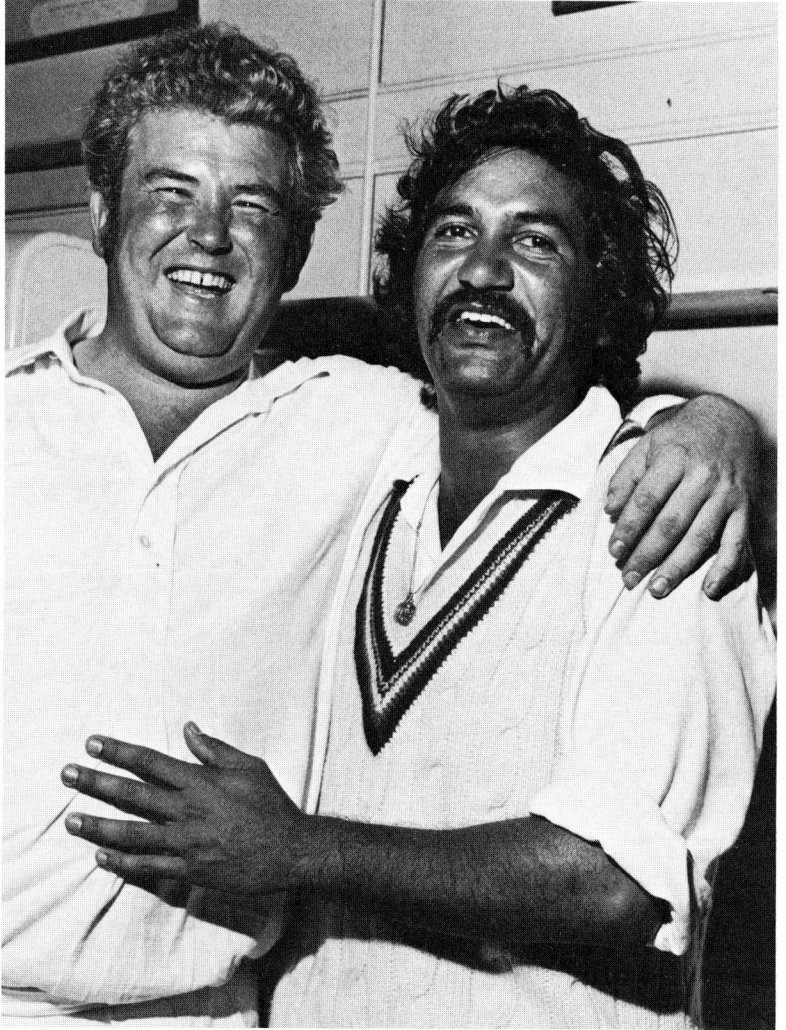

David Shepherd and Sadiq Mohammad in a happy mood.

edly he was an opening bowler. Richard Doughty, 21, of Bridlington, Yorkshire, on the ground staff at Lord's, wrote asking for a trial. He looked promising and the necessary registration forms were sent to Yorkshire, the County of his birth. They did not recognise him as a wicket keeper who had attended their nets for an unsuccessful trial. This now precipitated his attendance at their nets as a bowler. He was offered a contract on the spot, refused it and made his Gloucestershire debut against Somerset at Bristol.

Three Young Glosters established their places in the team before the season was over. The first of them, David Graveney, took over the captaincy from Mike Procter. He first captained the side in the John Player League game against Sussex at Hove

David Graveney took over the captaincy from Mike Procter in July 1981.

Robert ('Jack')
Russell.

on 5 July 1981, and then in the Championship against Glamorgan at the County Ground on 18 July. This side, which had gained only one Schweppes County Championship success at the beginning of the season responded by winning the first two games at the Cheltenham Festival and then another before the season was completed. In terms of 'history' an event occurred during the last day of the season against Leicestershire at Bristol which a few watchers recognised as a Bev Lyon declaration. In 1931 he had persuaded the Yorkshire captain to declare each first innings at 4 for 0, leaving the game to be fought for on the second innings. Now in 1981, on an equally rainy weekend, both captains forfeited an innings, Roger Tolchard the first Leicestershire and David Graveney the Gloucestershire second innings. However, history did not repeat itself. Ironically it was Michael Garnham, who had recently left the County for Leicestershire, who held out to deny a Gloucestershire victory.

Philip Bainbridge, 1,019 runs and 33 wickets, nominated as the country's 'Young Cricketer of the Year' and Chris Broad with 1,117 runs, both passed the 1,000 runs total for the first time; both were beginning to fulfil their exciting potential. John Childs (with a career best of 9 for 56 against Somerset at Bristol) was exploring the confines of the difficult and absorbing art that had inspired Charlie Parker much more than half a century ago and which he hoped one day would guide him to his Eldorado at the end of the left arm spinners' rainbow.

The wicket-keeper succession seemed to be assured with the debut of Robert 'Jack' Russell of Stroud against Sri Lanka at Bristol who took 7 catches and made a stumping in what must mark as a first-class record wicket-keeper debut.

Eighteen centuries and 8,687 runs were the batsmen's contribution to the first-class games of the 1981 season. Zaheer made another ten centuries and 2,306 of the runs. He headed the national averages with an average of 86.69. He had not played a single ball in May, made 1,016 runs in June from 1,490 balls in 1,488 minutes, passed 2,000 runs during the second week of August and it was not until the beginning of September that his average fell below 100 runs per innings. Throughout he had batted with supreme authority, seemingly oblivious to the problems and the batting failures around him – the loss of his wicket no more than a remote possibility. Perhaps now Gloucestershire will be referred to as Zaheershire!

Opposite: *Zaheer Abbas; it was reported in a Pakistan newspaper that a Gloucestershire village had been renamed after him!*

It was about this time that a Pakistan newspaper reported that Zaheer and Sadiq had been given a rare honour by Gloucestershire. Two villages had been renamed after them by 'suffixing their first names to them in recognition of their services to the County'. How about Sadiq-on-the-Wold or Mohammad-on-the-Marsh, perhaps Abbasford or Zaheer-on-Severn!

Nothing is forever. That just about sums up the 1982 stage of the Gloucestershire journey along their Road. 1981 had shown up the weaknesses on the field. The Club's confidence rested on two years of bumper profits and a settled stable management structure. Now this too was to be broken. The tremors erupted into a full explosion before 1982 was over.

A new season really begins directly the old one is over. What happened – and plenty had happened – in the months between the end of cricket in 1981 and the beginning in 1982 culminates in the Spring Annual General Meeting, and sets the scene for the coming season. The critics were given plenty of encouragement to support the persuasive theory that every organisation carries within it the seeds of its own destruction. Ken Graveney, who since 1947 had progressed from junior professional, to Captain and finally to Club Chairman was deposed at the Cheltenham A.G.M. to be replaced by Don Perry one of the leading sports authorities of the North of the County. Treasurer Dickie Rossiter who had been at the heart of the Club's finances since 1974 resigned. Alan Vaughan, Accountant, former Captain, and now Chairman of Westbury on Trym C.C. who had acted as the County Club's Assistant Treasurer, replaced him. Finally, towards the end of November, Tony Brown after a lifetime in Gloucestershire cricket left the club for a similar position with neighbouring Somerset.

David Graveney who had taken over the team following Mike Procter's departure was appointed Captain for 1982. So Mike Procter, the greatest match winner in the history of the Club, had limped off the Road in 1981. His tempestuous career in every dimension of the game was over. His figures for Gloucestershire are 14,441 runs, 833 wickets and 185 catches, but cold statistics can never relate to the excitement of watching him bat and bowl. Never again would we see that long run gathering momentum to the mid air explosive blast at the wicket. Cricket is the poorer with his passing.

242

Determination. Mike Procter who did so much for Gloucestershire and was the greatest match winner in the Club's history. Barry Meyer is umpire.

Brian Brain had also retired. But the opening attack problem did not end there. Alan Wilkins left arm third seamer had stepped up to share the attack in 1981 was unfit and did not

243

bowl a ball in 1982, and Australian Mike Whitney just did not appear in April. So before the season began all four opening bowlers had disappeared. John Shepherd, experienced West Indian and Kent batsman and bowler joined the Club. Although technically a third seam bowler he opened the bowling and proved to be the most effective. His partner, David Surridge (26), Hertfordshire and Cambridge U.C.C., had joined the Club in 1981, but missed that season through injury. All four of the seam bowlers' right arm and medium pace were soon exposed. The urgent need was for more pace. Franklin Da Costa Stephenson (23) burly Barbadian playing for Rawenstall, in the Lancashire League, was contracted. There were problems. Rawenstall had first call on his services. More seriously the new T.C.C.B. rule permitting only one new overseas cricketer to play in a game meant that if he played Sadiq or Zaheer could not.

The batting was just as thin. Z played in only seven matches but provided 811 runs and three centuries, two of them in the same match, 162 not out and 107 against Lancashire at Gloucester. His total of first-class centuries at the end of the season was 95, with 1983 to be his benefit year. The Young Glosters were

presented with their opportunity but failed to provide a consistent flow of runs and thus few targets for the bowlers. Two new batsmen advanced their claims. First, Paul Romaines (27) of Bishop Auckland, County Durham who had tried his luck with several other counties but felt he still had something to prove to himself. Perhaps he did. He made 74 in his first championship game against Yorkshire at Bradford and later 186 in the second innings against Warwickshire at Nuneaton. Tony Wright of Stevenage joined the Club in 1978 aged seventeen and made his debut in 1982 with 65 in the same game.

Do batsmen or bowlers win cricket matches for you? That question has always been at the centre of cricket debate. If statistics have any meaning then perhaps some Gloucestershire 1982 figures support the view that bowlers do. Hampshire with 46 batting but 74 bowling points finished third in the Championship while Gloucestershire with 46 and 55 were fifteenth. The overall Gloucestershire bowling and batting rates – almost 13 overs (74 balls) to take a wicket with 34.4 runs per wicket; and 27.6 runs per wicket with the bat. This was indeed stony ground for David Graveney in his first year as Captain. Success on the field is fundamental to a Club's welfare.

1982 also saw a dramatic change in the finances as the chart shows:

Year	Income	Expenditure	Profit or Loss + or −
1980	£357,325	£299,326	+£57,999
1981	£425,198	£383,332	+£41,866
1982	£343,670	£401,538	−£57,868

For many years Dr E. M. Grace administered the Club single-handed from his home, Park House, at Thornbury. He wrote all the correspondence and Committee Minutes, collected, listed and acknowledged the membership fees, organised the home matches, made arrangements and paid for the cricketers' travelling and hotels – and played cricket!

Running Gloucestershire cricket is now big business. The County wide representation of forty-four Council Members authorising the work of the Management Committee of fourteen set up with commendable foresight in 1919 still applied in 1981. These Gloucestershire cricket lovers form the various sub-committees but a movement towards a closer business type central authority is afoot. There is an inclination in some quarters that

Graham Wiltshire the Gloucestershire coach.

a management of, say, five members would tighten up the working of the Club. Traditions are not broken easily and it will prove difficult to bridge the uneasy divide between the democratic and business executive ethos of a County Cricket Club. The Secretary became the Secretary/Manager in 1971; some counties have already redesignated him the Chief Executive and that is only a step away from making him, or the Chairman, a Managing Director answerable to a Board. 1981 saw a strengthening in this direction with the appointment of Hugh Roberts as Financial Administrator.

The end of a season is always statistics time. I would not wish to end this stage of the Gloucestershire Road in a flurry of statistics but a brief look at the County's leading batting and bowling figures seems both relevant and interesting.

There is a perennial question in cricket – which is the more important, runs or wickets? Perhaps the safest answer would be to say that they both are. We are brought up to think in terms of cricket averages, runs against innings or wickets. There is another way, runs against balls received or bowled. This is the more significant – bowlers would say labour intensive – striking rate. To do this for the batsmen it is necessary to have available the specific scorebooks. Unfortunately Gloucestershire have only a few of the years before the First War, so we cannot compare fully statistically, say, W.G. and Wally Hammond. It is possible for bowlers if we remember that the over has not always been of six balls: pre 1889 it was 4 balls: 1899, 5 balls: 1900–1938, 6 balls: 1939, 8 balls: 1945 onwards, 6 balls.

Here are suggested the leading batsmen, bowlers, all rounders, wicket keepers, best teams of Gloucestershire born and all comers statistically:

BATTING

		Runs		Career
		G.C.C.C.	Career	Average
C. J. Barnett	1927–48	21,222	25,389	32.72
*J. F. Crapp	1936–56	22,195	23,615	35.04
A. E. Dipper	1908–32	27,948	28,075	35.27
*G. M. Emmett	1936–59	22,806	25,602	31.41
W. G. Grace	1870–99	22,807	54,210 (1865–1908)	39.45
*T. W. Graveney	1948–60	19,705	47,793 (1948–1972)	44.92
*W. R. Hammond	1920–51	33,664	50,551	56.11

BATTING

Runs

		G.C.C.C.	Career	Career Average
G. L. Jessop	1894–1914	18,936	26,698	32.64
C. A. Milton	1948–74	30,218	32,150	33.74
R. B. Nicholls	1965–79	23,607	23,607	26.17
*M. J. Procter	1965–81	14,441	21,307	37.45
*D. M. Young	1949–64	23,400	24,555	30.69
*Zaheer Abbas	1972–82	14,440	30,069	52.84

*Denotes not Gloucestershire born.

BOWLING

Wickets

		G.C.C.C.	Career	Striking Rate Balls/ Wickets
D. A. Allen	1953–72	882	1,209	59.77
A. S. Brown	1953–76	1,223	1,230	57.83
C. C. Cook	1946–64	1,768	1,782	59.01
*E. G. Dennett	1903–26	2,082	2,147	46.06
T. W. J. Goddard	1922–52	2,862	2,979	46.34
W. G. Grace	1870–99	1,349	2,808 (1865–1908)	45.95
*G. E. E. Lambert	1938–57	908	917 (1938–1960)	57.94
J. B. Mortimore	1950–75	1,696	1,807	60.00
C. W. L. Parker	1903–35	3,170	3,278	44.87
*M. J. Procter	1965–81	833	1,310	45.95
F. G. Roberts	1887–1905	963	970	48.71
*R. A. Sinfield	1924–39	1,165	1,173	63.33
D. R. Smith	1956–70	1,159	1,250	50.63

*Denotes not Gloucestershire born.

The best major G.C.C.C. bowler striking rate – C. L. Townsend 39.78 balls per wicket.

WICKET KEEPERS – TOP TWO (*Career*)

		Caught	Stumped	Runs	Tests
J. H. Board	1891–1914	853	354	15,674	6
H. Smith	1912–35	451	266	13,413	1

ALL ROUNDERS (*Career*)

		Runs	Wickets	Catches	Stumped
A. S. Brown	1953–76	12,851	1,230	495	
W. G. Grace	1865–1908	54,210	2,808	862	5
G. L. Jessop	1894–1914	26,698	873	463	
J. B. Mortimore	1950–75	15,891	1,807	346	
*M. J. Procter	1965–81	21,307	1,370	312	
*R. A. Sinfield	1924–39	15,647	1,173	178	

Overleaf: The County Ground, Bristol, 1970. It is interesting to compare this picture with the one on page 51.

247

Top Teams?

GLOUCESTERSHIRE BORN XI   FULL GLOUCESTERSHIRE XI

Teams of 5 batsmen, one all rounder, wicket keeper, two opening bowlers, two spinners.

1. W. G. Grace (Capt.)	1. W. G. Grace (Capt.)
2. A. E. Dipper	2. A. E. Dipper
3. C. A. Milton	3. *W. R. Hammond
4. C. J. Barnett	4. *Zaheer Abbas
5. G. L. Jessop	5. *T. W. Graveney
6. J. B. Mortimore	6. *M. J. Procter
7. A. S. Brown	7. G. L. Jessop
8. J. H. Board (Wk.)	8. J. H. Board (Wk.)
9. F. G. Roberts	9. F. G. Roberts
10. T. W. J. Goddard	10. T. W. J. Goddard
11. C. W. L. Parker	11. C. W. L. Parker
12th Man C. L. Townsend	12th Man C. L. Townsend

*Denotes not Gloucestershire born.

For inclusion in an All England XI:
W. G. Grace

W. R. Hammond

For a World XI: W. G. Grace?

The modern cricket world is light years away from the game W.G. can justly claim to have made. Beards and the prevalent habit of 'chuntering' he would recognise, but since his day the game has gone through a bewildering cycle of evolution. There is much in the contemporary scene that would astonish him. Now TV cameras catch 'every blink' of a Test Match; umpires with light meters; cricketers hung around with jewellery, embracing at the fall of a wicket and engaging in other preposterous histrionics; batsmen and fielders in helmets, padded in every part of the anatomy, bowlers in bandeaux; all against a background of moronic chanting and rattling beer cans. May the old virtues at the heart of this absorbing and enchanting game never be lost.

Yesterday has gone. 'The moving finger writes; and having writ, moves on.' Soon it will be another spring and then another cricket season. Gloucestershire will be travelling on along their Road, with pride in their past but with a wavering confidence in their future.

Index